PRAISE FOR THOMAS BELLER

Praise for *J. D. Salinger: The Escape Artist*

"Irresistible ... endearing ... lyrical and precise. ... *J. D. Salinger* is the story of the resonance of its subject, but it is also the story of a generous, humorous, sensitive writer, which is to say Thomas Beller. Not much escapes him."—*The New York Times Book Review*

"Beller writes with intelligence and insight"—*Los Angeles Times*

"Beller offers a uniquely literary inquiry into the combatively reclusive and epically blocked author of *The Catcher in the Rye* and beloved short story collections. ... A fine and stirring portrait of a haunted literary artist."
—*Booklist* (starred review)

"Rather than writing a straightforward biography, Beller ... offers here an exceptionally well-researched, deeply felt, and thoughtful exploration of the elusive author's history, in which he probes Salinger's life and prickly familial ties, and their manifestation in his timeless characters and settings."—*Publishers Weekly*

"In this genre-bending nonfiction delight, a Tulane professor and contributor to *The New Yorker* tells a story of literary obsession, deftly folding a slim Salinger bio into a memoir of his own pursuit of the elusive literary icon."—*The Times-Picayune*

"The objective, exhaustive biographies of Salinger have been published. Beller supplies us with what's needed now—a book that shines with a deep personal passion for the writer."—Edmund White

"This mesmerizing brief biography captures the many sides of Salinger's complicated personality.... *J. D. Salinger* is hugely readable; I couldn't put it down."—Patricia Bosworth

"This book approaches J. D. Salinger's life and art from six or seven angles, all of them acute.... A wonderfully personal portrait, telling in every detail, gesture, remark, and reflection."—Daniel Menaker

"It's hard to imagine a more perfect pairing of author and subject than Thomas Beller and J. D. Salinger. This book is both a pleasure and an education."—Meghan Daum

Praise for *How to Be a Man: Scenes from a Protracted Boyhood*

"Beller casts himself as both hero and hapless sidekick—just the guide you want for a jaunt down memory lane."—Adena Spingarn, *Vogue*

"These quite marvelous and darkly hilarious personal essays derive their power from shameless honesty, often about the most shameful moments."—Phillip Lopate

"[Beller] is disarmingly self-deprecatory and gets his laughs, of which the book has a number, mainly at his own expense."—Jonathan Yardley, *Washington Post*

"An enjoyably mature read."—Gilbert Cruz, *Entertainment Weekly*

"[Beller] can write his butt off."—Donnell Alexander, *San Francisco Chronicle*

"His essays shimmer with comedy and insight and exuberance. I absolutely loved this book."—Jonathan Ames

Lost in the Game

Lost in
the Game

A Book about Basketball

DUKE UNIVERSITY PRESS
Durham and London
2022

Thomas Beller

Project editor: Lisa Lawley
Designed by A. Mattson Gallagher
Typeset in Arno Pro and Helvetica Neue
by Westchester Publishing Services

Library of Congress Cataloging-in-Publication Data
Names: Beller, THomas, author.
Title: Lost in the game : a book about basketball / THomas Beller.
Description: Durham : Duke University Press, 2022.
Identifiers: LCCN 2022029804 (print)
LCCN 2022029805 (ebook)
ISBN 9781478018834 (paperback)
ISBN 9781478016175 (hardcover)
ISBN 9781478023449 (ebook)
Subjects: LCSH: Basketball. | Basketball players. | BISAC: SPORTS &
RECREATION / Basketball | SPORTS & RECREATION/ Reference
Classification: LCC GV885 .B455 2022 (print) | LCC GV885 (ebook) |
DDC 796.323—dc23/eng/20220623
LC record available at https://lccn.loc.gov/2022029804
LC ebook record available at https://lccn.loc.gov/2022029805

Cover art: *Ingersoll Houses, Brooklyn, USA,* 2011. © Kevin
Couliau, kevincouliau.com.

For Elizabeth, Evangeline, and Alexander

Along the journey of our life half way I found myself again in a dark wood wherein the straight road no longer lay.

—Dante, *The Divine Comedy* (1472)

We said, "Hey, let's just go out there and get lost in the game and we will live with the results. Confidence and momentum is a real thing."

—Lou Williams, after leading the Los Angeles Clippers to victory after being down 31 midway through the third quarter against the reigning Champion Golden State Warriors (April 15, 2019)

We go to the playground in search of our fathers.

—John Edgar Wideman, *Hoop Roots* (2001)

CONTENTS

AAU	Amateur Athletic Union
CUNY	City University of New York
FIBA	International Basketball Federation
JCC	Jewish Community Center
MVP	Most Valuable Player
NBA	National Basketball Association
NCAA	National College Athletic Association
NYU	New York University
OKC	Oklahoma City Thunder
OMG	Old Man Game
PER	Player Efficiency Rating
PGA	Professional Golf Association
PPS	points per shot
UCLA	University of California, Los Angeles
U MASS	University of Massachusetts
USBL	United States Basketball League

ACKNOWLEDGMENTS

I would like to thank the following individuals and institutions for their insight and support in the writing of this book: Sasha Weiss, Michael Agger, David Remnick, Connie Rosenbloom, Frank Flaherty, Andrew Blauner, William Rhoden, Eryn Matthews, Whitney Donnhauser, Lilly Tuttle, Marco Roth, Mark Krotov, Elaina Richardson, Yaddo, Lorin Stein, Deirdre Foley-Mendelssohn, John Merz, Christian Martin, Veljko Vujačić, Jacob Margolies, Ben Golliver, Henry Abbott, Mike Singer, and Gerald Howard—as well as Lisa Lawley, Christopher Robinson, Laura Sell, and everyone at Duke University Press. An especially deep bow of gratitude to my editor, Dean Smith, and agent, Rob McQuilkin. Special thanks to Nicholas Hamburger for his sensitive and perceptive notes on the manuscript as it took shape.

Grateful acknowledgment is made to the publications in which some of the essays in this book first appeared, often in a somewhat different form:

The New Yorker: "Spree," "Damian Lillard's Game-Winning Shot," "The City Game?" "James Harden's Transcendent Step-Back," "Anthony Davis and the Plight of the Modern Big NBA Man," "The NBA Kaleidoscope," "Loitering Backstage at the NBA," "Here We Go Again: The Cavaliers-Warriors NBA Finals," "The Earth Is Round and Kyrie Irving," "The Pleasures of the Old Man Game," "The Warriors' Torrential Victory," and "French Math at the NBA Draft."

The New York Times: "The Court on Horatio Street" and "Most Definitely."

N+1: "Pandemic Playgrounds."

The Paris Review: "The Maserati Kid."

Action, Spectacle: "Bol Bol on an Escalator."

"Lost in the Game" is from the catalog for the Museum of the City of New York's exhibit *City/Game: Basketball in New York*, edited by William C. Rhoden (New York: Rizzoli Effects/Museum of the City of New York, 2020).

"The Court on Horatio Street" and "Most Definitely" are reprinted from *How to Be a Man: Scenes from a Protracted Boyhood* (New York: W. W. Norton, 2005).

INTRODUCTION

The other day I got into a screaming match with an enormous guy at the playground in Riverside Park. He was huge, burly, a kind of miniature Shaq. He was killing me in the post. And he was talking trash, louder and louder: a bully who sensed my weakness. But I yelled back; I held my own. That's what I have, that was my education, acquired on that very court when I was a kid and then refined at many others—playing hard, arguing, being loud when need be, being strong. Or trying to be. His team won, which was very annoying, since I did, in fact, back off and become more passive on the court—the old mental weakness. But afterward, we were friendly. Slapped hands. It turns out his hero is DeMarcus Cousins. This softened things, but still, I had to sit on a park bench on the way home, cooling down. I wrote to a friend, a former high school teammate from Brooklyn, and described the scene. The streetlamp turned on while I sat there texting. He responded, "I am so proud of you (and jealous) that you're still playing ball. It is a way to connect with the world around me that I miss in the most profound way."

Basketball—playing it and watching it and thinking about it—is a bigger part of my life now, as a grown man, than it was when I played on high school and college teams. And yet this book began back then, long before I knew I was writing a book about basketball. The sport always felt walled off from and apart from my real life. It felt illicit. At some point, in my thirties, I started calling the game my last vice. This was partly because I had by then given up so many others. (The circumstances by which I stopped drinking, or commenced the "break" which has now lasted over twenty years, were strangely wound up in basketball, as discussed in "The Nets.") But it was also in my thirties that I began to take the game more seriously.

Perhaps I was swept up by a phenomenon in our culture in which the midlife crisis now manifests not in sports cars and affairs but in sudden commitments to triathlons or CrossFit or some other way to push the body to the extreme and attempt to cheat time. Or maybe it was around then that I noticed that all this time spent playing ball was the equivalent of a drug.

I had always dismissed basketball as secondary to the real action of my life, which is probably in part why I never got very good at it. And yet it took up so much time! From practices and games during the winter months, when the sport moves indoors, to spring and summer, when it flourishes in playgrounds around the world where anyone can take an afternoon sojourn in the park, I enter the world of the playground and pickup ball with the sense of relief and enclosure with which I once entered bars. This book is an attempt to make sense of this phenomenon on both a personal level and a cultural level while providing a close read of the game as it ascended to what will surely be seen as a golden age with Steph and Lebron as the successors to Larry and Magic.

The book moves along two axes: the world of organized basketball and the world of pickup basketball. In terms of talent, money, and milieu, they are light-years apart. And yet the street game, and its attendant culture, is a wellspring of energy and innovation for National Basketball Association (NBA) players. And NBA players, by their embrace of that culture and milieu, connect their aura and talent to the world of playground ball. When, for example, you see footage of Kevin Durant draining buckets in his orange jersey at Rucker Park, the energy and elation feel mutual: Durant bestowing his All-World talent on the playground while he absorbs love, enthusiasm, and validation from that very playground. He is not from Harlem, but it is nevertheless a kind of homecoming.

Playground, here, is a euphemism—it is more than a patch of asphalt amid buildings or nestled beside a highway (as is often the case in New York City), though the structural origins of the basketball court, whether found in the city or the country, are interesting to ponder. Where there is a hoop there is a scene, a community, a neighborhood, a world. Rucker Park is known as the mecca, which is to say a shrine to which the faithful go to worship, but I contend that every playground where serious basketball is played is a kind of mecca that bestows blessings and acceptance on those who worship there.

Early on, right after I graduated from college, I had the experience of attending a few NBA games at Madison Square Garden as a journalist. The encounter with my college coach at one of these Knicks games is detailed in this book. I wasn't there as a beat writer, and I wasn't interested in being a sportswriter, or even a journalist. But it was a glimpse into the world of professional basketball, as well as the old, now almost prehistoric arrangements of arenas, before the multimedia big screens, the luxury boxes, and so forth. Most important, it provided an up-close look at the players themselves, not as figures in the distance or on a screen but in the corporeal present, these humans who are gods, and vice versa.

Almost three decades later, at the 2014 NBA All-Star Game in New Orleans, I reentered the world of the NBA with a press pass, for I had begun attending games regularly for the *New Yorker*. Because of my own literary predilections, I wrote as an outsider. But I was aware—mostly unconsciously—of the long tradition of sportswriting at the magazine in which the reporter functions as a kind of credentialed amateur, an outsider to the working press even if also a member of it. I was aware, in particular, of Roger Angell, with whom I had worked directly on short stories and nonfiction. His pencil passed over all of three or four paragraphs in this book, but his influence as a writer and editor goes beyond that.

This book is peppered with close reads of some of the most famous athletes in the world, interspersed with the undistinguished basketball adventures of the author. I was on the basketball team for ten years of my life, from middle school to high school to four years of college, a massive commitment of time and energy, even if my college, Vassar, was a small-time Division III program. After college, I continued to play, more out of habit than love, but it was not important to me, and for about three years, because of injury and a kind of depressive sloth and lack of care for my body, I stopped playing altogether. The main emotion I felt at the end of my college career was relief—my body, during the season, was always in some degree of pain. Perhaps the fact that I was always failing to live up to my potential as a player has made me sensitive to the strange secondary market in expectation that surrounds all the young talent in the basketball pipeline, which swirls with phrases like *ridiculous upside* and *high ceiling*. Maybe it has something to do with my fascination with those players invested with so much hope who are struggling to pan out and survive in the league—players like Lenny Cooke, Al-Farouq Aminu, or Bol Bol, to cite examples discussed in this book.

Similarly, my days playing pickup basketball, on the playgrounds of New York City and elsewhere, were and are exhilarating in part because they feel so perilous—the court as a source of insult to my pride and ego, if not physical injury, where every visit poses the question of whether I can overcome the old fears. When I was a kid and young man, the playground was a place of intense competition with players who were better and stronger than me and who were on their own territory, with me as an interloper, which is to say it was a largely black environment in which a white, weak, soft, very tall kid appeared. And continues to appear. No longer a kid. And finally, in middle age, not quite so emotionally fragile. And even in some instances liked and respected, a fact that gives me an unseemly amount of pleasure, I admit. But then, it's my experience that when someone shows up to play ball, no matter their height or physique, they have a reason to think they can play ball, and often they care passionately about the game.

That I kept going back to the court as a kid might be a story of masochism or of willpower, but the element I am most interested in is the story of basketball's mystical, spiritual allure—basketball as a drug, as a safe space, as a unique experience of time. Organized basketball is built around regimented and organized blocks of time: basketball practice in the afternoon or in the morning; the coach counting down from ten to zero as the team runs suicides (the drill is no longer called that, I have been informed) with the threat that if he reaches zero while someone is still running, everyone has to run again. Invariably that someone is the lumbering big man, the project, which is to say it was me. And then the games themselves, with the referees, the clock, the buzzer. Time here as cruel God, slightly fungible in late game situations when someone's finger has to press a button to stop or start the clock, but largely immutable and unforgiving.

Playground basketball, in contrast, is timeless. It exists on its own time, summer time; it's ruled by the sun, or by the night lights, if there are any, or by the willingness of those with a ball to keep shooting in the dark. The rules on the playground are implicit—universal, if variable. For if basketball is a global language, it has dialects. This is true at the highest level of the game, such as the Olympics, where the rules of the International Basketball Federation (FIBA) differ in small but significant ways from the NBA (ask Tim Duncan). And it is true at the playground level. Each court has its own rules, its own character and aura. But these are peripheral differences—the language of basketball translates everywhere it is played, among all who play it. To be a committed player or fan is to be part of a club that has members in every part of the globe.

I was recently asked if this book was about the history of the game. In a way it is, with a focus on the recent history. In 2014 the All-Star Game came to New Orleans, and I attended with a press pass and wrote about what I saw. I began covering the league soon after. The year 2014 was a significant juncture in the NBA. It saw the last great victory of the Spurs dynasty and the swan song of the Heatles team. That year was the dawn of the Splash Brothers' era, with Warriors coach Mark Jackson making the claim, mocked at the time, that the Stephen Curry–Klay Thompson backcourt was the best-shooting backcourt in history. At the end of the season, Jackson was replaced as coach by Steve Kerr, whose team, over the next years, would make Jackson's remark seem like a matter of fact. The spring of 2014 was also the first All-Star Game Kobe Bryant missed because of injury.

The way the league and its players were discussed was likewise changing rapidly—the focus on analytics and data dovetailed with the ever-expanding supply of video footage of all levels of the game and its distribution on social media, where this footage and data were put to use by amateur scouts/pundits/data analysts, to make their case for or against certain players and teams.

I had begun, around that time, to take my own basketball game more seriously. When I was a kid, we were told weight training would ruin our shot. Now the best NBA players post their workout videos online, and expert training has been largely democratized. Everyone can be their own six-million-dollar man or woman, with a body honed and enhanced by the latest in training techniques, without spending six million dollars. And then there is the feeling, or fact, that at some point in the twentieth century a group of people in middle age began to turn their energies toward the radical improvement of their own functional fitness. People in sweat suits and tennis shoes jogging around Central Park had once—in the long-ago dawn of fitness culture as a mass movement—been a novelty, and slightly absurd. In the twenty-first century there has been an explosion of gyms across the land, including CrossFit, to which I belonged. Everywhere you looked, oldsters were training for Ironman contests and triathlons, a form of survival through self-obliteration that any dedicated player of pickup basketball would recognize. Based on personal experience, the underachievers are the ones who are most motivated; converts are always the biggest zealots.

"Do you still play?" Bernard King asked me toward the end of a thrilling impromptu conversation we had at the opening of the Museum of the City of New York's exhibit *City/Game*. King was one of my earliest heroes. Dapper and sophisticated, he was indulging me with this question, I knew. I explained that I did, with more passion than ever, and then asked, "How about you?"

Now it was my turn to be polite. He waved me off. "Never."

I knew all about his incredible recovery from knee surgery, a return to All-Star form, the first person to do that after such a surgery. I had played once on the Tillary Street Court just down the street from the Fort Greene housing projects where he grew up in Brooklyn, a fact that I was well aware of at the time of that first visit, in 1983, and that lent the visit part of its drama and tension.

Serious athletes are always living at the precipice of permanent damage to their bodies, always living with pain or the recent memory of it. As we walked down the stairs, it was clear from King's gait that he was no longer playing. What I took from our exchange was that he no longer felt the desire, or maybe I should say the need. Instead, he told me of his intellectual pursuits, the writing of his memoir, *Game Face*. When I told him I enjoyed the documentary about his college career, *Bernie and Ernie*, he said he had brought the idea for the project to ESPN.

There is something compulsive about basketball. I love the detail, mythic in flavor, about the game's founder, James Naismith, reporting that he had once walked past a young boy throwing a ball into a basket and then a few hours later walked past the same boy, who was still tossing the ball at the basket. When he asked the boy why, the answer was, "To see if it goes in."

This feeling of a story being continuously written, a waterfall of balls splashing through nets, so to speak, ongoing and hypnotic, underpins this book. I got the title from a passing remark made by Lou Williams after he led the Clippers back from a twenty-eight-point halftime deficit against the defending-champion Warriors, whose roster that season featured not only Stephen Curry, Draymond Green, and Klay Thompson but Kevin Durant. Williams's phrase, uttered in response to a "How did you do it?" question from the television reporter after the game, contains a sense of the game as a refuge, a state of grace in the present moment, a thing in which to get lost. The game as a place where one might find a kind of redemption. The line that immediately follows "We just got lost in the game," said in a continuum of thought as though one naturally follows the other, was "Confidence and momentum is a real thing."

This book is an attempt to enter this flow—the flow of being lost in the game—both as a witness to the NBA spectacle and as a player in the global pickup game. The point of view—and the geography—reflects my life as a native New Yorker who moved to New Orleans in 2008 but who still spends a lot of time in New York City. Indeed, I am here now, and soon I will go down to play on the courts in Riverside Park.

The subject of fathers comes up in this book now and then. Or perhaps I should say the subject of absent fathers. "We went to the playground court to find our missing fathers," writes John Edgar Wideman in his book *Hoop Roots*. When I first read that line, I felt a shock of recognition. I also recognized that this identification is absurd: Wideman grew up in a black neighborhood in Pittsburgh and was a standout athlete. His game got him a scholarship at the University of Pennsylvania, where he was a basketball star. Most important, his father literally played basketball on the courts when he went to play. None of that applies to me—not the race or the talent, and certainly not the paternal legacy in basketball. The line that comes next, though, cannot help but resonate, if only as a possible explanation for why I—who lost my father at age nine—have been drawn to this environment so intensely. "We didn't find them, but we found a game, and the game served as a daddy of sorts."

It just so happens that in the past six months or so, my son, who until the age of nine had been emphatically uninterested in sports, has started to show an interest in the game of basketball. For years now I had brought him to NBA games, mostly Pelicans games. More recently, I have been bringing him to the courts—first in New Orleans and then in New York City. I will shoot with him, play a game against him, at times giving him space to shoot and at times smacking the ball out of the air. Sometimes there are pickup games with other kids, and his ability to navigate this unstructured, city space fills me with pride.

At some point I will peel off and play with the grown-ups. On occasion these games get a little heated. I have a strange identity in pickup games these days, a change that became more pronounced after the COVID break. "I want to be like you when I grow up," some young guy said to me after a game, and I was not sure if this was a compliment or an insult—if he was referring to the level of skill I demonstrated playing basketball, or the degree to which I was into it, being an antagonist, difficult, loud, competitive, all the things that in the proper measure make these games more fun. In either case, the message seemed to be one of surprise that I was so invested in the game. Because I talk now. I never did when I was younger. I was mute on the court. But now I speak a language I would describe as bellicose encouragement: calling out "We're good" or "We're fine," slapping teammates five if they hit shots, encouraging them to shoot when they are open, making little Nikola Jokić–like gestures with my chin or my hand, directing them to cut, setting screens to give them space. I have discovered the joy of giving other people confidence. A little of this can go a long way. I once was playing HORSE with Jason Kidd, as part of a magazine piece, and I was so nervous I kept missing. I mentioned this, jokingly, and he responded in his murmurous way that he could tell I had a good shot. Whatever polite expedience was behind this remark, there was a germ of sincerity, and hearing it from him was like a drug.

The joy of instilling confidence in a teammate is an extension of the joy of getting an assist, which I think matches or in some ways exceeds the pleasure of scoring. But I offer this support not from the sidelines but from on the court. A player, not a coach. Or maybe a player-coach. That may change, one day, but this book is written from the point of view of someone emphatically in the game. Someone working to improve their game. I am asked, sometimes, "Did you play basketball?" And I always respond, "I still play basketball."

When my own son was shooting around with me, I began to see this insistence on being a participant and not just an observer in a new light. I realized that my thoughts about basketball and fatherhood had been, up to that point, from the point of view of a kid who lost his father. I want to acknowledge that there is another story unfurling as well, in which I am on the court as a father.

And what kind of example am I setting?

A few days after that screaming match with baby DeMarcus Cousins I was at the playground with my son. I shot baskets with him, and then I went and entered the full-court game. Baby Boogie Cousins was in my face again, yelling, talking trash. He was so much stronger. He bullied me in the post, and I struggled to get mine on the other end. But I played hard and was able to maintain my dignity. Eventually we got into a shouting match, and I heard myself shouting, with violently cranky indignation, "I've been coming here since 1977!" I saw the boy nearby watching. We lost the game. I thought the boy handled it fine, or maybe he didn't register anything unusual.

But then on the walk home, he made some remarks about finding that guy and—I paraphrase—being violent. This was alarming. Also refreshing in its lack of guile. He wasn't playing it cool. He wanted revenge. Furthermore, he was only putting into words the feelings that had been coursing through me moments earlier, and that were only now beginning to abate. I made a speech about staying cool, about moderation, about love of the game, about the importance of leaving it all on the court, not bringing all the craziness home with you. He made fun of me for yelling, "I've been coming here since 1977!" I wondered, all the while, what sort of education this game, and this father, was passing along to the younger generation, and what basketball would mean to him, and what role I might play.

But that is a subject for another book.

Lost in the Game

The Court on Horatio Street

One day in the fall of 2002, when the weather had cooled and summer seemed to be over, I went down to my local basketball court, on Hudson Street between Horatio and Gansevoort Streets, where I had been going for seven years. The court, which is wedged between the West Village, where I live, and the Meatpacking District, is on the loose circuit of courts upon which players, as it were, like to play. But it looked a little emptier than usual. The players there were mostly those diehards whose compulsion to play basketball is somehow suspicious, less morbid than the derelict types sitting on the benches drinking something out of brown paper bags and waiting for their man, but its own kind of addiction nevertheless.

I played a few games, and then, after nearly everyone had gone home, I lingered to shoot around in the strangely early dusk.

The trance of the court, into which I had fallen so happily all summer long, was broken. I saw from the inside how the place must look from beyond the chain-link fence that surrounds it: a wide swatch of asphalt in the middle of the city, with dented hoops, a playground at one end, a softball diamond at the other, the whole thing populated by dog walkers, bench sitters, kids, parents, some derelict types, and guys in baggy shorts playing basketball, all in a space officially known as John A. Seravalli Park.

Just then the person I have come to call the Crazy Lady approached me, with an unusual expression on her face.

"Will you take one of these?" she said, handing me a flier. "It's really important."

The Crazy Lady, whose name, I later learned, is Lana, was not, in fact, crazy. She was just very brave, but the two qualities sometimes blur. I started thinking of her as the Crazy Lady when I arrived at the court one afternoon and found her at the center of a mob of basketball players, defending her kids and their friends against what are normally understood to be the laws of the playground.

The issue, as is so often the case, was real estate. There is a point in the afternoon when a critical mass of players have arrived, and the half-court games move over to the full court. Lana's kids were shooting on the full-court basket when they were suddenly overrun by the players, all of them itchy to get their hands on the ball.

Lana has frizzy gray hair, wears sandals and jeans, and smokes cigarettes. Her face often registers a "What in God's name is next?" expression that I associate with city parents. The day of the turf war, I arrived to find her standing in the middle of the full court, a cigarette in one hand, a cell phone in the other, and, like Gandhi on the train in South Africa, refusing to move. Words were exchanged. Voices were raised. Finally, a half-court basket was secured for the kids, and, like refugees given a new homeland, they were ushered to their basket before Lana yielded the full court to the mob.

This autumn day, however, she approached me with a stack of fliers in her arm and an odd look on her face. According to the flier, the Parks Department was considering a proposal to tear up the playground, resurface it with artificial turf, and turn it into a private softball field. A nearby private school would help pay for the renovation. The gates would be padlocked, the ground would be green, and there would be soccer practice by day and Little League games by night. Who could argue with that? Quite a few people, apparently. But the tenor of the flier, and the fact that a community board meeting had been arranged to discuss the proposal, suggested that, unknown to us, wheels had been turning for some time. All summer we had been involved in the drama of our playground while, just like in a horror movie, a huge monster was almost upon us.

Now it's spring. On the first nice day I went down to the court. There was a game in progress at each of the three half-courts, and a crowd of people waiting to play.

Arriving at a basketball court is a seemingly casual thing, but who actually gets to play is determined by a number of Byzantine rituals involving such things as how well known you are to the regulars, how well respected your game is, how you look, what color you are (and there is a very wide range of colors), how you dress, walk, talk.

But these rules are not written down. They are implicit. They incorporate the rules that pertain to the world outside the playground—the rules enforced by the police, for example—but there are variations, additions, and deletions, and no one on hand with a clipboard and a whistle to enforce them.

This is not a gym. One of the more important rules is that, in certain circumstances, there are no rules.

That first day, everyone was in an unusually friendly mood. I slapped people five. Vague communications were made, along the lines of "How you been?," answered by various words and sounds that equated with "Good."

I saw a guy I recognized go by on a bike, a fiercely quick, whippet-thin kid the color of Turkish coffee whom I have privately nicknamed the Assassin, in part because he is so lethal on offense and in part because he usually wears the expression of someone who is prepared to kill you. Most basketball players exist in a state of mild irritation, like magicians who cannot get a certain trick to go just right. Street ball elevates this irritation to a style, and a lot of people on the court sport a homeboy version of the Travis Bickle line "You talkin' to me?" as though they are just waiting for someone to tick them off.

"You been playin' ball this winter?" someone asked the guy on the bike.

"Yeah," he replied. "In a way."

The reply was so conversational that I had a hard time equating it with the nasty style he had on the court, where he usually wore a white do-rag that made him look like a member of the hip-hop division of the Foreign Legion. This day, on his bike, he seemed like a sweet guy only a few years past teenagerdom.

Glancing around the playground, I realized I knew a lot of the guys there. I know if they are good in the clutch or if they choke. I know how they smile when they mean it, and how they smile when they are faking it, and how they look when they are trying desperately not to smile because they just made a great move but don't want to make it look like a big deal.

I know what it takes to stop them and what they'll do to stop me. What I don't know is their names, other than a first name or nickname. I don't know how old they are or how they make a living.

I came to appreciate the strangeness of this dynamic a long time ago, in the events surrounding a guy named Rich. He was a longtime regular at the court on which I grew up playing at Riverside Park on Seventy-Sixth Street. Rich used to arrive in a shroud of silence, carrying a big shoulder bag. He was very fat. Upon arriving, he would stake out a considerable amount of asphalt (a shade of gray as distinctively New York as a yellow taxi) and elaborately change into a pair of immaculate white tube socks. Then came his game sneakers.

Once he got changed, he always made sure he was a captain so he could pick his team. He did this as judiciously as any NBA general manager. The thing about these street games is that if you win, you play again. If you lose, you watch. Considering the time and effort involved in getting to the playground in the first place, there was a lot at stake in winning. Rich wanted to win. Therefore, he always refused to put me on his team.

Rich was a trash-talker. He wore a plastic mouth guard, like a football player, but spent half the game with it sticking halfway out of his mouth as he did his running commentary. The commentary was usually about the ineffectiveness of the man guarding him. He would use his bulk to bounce you out of the way and get room for his shot. After it went in, he would remove his mouthpiece and tell you how useless you were.

It takes no effort for me to recall how Rich's body felt when I banged into him in a game. The sound of his voice, the way he ran, the speed with which he shifted from being caustic to being, if the word can be applied to basketball, sweet: all that comes to mind easily. He's a perfect example of how, on the basketball court, you can know someone intimately and not know him at all.

One day I went to the court, and Rich wasn't there. I didn't notice his absence until I heard some guys talking about him. "When they showed his picture on the late news, I didn't recognize him," one said. "Then I switched to Channel 11 and saw their picture."

It took me a few seconds to realize I had seen Rich that day too. I'd stopped at a newsstand to stare at the picture of a dead body lying in a pool of blood that was on the cover of both the *Daily News* and the *New York*

Post. In spite of the smudgy image, there had been something disturbingly intimate about the picture. Now I knew why.

Rich, it turns out, was a token-booth clerk at the West 145th Street subway station. He was shot dead during a robbery, when he had gone to collect the tokens. He earned $30,000 a year. He worked a 6 a.m.–to–2 p.m. shift, which meant that all those years I had seen him shortly after he got off work.

Meanwhile, nothing changed at the court. The culture of street ball in New York is like the city's population. Some people are fixtures as permanent as a tree. Others show up out of the blue and then, after a week or a month or a couple of years, disappear without explanation, though usually for reasons less tragic than those that explain the disappearance of Rich.

My game got underway.

I had on my team Monsieur M, a skinny man arrived not long ago from Haiti who speaks hip-hop with a French accent. He can jump to the moon, but he has not yet learned not to smile. He doesn't use his smile as a weapon of contempt.

Then there was the Laughing Man. Only a month earlier, he had suffered a dislocated thumb. "I broke my thumb!" he called out, and, in a continuation of the play, ran right out of the playground toward St. Vincent's Hospital. A month later he was back, with white tape around his injured finger, in his irrepressibly good mood.

The Laughing Man has one of those iron-hard upper bodies (he usually plays without a shirt), and he can jump quickly; he's like a socially well-adjusted Dennis Rodman, with a touch of Karl Malone. The Laughing Man is also a father. A little girl who was standing near him one day as he changed into his sneakers and socks announced loudly, "Daddy, those socks stinky!"

Our third member is a young man named D. He has the baggiest shorts on the court and, when he can bring himself to shoot it, a nice jump shot. But in games, with the pressure on, D tends to, shall we say, withdraw. The painful disparity between the basketball opera in his head and the game on the court makes him sullen. He's probably the only guy about whom one could say, "He doesn't shoot enough."

The fourth member of my team is me. At six feet, five and a half inches, with a high school and Division III college career behind me (Vassar!),

I am, in my own way, a basketball poster boy. In every basketball poster there are two essential components: the first is someone flying through the air in the middle of some amazing, gravity-defying move, usually a dunk. The second is the person, often partially obscured, being dunked on. I fulfill the latter role.

We won our first game. Monsieur M was the star of the show, skying for rebounds and hitting his jump shot. The team we beat comprised guys of whom I could give thumbnail sketches, quick scouting reports and some essential details about personality, and whose names I hardly knew.

The next team was a tough, athletic squad that comprised longtime locals, among them the Litigator. His real name was Dennis, but he was the Litigator to me because he was always manipulating the score and arguing calls. Once, when I referred to him as the Litigator out loud, a guy on the sidelines said, "What are you talking about? He works in a bodega."

My team had no litigators. None of us could argue, least of all me. On the court I am mute. What words I do say hardly count as language; a transcript would sound vaguely pornographic: "Yes, yes! That's right! Give it to me! Here! Come on!"

We played hard in our second game. Monsieur M! I loved him! His jump shot looked like a shot put; he'd take two massive dribbles, lift off with both feet, and throw toward the rim, but the shot was falling. The Laughing Man rolled to the hoop, bruising everyone around him; I had my rebounds and short jumpers. Then Monsieur M unleashed a series of his funny jump shots, and we won. I wandered off, exultant. Then, for the first time since last fall, I saw Lana.

Over the autumn and winter, the outlook for the court had gone from bleak to cautiously sunny.

A meeting had been called by Community Board 2 to discuss the fate of the court. The day of the meeting was a spectacular Indian summer day, and the court was mobbed. Each of the half-court baskets had two teams waiting to play, the full court was packed, and no one was paying attention to the fliers about the meeting that had been taped here and there around the park.

But as six o'clock approached, there was a giant mood swing. Some of the regulars said they were going, and at the last moment a large contingent of sweaty guys in shorts headed for a cramped room in an NYU building, where the meeting took place.

"It was immediately apparent that this was an incredible turnout for a Community Board 2 parks and recreation committee hearing, possibly the best-attended hearing the committee had ever seen," a friend emailed afterward. The plan to privatize the court and resurface it with artificial turf was abandoned in the face of community opposition.

As Lana and I chatted, I noticed the new hotel, the w Hotel, that was rapidly rising on a former parking lot across the street from the court. Some of the rooms will have a view of the Meatpacking District, others of the West Village, and still others of Chelsea. Some guests will look out and see, right across the street, a big stretch of not very pretty asphalt on which people are jumping around in baggy shorts, playing basketball. If they see that, they'll know they're in New York.

It was a rosy dusk. The court cleared. I practiced some dunks. I bounced the ball in a trance, vowing to get skinny, to be strong, to move around the city and play at other courts, so that the whole fluctuating but familiar family of basketball junkies who go to Horatio Street don't get too familiar. I promised myself not to disappear too far down the rabbit hole of street basketball, walked in circles bouncing the ball, and took foul shots in the soft and almost gauzy darkening heat. I was wretched, sticky, dirty, thirsty, thrilled. Finally, I went home.

—2003

A year or two after the events described above, a large engineering project commenced. A huge wall was erected across a portion of the park, behind which heavy machinery and large concrete pipes were assembled.

I would learn—years later, when I thought to ask—that this project was part of the building of New York's Tunnel Number 3, a massive, multidecade feat of engineering in the cause of enlarging and improving New York's water system. But at the time it seemed like a dubious incursion, as though the force that wanted to padlock the park would now achieve its ends through more subterranean means—literally in this case, as the project involved building a shaft hundreds of feet into the ground and installing a huge refrigeration unit whose purpose was to freeze the ground as a way of stabilizing it. I didn't know anything about that at the time. I simply observed that the playground, still open to the public, had been slightly maimed—there were now only two half-court baskets instead of three. An invisible layer of grit and sand covered the ground. Or at least it felt that way. But the same general population, many of whom came from the housing projects in Chelsea, and all of whom belonged to the large, amorphous congregation of basketball, still used it.

The water main project made the remaining open space, a kind of asphalt meadow lined with backboards and hoops, seem even more transitory and negotiable than it already was. It had once been a softball field, if one can call an expanse of asphalt a field. This was its own source of contention, as you always had to keep one ear alert for the thwack of a long ball while playing basketball, so you could look to see if a softball was streaking toward your head. Every now and then an especially hard-hit ball would clear the high chain-link fence and plop into the playground where babies and toddlers roamed, and I think this was what eventually got the softball games banned.

This vast expanse of asphalt had always functioned as a kind of geographical ellipsis in the self-protecting bafflements of the West Village's syntax, but now it felt like a prelude to its own destruction. The fact that the digging and the machines were all hidden behind a huge concrete wall of a raw gray color was probably better than there not being any wall at all, but it nevertheless felt like a violation. There was a faint echo of the Berlin Wall in this wall's scale and color.

After a couple of years, the water main project was finally finished. At some point thereafter came the renovation that destroyed the whole place in the name of saving it. What is amazing to me, in hindsight, was how the slow-motion nature of events had the effect of making it all imperceptible. When I read the following passage, in Louis Menand's book of cultural criticism, American Studies, I thought of the park:

> Everyone has had the experience of driving past work crews on the highway. You see five guys sipping coffee and watching one man with a pick while he hacks halfheartedly at some gravel. You suspect that in five minutes the man with the pick will also be on a coffee break. Six months later, there's a new road....
>
> History is the same. The critical massing of conditions that enables a particular way of life to come into being is almost impossible to detect while it is happening, and so is its deterioration. The world just rolls over, without anyone noticing exactly when, and a new set of circumstances is put in place.

The park closed down entirely for about two years. When it reopened, it was still a place to play basketball, or so it seemed. The three hoops where the half-court games were played—which had faced west—had been moved and now faced north. More important, they had been lowered, to be more suitable for little kids. The full court was still there, the huge blank face of the building behind it rising up, but they reoriented it from north–south to east–west. I am sure someone had a reason, but the effect was to uproot the sense of place, of continuity. The lowered rims were a cruel irony; seemingly a concession to the needs of kids, they were in practice a concession to parents. And a certain kind of parent. All of it raised the question: who was this gleaming park for?

I discussed this with someone who had played there, and he spoke emphatically about how they had ruined the court by building these low rims "for kids." He said the word contemptuously, though in fairness to him I don't think the contempt was for kids so much as for their coddling: making the rims lower, coming down to the kids' level, as opposed to the kids reaching to attain the strength to shoot on a regulation rim. That they rearranged the placement of these hoops added to the feeling that part of what was going on was a complete erasure and eradication of the old world of that court. What resulted was a variation of Yogi Berra's famous remark about a popular bar: "No one goes there anymore, it's too popular." The variation being that after the park's renovation, no one went there to play basketball.

When I encountered a line in a Ross Gay poem about a beloved playground being closed down,

> because of complaints to the city
> from the condo owners
> across the street
> who did not want to hear god forbid
>
> all that Negro gathering
> and celebration and care and delight
> every goddamn weekend morning,

I wondered if that formulation applied to the Court on Horatio Street. But by then I had moved out of the neighborhood.

Spree

Sometimes, late at night, I Google Latrell Sprewell. I don't really know why. Some vague longing. It's been going on since he slipped out of the NBA, and the public eye, in 2005. At first I was looking for news of his return. After a while I was looking for any news at all. One would have thought that the recent first-round matchup between the Heat and the Knicks would have been the occasion for an update, but this was not the case.

Sprewell's playing days ended abruptly. The cause was a self-inflicted wound. He once broke his hand under mysterious circumstances while he was a Knick, but this was more symbolic and therefore more damaging: he blithely turned down a three-year contract of $21 million from the Minnesota Timberwolves, saying—brace yourself—that he had "a family to feed." The quote has been the gift that keeps on giving to every moralizing sportswriter in America. It was like sending them a dartboard with his face on it. They still have it on the wall, years later.

The "family to feed" debacle served to return to prominence the story of Sprewell choking P. J. Carlesimo, his coach on the Golden State Warriors. In 1997 he was suspended for the rest of the season and then traded to New York.

Sprewell experienced a renaissance with the New York Knicks, and the Knicks experienced a renaissance with Sprewell. There are many New Yorkers who love Spree, but it's a silent majority, a strangely private love, perhaps because of its irrationality, which I now want to express.

Sprewell's greatest moment with the Knicks was back in the news a few weeks ago, when the Knicks and Miami Heat were going head to head. The teams met in 1999 under similar circumstances: the Heat were heavily favored, the season was shortened by a strike, and a new star was taking control of a Knicks team (Sprewell then, Carmelo Anthony now). Then and now, there was an opaque power struggle in the Knicks organization that resulted in somebody getting fired. This happens practically every year with the Knicks, but it still bears mentioning. In 1999 it was General Manager Ernie Grunfeld; this year it was Coach Mike D'Antoni.

Because of these echoes, video clips from that earlier series have been wafting through *SportsCenter* and around the internet. The images were a little jarring, partly because many of the stars are still with us. Pat Riley, whose shrewd face has now taken on a patina of grandfatherly sagacity, pops onto the screen in all his sleek, cuckolding glory, the betrayer who notified the Knicks of his departure by fax—and left them for Miami.

Patrick Ewing, the key figure of the modern Knicks era, is seen gamely soldiering through the season only to be sidelined with an injury when the playoffs began. As if his mythic aura of thwarted promise wasn't strong enough, he went down with a ruptured Achilles.

And Jeff Van Gundy! Now he's a humorous, blunt-talking television commentator comfortable enough with his baldness to make self-mocking commercials about toupees. Back then, he was a prodigy and a protégé of Riley, for whom Jeff's brother Stan worked in Miami. I was happy to see, on national television, the old clip of Van Gundy clinging to Alonzo Mourning's leg like an attacking Chihuahua while Mourning exchanged blows with Charles Oakley at center court, in the Garden. There was a brief shot of him just afterward, uncharacteristically aflame, his hair mussed. Hair? Van Gundy had JFK hair. By this, I don't mean that his hair was like JFK's hair but rather that the press treated Van Gundy's ghastly looking hair implants with the same discretion that they once treated JFK's affairs.

But the most significant player from this era has also been the most conspicuously absent from the retrospective: Latrell. It's almost as though he is an unmentionable, unassimilable figure.

Even in basketball terms he's hard to discuss. The Knicks had never really had a player like Latrell. John Starks, his closest antecedent, had some of that reckless abandon—hence "The Dunk"—but one rooted for him in part out of a sense of his sweetness. Latrell was in some unclassified category. Though obviously not nearly as offensively skilled as the all-time great wingmen of his generation, Michael Jordan and Kobe Bryant, he had comparable athleticism, played defense at Jordan's level, and, most important, had a wildly conspicuous will to power that was an inspiration to anyone who watched him play.

I still remember when I first saw his game—a fast break in an All-Star Game in the mid-1990s. He had an Afro, was wire thin, and didn't so much dunk the ball as attack the rim like some kind of velociraptor who wanted to tear it off and take it elsewhere to eat. I imagined him cackling as he ran back on defense. It was a bit frightening.

But to understand the importance of Latrell, and the feelings he evokes, one must go not just to the videotape but to the mood of the franchise, and the city, in 1999.

I remember meeting with a friend a few weeks into the new millennium, a few months before the bottom fell out of the dot-com boom. The Knicks season was underway. Ewing was back for what turned out to be his last season as a Knick. Sprewell, already canonized, was leading. To say that he had rehabilitated his image from the choking incident is to miss the point. A lot of people liked him for it. It was a breathtaking act of defiance, and it fit the mood of the city at the time.

My friend worked at a Silicon Alley start-up. I had gone to see him for advice about a website. He listened to me politely. When I was finished talking, he leaned forward with a gleam in his eye, as though he was going to impart some deep bit of wisdom. "Choke the coach," he said matter-of-factly. He repeated it about ten times, pounding his fist, getting to his feet, getting louder each time. It reminded me of the song "Alice's Restaurant," when everyone starts jumping around yelling, "I want to kill!"

He wasn't even a basketball fan.

The Knicks had ascended to unexpected heights in the spring of 1999, the first eighth seed to advance all the way to the finals. They lost in five games to the San Antonio Spurs, whose imposing front line of David Robinson and Tim Duncan was nicknamed the Twin Towers.

Larry Johnson, Marcus Camby, Allan Houston, and the rest of the team were all integral to the run. When Houston's shot bounced on the front of the rim and dropped in to win the Miami series, he ran the length of the court before allowing himself to exhale and throw a roundhouse punch, as though knocking out once and for all his reputation for being soft. But the glorious march to the finals was driven by Latrell. He set the tone.

Using a word as nebulous as *tone* when assessing a basketball player is almost heretical these days. It's the era of analytics, money ball, and basketball conferences at MIT. I'm confident that the numbers would bear out my claim about Latrell's significance, at least to a point. But what makes me love him goes beyond basketball.

There was something about Latrell that was from another time. It's not so much that he had an old soul. It's more that his game, and especially his game face, was Old Testament. There was something harsh and unforgiving about him. He had a face that had seen the plagues and the parting of the Red Sea. He was leading the Knicks out of the desert.

I somehow got on the subject of Sprewell with the author Scott Spencer, who told me that he had pitched Sprewell as a subject to Jann Wenner back when Sprewell was a Knick. He said that Wenner lowered his forehead to his hand and said, "You're the fourth middle-aged Jew who has pitched Sprewell to me this week."

All this is old news. The new news about Latrell, when it pops up, is always bad, sometimes comically, surreally so, such as when it was reported, in 2008, that Sprewell's yacht, *Milwaukee's Best*, had run aground. He reportedly refused to call for a tow in the conventional manner and insisted on hiring a fishing trawler to help pull it free.

Otherwise, there is little comic relief: the mother of his children sued. His house, or one of them, was foreclosed on. There are similar tidbits. Otherwise, nothing. Latrell, that soft-spoken, ferocious savior, has retreated into a silence that is tinged with grandeur for its totality.

His legacy in the imagination of the sportswriters of America is the choke and the quote. But when I quiz fellow Knicks fans on their favorite players, they usually mention Spree. There is something about him that provokes devotion.

I always excitedly ask them why, as though his appeal is a mystery. Could it have something to do with the fact that when he returned to Madison Square Garden after he had been traded to the Timberwolves, he turned to the courtside seats of Knicks owner James Dolan, whose ineptness is exceeded only by his control-freak tendencies, and unleashed a stream of invective and curses that was apparently shocking in its vulgarity? That he did this with a minute to go in the game after draining a three-point shot? That he did it on the way to a win in which he scored the most points ever by a former Knick playing back in the Garden for the first time since his trade? James Dolan has not done a great job as owner of the Knicks. One senses that very few people say this to his face. Latrell did.

All of his virtues were most on display in Game 5 of the NBA Finals against San Antonio in 1999, when the Knicks seemed to be lost. There were a couple of possessions toward the end when there seemed to be no hope except in the eyes and the face of Latrell, who coolly drained a couple of threes to keep them in the game. Shouldn't one's cherished memories of games be of victories? They lost that game and that series.

On the last play, the game still up for grabs, Latrell got a difficult pass under the basket and went up for a last-second fallaway shot as Duncan and Robinson converged on him, arms extended. He missed. In that last moment you could hardly see Latrell. The tips of his fingers, his legs kicking out as he fell backward, like a man falling overboard, trying to do the impossible. Failing, but trying. Doing a very good job. No one writes about that. The shot bounced off the rim. Then it was over.

—2012

In the years since this piece was written Sprewell has emerged into public view. That the specific context of his emergence is shot through with the twin strains of violence and the incompetence of Knicks owner James Dolan is not exactly surprising, but the symmetry should be acknowledged: Sprewell was at last welcomed back into the Knicks family, and into Madison Square Garden, literally into a front-row seat, when Dolan was frantically trying to disentangle himself from the fallout of the Charles Oakley scandal. This featured Dolan's security forces physically subduing and handcuffing Oakley, the former enforcer during the Knicks' Ewing-era glory years in the 1990s, in the middle of a Knicks game at the Garden. The crowd booed as Oakley was led away. Oakley's offense, roughly summarized, was being disrespectful to Dolan from his seat in the Garden. Surely nothing as caustic and profane as what Sprewell shouted to Dolan's face as a player, raining buckets on the Knicks on his return, but sufficient to create an ugly scene. As a way of softening up his image, Dolan summoned Sprewell. On a visit to the Garden in January 2020, my first visit in years, I visited the gift shop. The vintage jerseys most prominently displayed were those of Ewing and Sprewell.

More recently, I found myself at an event next to a young professor of dance who had grown up in Milwaukee. When I discovered this fact, I introduced the topic of Latrell. She listened to me talk about him for a minute or two and then, a cool customer, mentioned that though she didn't know him personally, her family and his family were acquainted. When I expressed interest in this fact, she went on to explain that the black community in Milwaukee is very small. She explained that it is contained in a space that is physically isolated from the rest of city, making it difficult to commute to jobs by public transportation. She said that it is severely policed. She had family members on the Milwaukee police force, and this was helpful during the many times she was pulled over while driving her car, but she was nevertheless frequently pulled over for no reason. She said she hadn't realized the degree to which she had internalized this as normal until she moved to Los Angeles and found herself much more relaxed while driving as a black woman. All of this, she said, led to feelings of pent-up rage and also self-sabotage. She didn't present any of it by way of excusing or even explaining Latrell. She wasn't terribly interested in basketball, though she did say that Giannis Antetokounmpo and the Bucks had been a huge source of pride. But she felt the need to point these things out. An accomplished dancer, she had started ballet at thirteen. I had mentioned, when we first started talking, that thirteen was late to start ballet.

"But I had a talent," she replied. Now she segued from the idea of self-sabotage—"I have a family to feed"—to those ballet lessons. She said that for the first weeks that her mother drove her the long distance to the ballet school, she would get dropped off but wouldn't go to class. Instead, she hid in the bathroom.

"And what did your mother say about that?" I asked.

"Oh! She never knew. Another kind of self-sabotage," she said.

And, she added, she did eventually get out of the bathroom and start going to class, where, it went without saying, the aforementioned talent was discovered.

Damian Lillard's Game-Winning Shot

The nature of basketball is such that its most cathartic moment—when the ball goes decisively and irretrievably through the hoop—is the same every time. The ball piercing the basket is both a discrete event and a continuous waterfall of motion that, for active players, is constant throughout their careers. They shoot in practice; they shoot in the game; they shoot and shoot and shoot. The motion becomes so ingrained in their muscle memory that the gesture requires only its activation; everything else—the elevation, the aiming at the basket, the cocking of the elbow, and the follow-through of the hand—is programmed.

I found myself thinking about the waterfall of shots in the wake of one of the more dramatic ones in recent NBA history: Damian Lillard, of the Portland Trail Blazers, hitting the game-winning, series-ending shot against the Oklahoma City Thunder in Game 5. He shot the ball from thirty-seven feet out, with 1.7 seconds on the clock, over the outstretched arms of Paul George, one of the league's best defenders, and it splashed through the net as the buzzer sounded.

The blocking of the play resembled a mostly empty chessboard at the endgame stage: Lillard is alone near half-court while the four other Blazers and their defenders are spread out on the perimeter, far away. Lillard looks toward the teammate nearest to him on his left, Al-Farouq Aminu (the speaker of the most chillingly profound remark I have ever heard directly from an NBA player: "Your body is your business"), and summons him. The conventional play here would be to set a screen so that a lesser defender has to switch over to Lillard.

But then Lillard changes his mind and waves Aminu off, not with an extravagant arm movement but with a smaller gesture, using his right hand. The first signal to Aminu is a beckoning: come here. But then, with the compact precision of an assembly-line robot, he rotates his wrist and, making the same motion but now in reverse, waves him away. As with so much that Lillard does, the whole thing happens so quickly that Aminu barely has a chance to react.

Now Lillard and George are alone near the center court. Then Lillard does the thing that has fascinated me most about his basketball style. Even more than his stellar drives to the basket where he curls into himself, only to extend his arms out at the last possible moment to release the shot; even more than the remarkable efficiency of motion in his piercing, long-range jump shot; even more than his Swiss Army knife versatility—in 2014 he became the first player to participate in every single event (the skills challenge, the dunk contest, the three-point-shooting contest, the rising-stars challenge) in an All-Star Game—what has most captured my imagination about Lillard is the way that he will sometimes stand very still with the ball. There is a tensile, almost vibratory quality to this momentary pause.

The shot that he took in Game 5 came off the dribble, but it, too, had this quality of pressure accumulated, unseen and then seen. But not believed. Everything about the shot made you question your own eyes. This included the sight of Lillard, normally so taciturn, turning around to wave goodbye to the Oklahoma City Thunder. The wave might endure as a more iconic image than the shot itself. The whole arena is on its feet in a frenzy; his teammates are all rushing toward him, as are some members of the crowd in the front row, but like a surfer with the wave closing around him, he is still in his own space when he turns to wave goodbye.

Lillard is a three-time All-Star and a first-team NBA point guard, and yet he has remained a stealthy figure who always seems to be hovering just outside a charmed inner circle of superstars. Part of the drama of his shot involved the way that Oklahoma City's two stars, Paul George and Russell Westbrook, have, in particular, treated Lillard with a palpable disdain. A further ripple in the iconic-image department came in the form of a photograph taken just as Lillard extricated himself from the swarm of delirious players who had piled on top of him. The look on his face is so inscrutable and rich. There is a hint of joy, without question, and a hint of defiance, since all these celebrations, even the ones the amateurs make alone, when it's just them and the ball and a hoop and the endless narrative loop of them taking and making shots, are stories of redemption.

Yet behind the singularity of Lillard's shot itself was the endless waterfall of shots taken in practice, chucked up during games, the shots discussed, watched on film, dreamed of with either pleasure or horror—but mostly just shots, "getting up shots," practicing shots, over and over, endlessly. Repetition as religion. The game continues; the shots go up and splash down like water. But for a moment, after that shot, the waterfall ceased. It was so definitive as to briefly stop basketball time.

—2019

The City Game

On the way in from the airport, late one night, my taxi lowered into the Manhattan landscape and came to a stop at a red light at Ninety-Seventh Street, just off Second Avenue. There is a playground there, and when I looked out the window, I saw a man shooting a basketball by himself. The court was a barren, lonely place at that hour, lit by some nearby streetlights, but his presence redeemed it. He was a heavy man, dressed in gray sweats, and for a moment I imagined that he was a once talented player who had gone to seed, now moved by some personal crisis to revisit his old skills near midnight.

After a moment of watching, it seemed clear that he had never had much in the way of skills. I then imagined that he had recently made a resolution to lose weight. He was moving quickly to get his own rebound, dribbling energetically, and I decided that this late-night cameo appearance signaled that he was in the manic phase of his resolution, that he was pushing himself too hard, that he would diet and work out like this for four days and then pull a muscle. By the end of the week, he would be eating pound cake out of the box.

For once, I was grateful for an interminable red light. The man was undaunted, rhythmic. His movements suggested some interior fantasy was in progress. I wondered what it was as the cab pulled away.

Location is important in basketball, and yet it's not—you can play anywhere, and in the act of playing you forget where you are. I make a point of playing basketball whenever I travel to a new place. There is an outdoor court in Paradise Valley, Montana, that has stayed with me. And there is a hoop in a parking lot in Phnom Penh, next to an apartment building with balconies on which, as I shot around there, in 1994, little kids appeared. More and more of these kids materialized as my workout continued, all of them practicing their English, which seemed to consist of one word: "Hello." They murmured it, softly at first, then louder. It was like playing in front of a flock of gently cooing birds that slowly, gradually, morphed into crazy American basketball fans, all of them shouting, "Hello!"

Basketball is a sport that contains many games. The one we watch on television is only one variation. Basketball can be played alone or in groups. Indoors or outdoors. Full court, half-court, or no court. The NBA players who play abroad must adjust to the rules of the league's European counterpart, FIBA. (The famously taciturn Tim Duncan offered his two cents on this variation of the international game at the end of the 2004 Olympics: "FIBA sucks.") Was the guy I saw shooting around by himself in the dark on Ninety-Seventh Street playing basketball? To quote a favorite phrase of the former Knick John Starks, "Most definitely."

When another former Knick, Bill Bradley, ran for Senate in New Jersey, his television commercials ended with him tossing a crumpled piece of paper into a tiny basketball hoop affixed to a garbage pail. Is throwing something into a trash can—with or without a tiny hoop attached—basketball? You could make the case. In the documentary *Doin' It in the Park: Pick-Up Basketball, NYC*, made by Robert (Bobbito) García and Kevin Couliau, an old-timer in Harlem recalls seeing the local playground courts so crowded with serious players that the kids were forced into a kind of apprenticeship, in which they would shoot hoops into a garbage can off to the side.

The culture of New York City playground basketball looms large in the history of the NBA. Several generations of the game's greatest players owe their basketball education, in part, to New York's Department of Parks and Recreation. So it was appropriate that the NBA used the occasion of the 2015 All-Star Game, which was played at Madison Square Garden, to commemorate this fact with a magnificently detailed map (and an app) titled "A History of New York City Basketball." The map is filled with notable places, and each of the five boroughs has its own section, along with special categories for "point guards" and "playgrounds." It seems right that these subjects should be highlighted. Street ball and ball handling are entwined. New York is, or was, known for its fierce point guards. The video takes you through the history: Bob Cousy, Dick McGuire, Tiny Archibald, Pearl Washington, Rod Strickland, Kenny Smith, Kenny Anderson, Mark Jackson, Rafer Alston, Stephon Marbury, Jamaal Tinsley, Kemba Walker.

The segment on Manhattan is mostly focused on the borough's most famous product, introduced as perhaps the greatest player ever to play the game: Kareem Abdul-Jabbar. When he says, "I was raised in Manhattan, so I learned the game right in the heart of the city," it is understood, even before the clip cuts away to a shot of the court at 140th Street and St. Nicholas Avenue, that he is referring to his local playground. "I never consciously made a connection between basketball and how it is tied to life in New York City," he says, while the camera pans across the court in morning light. "But I grew up in it, and I was part of it." The implication is that the playground is the primal scene of Abdul-Jabbar's basketball initiation and education.

As much as I enjoyed the history lesson from the NBA, it further crystallized my feeling that this was a historical moment that has been eclipsed. Street ball in New York is in decline. I have observed, in the past decade, one playground after another—where, once, you could have shown up in the mid- to late afternoon and found a group of fairly skilled players of different ages battling—become depopulated. I am not talking about a mass extinction. There are still lots of playgrounds with lots of good players—but fewer playgrounds, and fewer players, and the ones who show up seem older. Kareem's playground, for example, had just a few desultory players shooting by themselves on a recent afternoon. A river that runs low will sometimes run dry.

That the basketball courts of New York's playgrounds are not as popular as they once were is an observation based firmly on evidence that is anecdotal and totally unscientific. Furthermore, even this evidence is mostly limited to Manhattan. So perhaps these are all Manhattan problems. When I read a report in the *Times* on the people who buy condos in the Time Warner Center—in brief, extremely rich and not from here—I wasn't thinking about basketball, but it now occurs to me that the Time Warner Center is less than ten blocks from the projects that provided a fair number of the players at my own childhood basketball court, in Riverside Park at Seventy-Sixth Street. Can billionaires play ball? That is a different city game.

I am not claiming that the city's courts are empty, exactly—up on St. Nicholas Terrace, about ten blocks from where Kareem played, there was a respectable half-court game underway when I visited, but no one had next. One court over, however, was the scene of a roiling game of full court, comprising mostly kids. The place was not abandoned, yet this was not the world of highly competitive basketball in which so many NBA talents were forged. The remodeled courts on Horatio Street and Hudson (where Joakim Noah, age fourteen, a human pencil with an Afro smushed under a backward baseball cap which he wore throughout the game, dunked on me) are now devoid of pickup basketball in the afternoons. That court had been closed for renovations for some time, so perhaps it's a special case. The Tompkins Square Park courts have been rearranged and now seem depleted; the courts at Twentieth and Second Avenue, where a lot of the Tompkins Square Park crowd sought refuge, are now barren.

I don't even live in New York anymore. I'm there for a few weeks over the winter holidays and for a couple of months in the summer. Was I being paranoid? Was this just nostalgia, a projection of that terrible undertow of feeling that the world of your childhood is vanishing, which is unique to no sport or city?

I can argue against my own case: the court in Central Park (there is one, on the north side of the Great Lawn) is busy; the new courts down by Battery Park City, on the river, both half-court and full court, are populated by players from all over the city, as are the courts in the magnificent Brooklyn Bridge Park. Yet the feeling that I've gotten from playing playground basketball in New York in the past several years is that something has changed. The mystery concerns the youth. Where are the youth? Playing video games at home? Playing soccer?

My life as a street-ball player began when I was twelve years old. It was the middle of winter. I was at the basketball court in Riverside Park, at Seventy-Sixth Street. It was a bright day and freezing cold, the sort of weather where enormous sheets of ice might be floating on the Hudson. It's so cold that the asphalt on which I bounce the ball is dusted white with salt and frost. It catches the sun's glare. I look down at the ball, and at my hands, which are buried in black wool gloves. Around me, a vast expanse of empty courts. I see these images, and the white clouds from my breath, as though I were watching Super 8 footage. Sunstruck, silent, magical—it's freezing cold, but I am lost in a fantasy of buzzer-beating shots, variations on the same imagined heroics, the naked orange rim framing a circle of blue sky, which I seek to fill over and over. The hypnotic, syncopated sound of the bouncing ball.

I was on the junior-varsity basketball team and had a number of years playing in school gyms. But this was the first time that I thought of that patch of asphalt as a resource in my life, a place to which I could retreat and seek solace. On that freezing-cold day in 1977, I was all alone.

Perhaps the city game is in eclipse because the talent pool is now global. As the journalist Rick Telander showed us in his 1974 book, *Heaven Is a Playground*, there was a moment in the early 1970s when colleges around the country realized that they could tap into New York City's street-ball talent. In the ESPN *30 for 30* episode on Bernard King, he recalled seeing an assistant coach from the University of Tennessee show up at the Fort Greene housing projects, where King lived. He peered out the window at the man in the plaid jacket and thought, "Does this guy have any idea of where he is?" This recruiting revolution took place, at least in part, owing to the efforts of Rodney Parker, a playground-basketball impresario whose day job was scalping tickets at Mets and Knicks games and who became a kind of unofficial agent, working the phones and shopping local New York City talent to college coaches around the country. Previously, they recruited in their own region.

This exporting of playground talent from New York to the provinces no longer happens, or maybe it is no longer conspicuous. Why? Perhaps the very thing that once made New York ball players so special—their moves, their toughness, their creativity in getting into the paint—is now, somehow, a hindrance. In *Doin' It in the Park*, García and Couliau postulate that New York produced so many great ball-handling guards because New York is the birthplace of the improvised game "21," which is a kind of basketball version of "kill the carrier." Toughness and singularity of vision are what the city breeds in its players.

You see basketball courts everywhere in New York. They are prehistoric manifestations of the city—like old-growth forests. But they did not grow. Someone put them there. The person who put most of them there—the unlikely patron saint of New York as basketball mecca—was Robert Moses. According to Alex Garvin, author of *The Planning Game*, New York has more public parks, by far, than any other city in the country. More than Chicago, which built a lot of playgrounds. More than Los

Angeles. Twenty-five percent of New York's territory is devoted to public parks, the largest percentage of any city in America.

In *Doin' It in the Park*, García and Couliau interview scores of players from multiple generations, all of whom strive to find words for what makes street ball special. The speakers are not famous, exactly, but we understand them to be legends, if only from their nicknames: Shammgod, Sundance, Homicide, Fly. We hear from God Shammgod, famous for inventing a dribble move that bears his name, who declares, "I never had a more rush, to this day, since the first time I played street basketball." Kenny "The Jet" Smith says, "My most vivid memory . . . EVER . . . is the first day I won on the three-on-three in the back."

My first winter of dribbling in gloves gave way to spring. Other people appeared at the court in Riverside Park. I was tall, skinny, uncoordinated. Against common sense and good judgment, I tried to play in these games. I am still trying. I felt as if I had immigrated to another country and had no choice but simply to marinate in this foreign culture until I understood it and was accepted. It's been a long wait.

I played with guys whose nicknames were Birdie, Puppet, Red, Vio. I would arrive at the court and ask who had next. When I found that person, I would say, "You have your five?"

They would usually nod, yes, and sometimes look me straight in the eye as though they were hoping I grasped that this was a bald-faced lie and wanted to see the insult register in my expression. But I came back. There was one guy, Rudy, who was a writer for TV. He always seemed a bit depressed. It was a loud, buoyant scene but also crazed, somehow.

Birdie was a kind of basketball dandy—a very good shot, quick, hated contact, danced away from it. Puppet was a wild delinquent with athletic talent. (I have not the slightest idea why he was called Puppet. I never dared ask.) Red was an old alcoholic who talked trash nonstop, wore outrageously large kneepads, and had a curious glamour around him and his creaky game; in his insistence on getting the ball, there was a suggestion of long-past glory, which he could still, now and then, approach. Vio was loud, very good in a Charles Barkley sort of way—strong, aggressive, constantly talking. He stopped showing up at some point. A year or so later, I heard that he had been thrown down an elevator shaft. He survived, I was told, but his legs didn't.

My role in this game was as a kind of crash-test dummy—though with a mouth. Once in a while, I got punched. Sometimes, dunked on. But sometimes people would offer me tips. Keep the ball above your head! Don't dribble! I was always told to go down low. It was as though the post—that spot on the court near the basket—was a prison. It took me twenty years to break out with an assist from the Unicorns and my own dogged practice from behind the three-point line. Meanwhile, people still talk to me as though I am a project. I don't know why. I used to hate it. Now I like it. It makes me feel as if I still have upside. Upside is not optimism; it's potential. What you do with it hangs in the balance. The story is not finished. Do you have heart?

I didn't have heart. What I had was a kind of dogged masochism that kept me coming back. What is it about basketball? Alexander Wolff, in his book *Big Game, Small World*, reports on this addictive mystery at the heart of the game, first observed by its founder, James Naismith, who walked past a young person throwing a ball into a basket and, an hour later, saw the same boy, still shooting. "I stopped and asked him why he was practicing so long," Naismith wrote. "The boy answered that he did not know, but that he just liked to see if he could make a basket every time he threw the ball."

I kept throwing myself into this maelstrom. I would show up, ask who had next, be told by various people that they had their team, only to discover that they were holding out for better players. This was my idea of fun? It's almost like some part of me craved being defeated and abused. But at the same time, I got better. I survived. It taught me something— how to be a jerk, in part. But other, more valuable things too. Certain ball-handling moves, flow, postures, phrases ("You reach, I teach"). Most of all, the pleasure in the flow of the game, the unruly sense of possibility in a world with no immediate adult supervision, where anything could happen. My favorite scene in *Doin' It in the Park* is the first one, when a fierce game of one-on-one draws a crowd. Among them is a loud, funny guy who could be described as a comedian, a heckler, a drunk guy, or a dangerous individual. He paces, shouts, makes a fool of himself. He is funny but also a bit scary. The sense of being in the presence of some unmanaged force, in a place where there is no front desk at which to complain, is upsetting and kind of thrilling.

Compare this to a scene from the summer of 2015 in Riverside Park, at Seventy-Sixth Street, on a Saturday, late morning, a time when the place was once packed with players and games. Now it was empty except for two groups. One was an old, lean firecracker taking shots; he popped an Achilles a while back, he told me, and no longer plays, but my impression from his movements was that he was once pretty good. I shot around with him while, a few courts away, Rob Sergeant, a formidable figure, who once played professional basketball in Europe, worked out a kid who was maybe twelve, or ten, or eight, with no apparent physical gifts. I had spoken with Sergeant before, amazed to see him doing a thriving business coaching schmucks like the former me for eighty dollars an hour.

Would I have been a better basketball player had I received one-on-one personal training from a top-level athlete as opposed to being smacked around endlessly and trash-talked by Rich, Otto, Tweety, Vio, Red, and Puppet? Probably. And yet something about this picture seemed off. My daughter wandered over, and somehow Nelson, the guy I was shooting with, got onto the subject of stickball, which he explained to her, and in so doing conjured a teeming, unsupervised world of childhood. It sounded as remote, now, as it would have been for me, as a kid, to hear of women with parasols and men with wide-brimmed hats.

The moment when I first glimpsed this problem has stayed with me: it was a few years ago, and I was taking my daughter to camp at Riverside Church, the home of a famous Amateur Athletic Union team, the Hawks, who are enough of an icon that they get a dot on the NBA's All-Star map. I was locking up my bike when three young guys sauntered past, lanky, lean, age fourteen or fifteen. They wore socks and open-toed athletic sandals and baggy shorts and had bags over their shoulders—the basketball-prodigy look. The "I don't play on concrete because it hurts your knees" look. I won't disparage any kid with potential for wanting to protect their assets. As Al-Farouq Aminu said, "Your body is your business."

The idea that the talent should avoid the concrete playgrounds isn't new: Bernard King never played at the Tillary Street courts up the street from where he lived; his brother Albert, the former NBA player, did. Something about the saunter of those young ballers made me follow them into the church lobby. I saw the staircase they took, and after dropping off my daughter at camp, I wound my way through the maze of hallways until I found myself at a small window overlooking a modest-sized basketball court. A bunch of players of different sizes were being put through a rigorous workout by a coach.

Ashton Coughlin—who played basketball for Collegiate, then Wesleyan, and was, at the time, working as a coach at Riverside Church—wandered down the hall just then, and I stopped him to ask a question. As punishment for chatting with me that day, he has had to deal with me writing to him every year or so with more questions and propositions about the mystery of youth vanishing from the city game. The answer, clearly, in addition to the influx of foreign billionaires at the Time Warner Center and everywhere else in New York, and video games, and whatever else, is that the players who are really interested in basketball are not playing on the playground. They are in the basketball version of pre-med.

But are all these guys enrolled in the basketball equivalent of pre-med really talented? Or are there other motives for funneling so many kids into this pre-professional structure? "The professionalization of the game is definitely part of it," Ashton wrote in response to my most recent volley of questions and theories. He pointed out that there is money for more people in organized sports and that there is none in street ball. "Coaches tell parents and their kids—even the ones who suck—'Hey, come work out with me.... Come to this camp.... Join this team,'" Ashton wrote. Such programs, he added, can make significant amounts of money by "taking kids from street ball and putting them in a 'safe,' organized environment."

He added, "It's hard for anyone, especially kids, to turn down an opportunity from someone saying, 'Hey, you're special. I believe in you. Let me help you improve.'"

And yet there is something about basketball's spirit, perhaps more so than any other sport, that seems to resist the professionalization of the game.

I was recently seated on a porch at a Mardi Gras party filled with children, and beside me, in another rocking chair, was a very large fellow who was also taking a break. His name, I learned, was Tommy. He was from Alabama and had a demolition company. It turns out that Tommy had two sons who played football at Alabama and then in the National Football League. Both were linemen. Their careers are over now, and I asked how they handled the transition, physically, out of being a professional athlete. Which is to say I asked, as delicately as possible, if they got fat. He said one did and one didn't, and then, somehow, we got on a riff about football and basketball. "Football, especially if you are a lineman, is something you have to approach as work," he said. "And basketball, I always thought, was something you play."

—2015

Recently, while rolling along in bumper-to-bumper traffic on the West Side Highway, I thought I heard the voice of Giannis Antetokounmpo. But when I turned to look at the guy in the car next to me, chatting on the phone with his window down, it was not the two-time Most Valuable Player and, at that moment, recent Finals MVP *and champion. But it sounded like him. Similar accent. It put me in mind of my visit to the ancestral Kareem courts. On the day I went and played there, I played in a half-court game with a guy who, at one point, swung the ball low after he picked up his dribble on the way to a layup and said, "I learned that from John Wall at his camp." He was good. And in evoking Wall, he was evoking a blue chip name who had come through the blue chip factory. Looking away from the guy who could have been Giannis, my thoughts drifted to the adjoining court, where a bunch of young kids had been playing a chaotic, full-court game that mostly involved everyone sprinting up and down the court and heaving the ball at the basket. Fun, barely controlled chaos. But it wasn't really basketball.*

I somehow got the impression—I may have asked a bystander, or maybe it was something about the language being spoken—that these kids were mostly from Senegal. I watched them for thirty seconds, if that, and went on my way. They were having fun, but it didn't occur to me that such a game would produce a basketball player who might go on to play at the highest level of the game. Six years later I was sure it was Giannis Antetokounmpo stuck in traffic next to me.

I had seen him at the NBA *Africa party at the 2014 All-Star Game. He was pointed out to me across a dark room full of* NBA *luminaries. Giannis standing beside his brothers and his father. I had looked at him closely, observed his skinny youth accentuated by the way the sleeves of his jacket were too short, revealing his bony wrists. Keep your eye on that guy, I was told back in 2014.*

Now I was so steeped in Giannis, his game, his smile, his story, his voice, that I might have mistaken a guy stuck in traffic for him—though in fairness, Giannis has always been a man of the street, literally, in his youth, as a street vendor and then as a young player, famously running through the streets on his way to practice his rookie year because he had just wired the entirety of his first paycheck back to his family and had no money left over for a taxi. But then it occurred to me that the accent of the guy in the car next to me was a lot like the voices I heard in that chaotic game up on the Kareem Abdul-Jabbar ancestral playground (only a mile or so from where I was in that moment) and that the chaotic, free-flowing game, full of laughter that I had discounted as never being likely to produce basketball players, probably deserves another look in my memory before being dismissed. The phrase city game *always implied, for me, an American city—New York in particular. Both of those assumptions need to be revised.*

James Harden's Transcendent Step-Back

James Harden sent a shiver through the NBA a few weeks ago. He led his team, the Houston Rockets, back from a twenty-point deficit to beat the Golden State Warriors, the defending champions, on their home court. He did this by hitting a three-point shot with seconds left to send the game into overtime. And then, in overtime, with two of the league's best defenders, Klay Thompson and Draymond Green, floating in the air on either side of him, with their outstretched hands leaving a seam no bigger than the width of the ball, Harden hit a three-pointer to win it. He scored forty-four points in the game, with ten rebounds and fifteen assists. It was the sixth straight win since Harden's co-star, Chris Paul, went down with a hamstring injury, a span in which Harden had been averaging forty-two points per game. It turns out to have been a prelude to his playing in the subsequent weeks, which has continued to be dazzling, up to and including his sixty-one points in a victory over the Knicks, at Madison Square Garden, on Wednesday night.

There have been many strange milestones and records during this stretch, which may one day come to seem something like Joe DiMaggio's fifty-six-game hitting streak. (Though it's hard to imagine a nation turning its troubled eyes to Harden.) One stat I enjoy pondering is that only one player has ever averaged more than Harden's current January average of 45.3: Wilt Chamberlain, who did it five times.

But these game-winning shots and gaudy statistics, scintillating as they are, only hint at the pleasures of watching Harden play. His very movements are strange and unusual, even obscene. His game can seem—in some visceral way, having to do with his body language, his beard, the way he deploys his arms and legs with such litigious ingenuity that players have taken to guarding him with their hands held up in the air, as though someone just shouted, "This is a stickup!"—profane.

A friend and former high school teammate of mine, John Merz, who belongs to what is surely a small club of former basketball junkies who are now reverends, said, of Harden, "His step-back is driving me crazy. This lunging backward for the three-point line is becoming carnivalesque. It has completely changed the balance between the inside and outside dialectic of basketball. Those two things were always in delicate relation, but now it's gone. The game of basketball was meant to be played moving toward the basket."

Ronnie Nunn, a former director of NBA officials, has emerged as a kind of defender of Harden's step-back, which many people see as a travel. It is a travel, sometimes, Nunn told me, when he does "a double step-back." But, most of the time, Harden's carefully calibrated move is legal. "Calling travel is about a dance," Nunn said. "Once you understand the rhythm of it, you can determine whether it's legal or not. It's really not about counting steps anymore once you see it. Just know the rhythm." Harden's rhythm, as Nunn has described it, is 0–1–2: "A waltz." I always thought that the rhythm of the step-back was a kind of salsa. I showed videos of Harden's step-back to Laura Stein, of the Dancing Grounds dance school in New Orleans. She thought that it resembled hip-hop footwork, with its wide step and change of direction, "like a top-rock in breakdancing."

Harden didn't invent the step-back, and at this point it seems that nearly every NBA player has a version of it, including centers like Joel Embiid. If you watch Kristaps Porziņģis's draft workout video from 2015, you will see, amid the rapid succession of jump shots and dunks, the seven-foot-three Latvian taking two giant, elongated step-backs. Yet Harden has made it his own, crystallized its impact on the game. Everywhere you go, you will see players practicing the step-back move. And it's always unique; everyone has their own version. Playing pickup basketball last summer at Pier 2 in Brooklyn, I had to laugh at the flamboyant theatricality of this one kid's step-back. It was so over-the-top. The self-congratulatory way he cocked his head at the end was part of the Harden influence too. And, to the kid's credit, it worked. He kept leaping dramatically back. The ball kept going in. I see some version of this on every playground and at every gym. I practice it, ridiculously, myself.

Harden's step-back has entered new territory this season. "He took 0.9 step-back threes per game in 2016–17 and 2.4 last season," according to Andrew Sharp's 2019 piece in *Sports Illustrated*. This season he is taking more than six every game. Harden has changed the way the game is played in ways that remind me of Michael Jordan and Allen Iverson. Jordan's game fetishized his air time. The poster-worthy dunk from the foul line became the fantasy object of players the world over. Iverson made a fetish of the crossover. He managed to take the aesthetic of hip-hop and translate it into basketball. Breaking your opponents' ankles became basketball's ecstatic accomplishment under Iverson's reign.

A kind of changing of the guard occurred between Jordan and Iverson, in the spring of 1997—at the start of Iverson's career and near the end of Jordan's. It happened in one play. Iverson is guarded by Jordan at the top of the key. In the video you can hear Phil Jackson's voice, nearly drunk with confidence after his first run of championships, calling out to Jordan to pick up Iverson. There is something about his tone of voice that suggests the power at his disposal, in Jordan.

Iverson crosses once, to his left, then brings it back. Then he does it again, this time with more force. Jordan lunges, misses. (I feel as though I am telling a story from Greek mythology.) The great Jordan was now off balance, out of position, and this feisty and very quick newcomer was alone with the ball at the top of the key. But as Iverson would later remark, such was Jordan's skill that he recovered in time to leap toward the ball and nearly block Iverson's shot. But he didn't. The ball leaves Iverson's hands and swishes through the net. There is a nearly Sistine Chapel–like frisson to the moment, two fingertips just grazing each other.

Harden has taken Iverson's template and embellished it. Most of the copious baskets Harden has been making this month are unassisted. One man on an island, creating his own shot, as Iverson did against Jordan. And, like Iverson, there is a lot of dribbling. The feeling is of a player dancing with himself. Harden likes to lower his body, with one leg forward and one behind, and dribble the ball rapidly back and forth, instilling terror. Then he lunges and either continues to the basket, to score or get fouled (or both), or steps back. Once he has created his space, he pauses. The beard seems to jut forth a bit, taunting. It happens in a split second, but it is an unmistakable effect of the overall move. That one little hesitation has a practical element—it is Harden gathering balance before rising to shoot—but, psychologically, it is devastating. One can't help but wonder if this is why he so often draws fouls on these long-range bombs—the defender throwing himself at Harden with kamikaze conviction, anything to prevent another highlight-reel step-back from swishing through the net.

That Harden's game is an evolution of Iverson's came into focus a couple of years ago, when I was watching a video of Iverson highlights and, for the first time, Iverson's game seemed antique. At first I thought that it was because of all the long twos that Iverson took. Long two-point shots are now the equivalent of drinking beer after a game and thinking that it hydrates you. Analytics have revealed that the greatest efficiencies are to be found in three-point shots, foul shots, and shots at the rim. But my response was more visceral than that—something about Iverson's game appeared dated. It had always seemed timeless.

I finally realized that the famous Iverson crossover—so fluid, stylish, and fierce, the apotheosis of street ball's swagger at the NBA level—now felt incomplete. Iverson would cross and then either rise for the shot or dart toward the rim. Something was missing. And then I realized what was missing was the sudden launching away from the rim, which is the effect of the step-back.

We all know that athletes operating at the highest levels need to summon nearly sociopathic levels of confidence. After Harden hits that game-winning shot against the Warriors, he falls down, and then, like a Russian Cossack dancer, he pushes himself up into a squat position and, even before he starts standing up, enunciates a string of curse words directed at Draymond Green that emanate from within the cave of his beard. Green, who is charming in his own way, had surely said and done much to earn the retort. And then, moments later, Harden, surrounded by his exultant teammates, waves a single finger at them, scolding them, reminding them that there is still a second and change on the clock. When the Warriors' final shot bounces off the rim and the win is sealed, he is mobbed again and flashes two fingers. It took me a moment to realize that he was referring to the MVP Award, which he won last year. He was saying that he was going to win it two years in a row.

In spite of Harden's heroics, the game's most memorable play, which I have returned to many times, took place with exactly three minutes and forty-five seconds to go in the third quarter. The Warriors are still leading by eleven points. Harden brings the ball across half-court, moves hastily to the three-point line, and seems to consider taking a three-point shot. He is being guarded by Kevin Durant and—you can almost see the thought bloom—has a better idea. He hands the ball to Gerald Green, who is being guarded by Stephen Curry. Green immediately hands the ball back to Harden and sets a pick on Durant.

Curry, a two-time MVP, switches on Harden, the reigning MVP, while Green jogs away toward the opposite side of the court. Durant, also a former MVP—these guys are really good at basketball!—opens his defensive stance so he has a view of both Green, who is his responsibility, and the ball. But then Durant stops moving and looks directly at the suddenly isolated pair of players, Curry and Harden, with concern. Curry flicks his hand toward Durant in a way that suggests that he needs no help. "Go guard your man" is the message. There is something touching in Durant's reluctance to leave the scene altogether. His friend and teammate Curry is now on an island with Harden. It's like seeing your friend in need while having to take care of yourself. What to do?

Durant, after a moment of worry, moves toward Green, leaving Curry to his fate. Durant's face becomes stony, abstract, and he isn't looking at Green or at the ball; it's almost as though he is trying to put the decision he just made out of his mind. Then Harden, dribbling from his left hand to right, briefly loses the ball. An unforced error. He has to take a few steps away from the basket to gather it. Curry gets right up on him, pressing his advantage. The sun comes out for Durant, unfreezes him. Now he is engaged, watching the play, calling out encouragement to his teammate. Maybe it won't end badly.

But it does end badly, for Curry. Harden regains control, dribbles between his legs, lunges forward with two hard dribbles, and then does his trick, which is to stop very suddenly and push off in the opposite direction. The third dribble is essentially a crossover, except, instead of moving the ball from one side of the body to the other, like Iverson, Harden moves it forward to backward. To accelerate faster than another player is an obvious advantage, but Harden has shown us the other side of this equation. He is a genius at deceleration. The move sends Curry reeling.

Harden pulls up for a short-range shot that goes in. It wasn't nearly as spectacular as his later heroics in the game, but the point in the play where he lost the ball contained a delicious moment: his right hand reaches to dribble the ball, but, instead of meeting a ball, the hand finds only air. It flutters with a rapid hummingbird motion that was, I felt, like getting a glimpse into the inside of a watch, seeing the many cylinders and counterweights spinning madly in tension with each other. One senses, in this moment of disequilibrium, the remarkable balance within Harden and everything he does on the basketball court.

—2019

Homicide at the Playground

Poke, poke, poke went his finger against my head. I was playing basketball at my local basketball court, and some static had developed between me and a guy nicknamed Homicide. I stared straight ahead, trying to ignore his jabbing finger. "You stink!" he yelled, barking right into my face. "You know that?"

He was six feet three, not as tall as me, but much stronger, a white guy with a crew cut, a gangster roll, and a smooth hip-hop lexicon. If he was merely a criminal, this would be bad, but he was also a good basketball player. He wore a West 4th Street team shirt. All the neighborhood guys at the park seemed to know him. But although I had come to this playground for upward of five years, I had seen him for the first time just a few weeks earlier. As I stood there mutely absorbing abuse, my only thought was, "Where has he been for the past five years?"

The most prominent and disturbing clue to this question was that everyone called him Homicide. To make matters worse, some guys abbreviated it to Homo. Pronounced hah-mo, as in *homicide*, not hoe-moe, as in *homosexual*. I was equally petrified by the fear of this potential psychopath and the possibility that I would be unable to restrain myself from saying the one, obvious, thing that would set him off.

Poke, poke, poke. I stared straight ahead and wondered if he was holding his fingers in the shape of a gun.

At last play resumed. We were guarding each other. Every time either of us touched the ball everyone backed off a step. We existed in a halo of personal antagonism and potential violence. All the touches were his. "Big man is weak!" he yelled every time he scored, which was nearly every time he touched the ball. My heart palpitated, and I felt as though I might collapse from fear and shame, but finally my game showed up. I scored a couple of times, and then I blocked Homicide's shot.

On the next play, fighting for position, he elbowed me in the chest while planting his leg behind mine. I went crashing down, and, less out of antagonism than reflex, I threw my arm out and in this way took him down with me. I was saved by the freakish sound of my head hitting the pavement. Closer to a pop than a thud, and clearly unnatural. After a half-beat pause, all the players rushed over, intervened, though not before Homicide got in another elbow in my throat. I had no idea what their relationship to this guy was, but they all knew his name.

Historically speaking, when abused in this way, by criminals, bullies, the police, I let loose with a stream of argument, as though the proper response to a brutal display of force was parliamentary debate. This resulted, almost every time, in my getting punched in the face. But now, since I'd been elbowed in the throat, I couldn't talk. I walked it off in silence, and the game went on.

I saw him regularly in the next few weeks. I had to force myself to go to the courts, worrying he would be there. I had never laid eyes on him for five years, and now all of a sudden he was a fixture. Every explanation for this was, from my point of view, or simply that of someone with my interests at heart, bad. Nevertheless, I went. This was my basketball court. A public space. If I wanted to play, I was going to play.

The strange thing was—though maybe this was inevitable—in the following weeks, Homicide and I became, if not exactly friends, then communicants. I showed up to play. He dunked a lot, often on me; I always played him hard. I got mine too. After a full summer occupying the same cosmology—our neighborhood basketball court—he was able to acknowledge me without rancor. We slapped each other five after games; what he was offering wasn't exactly respect; it was more as if I were a village idiot of whom he had grown fond. I, in turn, felt the horrible love that emanates from the bullied soul who has been spared further abuse. But I kept all that insanity inside. I showed up and played my game. I didn't back off. This sounds as though I am writing about my teenage years, when these matters have outsize importance. But I was thirty-five years old at the time of these events. Only in my early fifties, still an avid player, did I acquire enough confidence and fortitude—and also physical strength—to withstand this kind of bullying behavior, mostly, and to take joy in being the person who instilled confidence in my teammates, telling them "We good," clapping, controlling the ball when we needed to, scoring in the clutch. Not always, but often enough. Showing confidence as a way of being confident.

It always feels like a fresh revelation, even if it is a commonplace, that so much of sports is psychological. I was fascinated to hear that during the 2020 Olympics Gregg Popovich used the phrase *Strong Faces* when exhorting his team when they were down by fifteen points in the second quarter against Australia. "I copied that from Coach K," said Popovich, referencing the longtime coach of the United States national team, Mike Krzyzewski. "Play on to the next play. You don't react to a teammate's turnover or the referee's call. The fact that you miss a shot? Nobody cares. You don't have that right. You're responsible to your team to move on to the next play. And he called it 'Strong Faces.'"

A college coach speaking of the need to project confidence, even to blue chip players, makes sense. But this was Greg Popovich talking to players like Kevin Durant and Damian Lillard as well as a bevy of players who had just played in the NBA finals, including Jrue Holiday and Kris Middleton, who had won.

Basketball in America has two fundamentally discrete seasons, winter and summer. This makes it unique among the major sports. Hockey is a winter sport. Baseball is a summer sport. Football, admittedly, is played and speculated about all year, but its center of gravity is fall and early winter.

Men's basketball, however, is a winter sport for everybody playing organized team ball—from junior varsity on up to the NBA. I played in high school and college, and in those years the phrase *pregame warm-ups* was to be taken literally, because the gym and the locker room were usually freezing. To this day, when I still think of the seminal basketball movie *Hoop Dreams*, what I remember is the long commute over Chicago's frozen tundra that one of the movie's two aspirants made every morning in order to play for the big-time high school coach on the other side of town. You forget this watching TV, but basketball players spend a lot of time in the cold.

The other side of this coin is the great wellspring of basketball joy that bears fruit in the warm weather: pickup basketball in the park. For many people who actively play the game, basketball is a summer sport.

I've always had a nearly addictive relationship with playground hoops. I tend to see my local playground the way some people see their local bar. Since I've stopped going to bars, or at least stopped drinking in them, the feelings toward pickup basketball have intensified.

My initial encounter with street basketball took place in winter, when I was twelve. A frigid session bouncing the ball. A bright day. I wore gloves and could see my breath. I was alone on the court at Seventy-Sixth Street and Riverside Drive. It was the beginning of something. It's possible that part of my initial attraction to basketball had to do with just how deep you can get into the game while alone. This is what every kid with access to a hoop has in common with every superstar—from Bill Bradley to Kobe— who has put in thousands of hours alone with the ball—the playing out of elaborate fantasies, the court's emptiness suddenly populated with shapes and stories of phantom defenders who are defeated by vicious crossovers, the hitting of last-second shots over and over and over. In the ensuing *petite morte*, confetti rains down from the rafters and teammates are rushing onto the court to lift you on their shoulders. And then it all vanishes and begins again.

After the first winter of solitary basketball, spring came, and with it a development I hadn't really contemplated out there in the cold—other players. Specifically, three guys showed up early one afternoon, joking around and casually shooting the ball in what seemed like the street-ball version of spring training. They were, to my twelve-year-old eyes, formidably grown up. All of them were black.

One of them was wearing a sweatshirt with the homemade logo "Funk Mob." I now understand this was a reference to Parliament-Funkadelic. At the time I thought it was a kind of gang. Maybe a gang I could belong to. As it happens, they were the trio of players who dominated the action on that court in Riverside Park in the late 1970s. People called them by their names: Frank, Joe, and Otto Graham (the guy with the Funk Mob shirt). Most of the other denizens of that scene had nicknames I remember twenty-five years later—Puppet, Tweety, Red. I hovered at the edge of this garrulous world, frightened; for most of my early youth, playing competitive basketball was synonymous with pain.

There are usually clear hierarchies of skill at playgrounds—the old guys, or young kids, or out-of-shape guys are usually around C hoop. Then there is the B hoop and then an A hoop. Often the C hoop is just as fiercely competitive as the A hoop, just a lower level of skill. In Riverside Park, A hoop was the full court. I must have hung around the C hoop at that court for two years before I had the courage to get into a full-court game.

In the winter you are part of a team. In the summer you become a member in the impromptu congregation in the church of hoops. To play on the high school or college team is, after all, to join a preexisting context with its own structures, traditions, and, one hopes, funding. The street game comprises a community that is entirely improvised. Citizenship demands some skill, energy, talent, but mostly it is established by simply showing up. The funding is municipal, but this is an adult observation; for younger people, these playgrounds are the urban equivalent of old-growth forests.

Although I played organized basketball, street basketball was the center of my own basketball cosmology. It was where I felt at home, or rather where I felt most myself, as a basketball player, for better and for worse. The winter game was cold in every sense—the coaches drilled you in repetition; they wanted to squeeze as much of the unpredictability of the game out of it as possible. The street game was the opposite—the temperature was hot, everything flowed, there was unlimited improvisation, you could try all sorts of moves that would get you benched immediately if you tried it during the cold season.

In the summer, the city's fried asphalt courts give off a kind of energy. You become inured to the heat and the grit which in turn imbues you with a kind of hard, flexible strength. You have to stay loose. You're up against kids and geezers, pot smokers, drinkers, fitness freaks, guys who like to spit a lot, and lunatic ballers, many of whom look totally undistinguished as athletes until they start tossing the ball up and it goes into the hoop again and again and again, and you realize that this is it, their true talent, the magic trick they will never get sick of performing.

The democracy of playground basketball is one of the great things about the sport—you go down to the local court, see who is there, and get picked up for a game or call next if no one will have you. Or perhaps you are the kind of street-ball player who relishes the role of general manager, scouting players, telling people you have your team when you don't, keeping spots for more talented players in the current game who might lose and be available for drafting.

Looks are often deceiving. There was a guy named Elvis with whom I used to play on Horatio Street. I believe he delivered pizza for Little Caesars, for a while at least, and would come after work. I knew him when he was a little kid, and then one day he was a little man, a few inches over five feet. Suddenly he was amazing, a kind of Allen Iverson. The joy in his game, his quickness, toughness, and skills, his bad-ass, trash-talking laughter are with me years after I last laid eyes on him.

The playground is like family but one where strangers are always coming to sit in the living room. Sometimes these strangers will travel in packs, three buddies who have descended from uptown or Queens to check out the competition on this particular court. They muscle in, do their thing, and either prevail or get slapped down by the locals. And then there are the lone gunslingers who don't seem very impressive until they unleash their jump shot, or do their crossover, and you realize they have come loaded and they want to embarrass you. Suddenly the public court becomes small and personal. You are assigned a specific role, isolated one-on-one, the guy with the ball versus his defender, you, and the unspoken question arises again and again: What are you going to do now?

If a fight breaks out, there is nobody around with a whistle, no authority to appeal to, no gym teacher, not even the implicit threat of not being able to use the college gym, or the health club gym, or the y. Yes, there are always the police or concerned citizens, but they're on the other side of the fence. The higher power on the playground is the same one that prevails on the sidewalks of the city—that unseen fabric of shared assumptions that allows people to navigate around one another, a civility that rises to the surface out of an awareness that civility is the only higher power to turn to. If that doesn't work, you can try your luck with 911. There is a political contingent that feels intensely threatened by this civility and for this reason loudly laments, which is to say celebrates, every event that suggests city life as a kind of infernal hell.

Showing up to play basketball on a summer playground is a slightly peevish experience. Everyone arrives in a mood to insult and prepared to defend against insults, basketball related or otherwise. I like it; I think it's part of my addiction. It's not like I play ball to fight, but I crave the intensity, and one of my skills, for better and for worse, is to inject a bit of animosity into whatever casual pickup game I am in, if it feels too casual. In this way, one creates the atmosphere in which an enjoyable game can take place. My game is respected for this reason above all others. For a long time now, that has been my thing—to be intense, to play hard, to exhibit a certain smug satisfaction at hitting shots, to want to win, to relish nifty passes, to clap and congratulate my teammates, to be loud, to be in your face, to stir the pot so that the people I'm playing against feel annoyed and insulted, so they try harder. Afterward, everyone seems to feel the game has been better for it.

I've learned all this—both the ability to play at all and the ability to believe I can play—from years and years of playing on public basketball courts in various cities and locales. I was intrigued by a passing reference to the unofficial communities that spring up around a basketball hoop in J. D. Crabtree's *We Will Not Fade Away*, a book composed mostly of photographs of hoops from around the world. He called them "labyrinths." A labyrinth is something in which you can get lost. It has somewhat nightmarish connotations. But it is also a place within which you can find refuge, especially if you know your way around.

"I want to be like you when I grow up," a guy said to me in the immediate aftermath of a hard-fought game on Seventy-Sixth Street. Said in the immediate aftermath by a scrawny point guard with a good handle on the losing team. His age, like the intent of his comment, was ambiguous. He wore a ponytail and a Nets jersey with *Pierce* on the back. There were wisps of hair on his chin. It was unclear to me if his Nets jersey had been purchased a decade earlier during Paul Pierce's brief interlude as a Net or if it was off a thrift shop pile and ironic, the basketball equivalent of mom jeans. Or maybe the guy was one step away from being a bum. There was a homeless man I often saw that same summer wearing a Nets jersey with the name *Williams*. It took a few moments of concentration before I summoned up *Deron*.

"I want to be you when I grow up" could mean any number of things. But I choose it to mean that the joy of being lost in the game is a joy that doesn't have to be relinquished. It means that the ugliness of those scenes with Homicide and the many equivalents—though none so ominously named—have added up to something worthwhile.

—2021

Coach

It was halftime. I stepped out of the pressroom at Madison Square Garden and saw him walking toward me carrying a flimsy cardboard tray filled with hot dogs and beer. He had recognized me first, and his eyes were already on me by the time I saw him.

"Coach," I said instinctively. "I don't believe it."

"I can't believe it either," he said. "You've actually turned out to be good for something."

Denis Gallagher, the Vassar Brewers basketball coach for my last two years of college, now stood before me wearing a windbreaker, jeans, and sneakers. He was with a friend whom he didn't bother to introduce. He just looked at me with a bemused expression.

"Coach," I said again, staring with the same stupor I always seemed to display in his presence. "What are you doing here?"

"The same thing the other ten thousand people in this building are doing, you idiot!" he said.

Coach Gallagher spoke a language of insults warmly delivered. This was not my language. I could never seem to absorb his messages when he was enraged or, for that matter, when he was diagramming a play, but when he spoke sharply to me I always had the feeling that there was affection somewhere beneath it, or I liked to think so. For example, the time I showed up at practice after a game with my thumb wrapped up in white gauze and announced, "Coach, I broke my thumb," and he replied—or, should I say, cried out in fury, but perhaps an amused fury?—"Why did you go to the doctor?"

Now we stood face to face in the Garden. I wasn't used to interacting with him in civilian terms. I stared at him, a regular guy at a Knicks game.

"Of course I don't have seats as good as you," he continued. "I see you're a real big shot now."

It was my first time with a press pass at the Garden. I was filling in for a friend who covered the Knicks for the United Press International wire service. He had to be out of town for a while, and none of the other writers at UPI was enticed by the prospect of calling in the score at the end of every quarter of the Knicks game and filing a short article after the game with a few quotes culled from the locker room. It was Patrick Ewing's third year and Rick Pitino's first season as an NBA head coach. I jumped at the chance. When I was shown to my seat at the long, narrow table that ran along the court, opposite the team benches, I couldn't believe my luck. Even more amazing were the rotary phones that sat at intervals on this same narrow table.

These were the last years of the pre–luxury box era. Less than a decade later, David Remnick would begin a profile of Michael Jordan with the line, "Nearly all the old American basketball arenas have been abandoned or razed. . . ." The Garden's renovation was in 1992. That narrow table occupied valuable real estate that would be transformed into courtside seats. But that night the seat was mine, as was the phone.

I lifted the receiver to my ear. When I heard a dial tone, I began madly dialing every single person whose number I knew by heart so I could announce where I was and what I was doing. At some point in the half, a loose ball bounced toward me. I reached out with two hands and tried to catch it with the phone nestled against my ear. For a moment I could sense the gravitational pull the ball exerted on every eye in the arena. And because of this pressure, and also the phone, and also because I was not used to the experience of having a ball come careening directly at my face while attending a Knicks game, and maybe because of certain liabilities that on a basketball court might be called

"Butterfingers" I dropped the phone and also failed to catch the ball on the first try.

This must have been the moment when my old coach spotted me. I imagined what he might have said to his friend: "He *still* can't catch a basketball."

Later that night I had my first visit to the Knicks locker room. I witnessed Ewing, the sullen king, sitting on a low stool with ice packs taped to his knees. I watched as Dikembe Mutombo, preceded by his loud laughter, sauntered in wearing a gray two-piece suit and a black turtleneck. He was paying a visit to his fellow Georgetown alum. Out in the hallway, I stood in the tight little throng around Rick Pitino as he gave his postgame press conference under the bright TV lights. He was exuberant and energetic. Pitino's adventure with the Knicks lasted two seasons; a decade later he coached another two seasons for the Celtics, where he made his famous, now meme-worthy speech about how "Larry Bird is not walking through that door." But the NBA was not for Pitino, and vice versa. He made his name as a Hall of Fame college coach by taking Providence, led by his point guard Billy Donovan, to the Final Four. And then the years of success, and scandal, at Kentucky and Louisville. It would not have occurred to me, that night, to think of Coach Gallagher and Rick Pitino in terms relating one with the other.

The basketball coaches to whom I submitted for a couple of hours every day after school—starting in seventh grade and continuing, in an uninterrupted parade of years, until I graduated from college—exist with a remarkable lack of specificity in my memory. I assume I remember so little because there is very little, in terms of my own play in those years, that I wish to remember. I was a project. Tall and lanky but without much in the way of athleticism or coordination.

I recall only three incidents from the year that Bob Clark at the Riverdale Country School had me on his varsity team. The first and most positive was the shock of seeing my name posted on the typewritten list announcing the varsity team. The second was an attempt at an overhead pass during one chilly Saturday morning practice—it rose up in the air and plopped down ten feet in front of me, at which point the team burst out laughing. Coach Clark, normally subdued, got stern; he insisted it wasn't funny. Another memory involved me clowning around, putting the ball under my practice jersey. Suddenly a senior named John was in my face, seething with contempt. I thought he was going to hit me. He was a scrappy, stocky guy, the guy who dives for every ball and gets his minutes from playing ferocious defense. It took twenty years for it to occur to me that he was so mad at me for joking around because his younger brother, a freshman and the star of the team, was always joking around. The brother, a huge, blond, beaming gazelle of a boy, running around in the locker room in a jockstrap, laughing and snapping his towel, was an athlete of Division I caliber, if only he took it seriously.

At St. Ann's High School in Brooklyn, where I spent my senior year, the spirit of the school was so bohemian that sports were considered a joke. But the spirit of the school was such that everyone on the team was immersed in this relatively new music called hip-hop. The team's backup center, Tom Cushman, contributed the following lyric to rap history: "You have to fight / for your right / to party," sung by our classmate Michael Diamond.

And so, in this roundabout way, we took basketball very seriously; my teammates John Merz and Mark Pierson would iron their fat shoelaces and tell stories of pickup games in Brooklyn with Jack Ryan, the famous street-ball player who would remove his false teeth while on a fast break, spin the ball on his dentures, and then lay it in. I started at St. Ann's; it seemed natural that I would continue to play in college, at Vassar. But I didn't take it seriously.

For the most part Vassar didn't take sports seriously, either. Certainly not men's basketball. Vassar in the 1980s was still thought of, or remembered, as a girls' school. There was a rumored winning season sometime in the 1970s, but the team won just a handful of games my freshman and sophomore years. The coach for my first two years was a man named Sam Adams. He had been an assistant at the United States Military Academy—Army—against whose junior-varsity team we always had a preseason scrimmage. He had a connection to Bobby Knight, who had coached at Army before moving up the ladder. Every year Knight sent Adams an Indiana team poster.

This association with Bobby Knight might suggest that Adams was a fiery figure who motivated players by screaming and throwing chairs.

This was not the case. Coach Adams's most intense feature was his fine, smooth-as-silk, bright-blond hair, which he kept in a side part. He was neat and fastidious and rarely raised his voice. He was so mild that he rarely even *inflected* his voice. It was like having Jack Nicklaus as a basketball coach. After my sophomore year, partly in response to complaints from the players, Adams was let go. The athletic director at the time said, in response to our request, that firing Adams would be difficult because he always had his paperwork in on time and it was flawless. The secret life of a coach as bureaucrat and politician was revealed to us.

What is it with the put-upon, exasperated demeanor of basketball coaches? Football coaches have field marshal grandeur. Baseball managers sit like yogis, calculating how many relief pitchers can fit on the head of a pin (they've transcended the word *coach* altogether). But basketball coaches, my God, they look as though they have for years been trying to whittle down a giant tree with a penknife while a clock counts down to zero. The ones who aren't former players are often small, downright runty figures and have a physical energy made frantic from being packed into too small a package. The Van Gundy brothers, Stan and Jeff, for example; Tom Thibodeau is the current embodiment, but the legacy seems to go way back to Red Holzman, Red Auerbach, and beyond.

Gallagher was relatively young when he came to us as coach, and his natural resting face had a kind of innocence—chipmunk cheeks, a small mouth, and kindly eyes. The coach's sense of grievance had not entered into his expression. But this innocence simply made the transformation of his demeanor, when he was upset, all the more shocking. He had a temper. The team he inherited played in what was then a relatively new facility called Walker Field House.

Built in the rear of the small jewel-box campus, next to the golf course, Walker Field House looked like a series of medieval huts, the roof rising toward sharply pitched points in several places. The floor was a thin layer of tapioca-colored rubber laid over concrete. The ceiling was lined with wood panels. For four years I lay on my back during pregame stretches and stared at the knots in the wood. The bleachers were modest. During my freshman year, home games often were witnessed by a smattering of people, among whom a single figure stands out in my memory, just as he stood out during the games. His name was Sal LoBreglio, the father of one of my teammates. He was an ex-cop who wore a jacket and tie over his substantial and rather round frame and attended every game, even road games. He drove a Cadillac Seville. He was an enthusiastic clapper and yeller, especially when his son, John, did something good.

John LoBreglio was one of our stars. He was a gentle kid with a very nice jump shot and a level of Bronx-bred street toughness that emerged when necessary. John was also a very spiritual, academic-minded religion major who was to play an important role in the recruiting intrigues of later years. Those first two years under Sam Adams—all the shouts and cries during games and practice echoing through the huge tapioca interior of Walker Field House—are encapsulated, for me, by the almost spiritually lonely sound of Sal LoBreglio, the ex-cop, clapping and calling out encouragements.

Looking back on it, Sal LoBreglio was Coach Adams's alter ego—loud, dark, a little dangerous, ferociously optimistic, sticking up for us on one side of the court, while across the court our coach stood in his bright blondness observing our demise with mild disgust. The idea that Sal LoBreglio was a doppelgänger coach came to me in a bizarre realization during a road game, when Coach Adams somehow got lost on the way to the game. I say this hesitantly because it's been a long time, and Adams was very organized. Maybe it happened during Coach Gallagher's first year. At any rate, the team was there, but no coach. LoBreglio, either on his initiative or at our request, came down from his perch in the stands and took over. One of his executive decisions, which of course deeply endeared him to me, was to insert me, the underachiever, into the starting lineup.

Coach Gallagher's tenure as basketball coach began before I met him, when I received a letter sent to everyone on the team the summer before he started his job.

"If you want to be part of something special......," it began.

There may have been some sort of introductory pleasantry along the lines of "Hello, I am your new basketball coach," but Gallagher quickly moved on to a list of push-ups, running, sit-ups, and ball-handling drills that he expected us to do on our own.

"If you want to be part of something special......"

Today, anyone with a casual interest in the game has access to instructional and workout videos from coaches and basketball stars. A theme that runs through them all is the virtue, the necessity, of work. A person who was always in the gym was once referred to as a "gym rat." Now such a person is on a quest for an ascendance—spiritual, physical, and maybe even financial—to be achieved through hard work. The very idea of the gym, once thought of as a place to play the game, has been extended to include the weight room. "I will not be outworked" is a phrase from a Donovan Mitchell workout video that stuck with me because it captured the dedication to the grind that is now a badge of honor and an acknowledgment of what it takes to excel. "What would I be if I snoozed?" LeBron James mused in a recent commercial, as though yielding to the snooze button instead of rising for a dawn workout would have made all the difference for his great career. Perhaps it would have. I don't want to overstate the novelty of this—elite athletes have always put in the work. But it seemed less conspicuous. Even sleep is now understood to be an episode of molting during which the body can regenerate and consolidate the gains in muscle from all the work in the gym.

I now wish I had been more receptive to Gallagher's memo. But at the time I received it, Gallagher's list was a shocking intrusion of winter pain into summer leisure. Up to that point in my life, I had not put in the work.

Regarding my own play once Coach Gallagher's first season began, suffice it to say I was familiar with that collapsed blotch of red where his face should have been. When things went wrong during games his arms would go rigid at his sides and he would clench his fists into little balls. He had small hands. When clenched, they were no bigger than cue balls, it seemed. My problem was that I was inconsistent. I couldn't seem to grasp what was going on in practice. During games, I moved through the offensive sets like someone being given a crash course in the foxtrot or the waltz. Someone who is counting when they should be dancing. But sometimes things would come together and I would have an impressive game. I scored nineteen or twenty points at least once in all four seasons I played, in games where the total was usually in the sixties. After one of these showings Coach Gallagher came to me and said, "You could do that every night if you wanted to." And it strikes me now that the other half of that question was, "What's holding you back?"

I had the basketball equivalent of mental problems. I seemed to play best when I didn't have time to think. John LoBreglio recently sent me some digitized files of old VHS tapes from my freshman and sophomore years. There on the blurry video is a long, lanky guy who seems very concerned with making sure his shorts are properly tied. There I was at the foul line against Rensselaer Polytechnic Institute, missing two foul shots at the end of a game that we lost by one. I seem to be a second behind in every play on offense and defense. You could see the sense of relief in my body as I ran from one end of the court to the other, because for that short stretch of time it was clear what I was supposed to do: run to the other end of the court! It didn't help that 1980s basketball, especially college basketball, was a highly regimented and controlled game. This was the era when, with ten minutes left in the game, Dean Smith's University of North Carolina team would pull the ball out and run a four corners offense with a lead of just four or six points, the better to run out the clock. And yet I was amused to see that there was one moment on that ancient videotape when I looked pretty good: I grabbed a loose ball, drove to the basket, spun, and put up a shot with two defenders in my face. It went in. The shot was part of a broken play in which there was no time to perform the assigned dance steps, counting under your breath. You just danced.

Gallagher's manner was simultaneously extremely intense and mild mannered, and that juxtaposition seemed very human. Once, he shot some jump shots for a while after practice and showed impressive skills. We all watched in a kind of mortified amazement. He couldn't have been older than thirty. The basketball skills of coaches are like the sex lives of parents—you acknowledge their existence but the fewer specifics the better.

Early in his first season, my junior year, Gallagher made us write out our course list. The purpose of these lists was to allow him to monitor our academic activities and make sure we didn't screw up to a point where our eligibility was threatened.

I listed among my credits "Shakspear."

"There is an *e* at the end, you idiot!"

When I think of the voice, it sounds like Jackie Gleason as he is in *The Honeymooners* and *Smokey and the Bandit* and Don DeLillo's *Underworld*—an insult comic, a guy about to blow a gasket. But when I remember the face, I recall a glimmer of mischief. "You're an English major and you don't know how to spell Shakespeare? What do they teach you here?"

I felt a tiny pang of camaraderie. He had taught second-grade English at a public school and had been an English major too. This turned out to be our warmest moment for some time to come.

My arrival at Vassar coincided with the arrival of a prized recruit named Pete, who had done the very serious basketball thing of taking an extra year after high school at one of those supercompetitive basketball prep schools. He was a little over six feet and played point guard. My guess, now, is that Pete was the sort of talented player who can keep things under control and facilitate for the more talented players on his team. He could hit an open jump shot. He played with toughness. Pete was good, but he was no savior. Like a pro player who puts up great numbers in a contract year, Pete hit his peak the year before we met him. The contract was now signed, he was in college, and his best game was in the rearview mirror.

In the second year, there was another prize recruit. He came through LoBreglio. He knew Seamus Carey from the Woodlawn neighborhood in the Bronx. We were told he was really good. When he came through the doorway at Walker Field House I looked for his face and found it when my eyes adjusted downward. I don't trust the memory: too theatrical, Seamus coming through the door as though entering a saloon in the old West. But that was the emotional tenor from the moment he arrived. A new sheriff. He was a smoldering ember with black hair, Irish, a stocky five feet eight or so. My heart sank when I first saw him, but during our first pickup game, he demonstrated a degree of speed and something else—fearlessness, assertiveness—that put him in a different category than everyone else on the team. He went airborne with so much force. I don't mean to shrug off the parts of his game that relied on touch and finesse—jump shots, passing, and the like; he was good at it all—but there was a medieval barbarity to his play. He flew into the lane like a rock thrown by a catapult.

My understanding of the dynamic between Seamus and me on the court comes largely from my memory of a slow-motion replay of one specific pass. It occurred during our senior year, but I assume it applies to the three years we played together. It was an away game against NYU that was, improbably, televised on MSG 3. The announcers were Bruce Beck and Cal Ramsey. We lost that game badly. As often happened in our losses, I played well. Seamus played hard. I recall a sense of disgust and anger that came over him as the game slipped away. At one point he went after a loose ball, jumping over the chairs lined up at the end of our bench, knocking some over, rolling onto his back in the manner of a person well practiced in getting knocked down. He was down for only a moment before jumping to his feet.

Of the play in question, I have no firsthand memory. *Lost in the game* suggests a dreaminess and flow state, but it also suggests someone who has no idea what is going on and is struggling to keep up.

Watching a tape of the game, there was a slow-motion replay of Seamus driving into the lane. He leaves his feet. The NYU defenders turn to him, move toward him, and for a moment his face registers something almost like panic as the defenders' bodies converge on him. The natural thing to do would be to shoot the ball or dish it to the guy under the basket. Seamus keeps the ball. He stays in the air an extra beat. And then his arm emerges from the thicket of defenders. The ball is in his hand, which wraps behind the back of the last defender. The camera, on the baseline, stays with the ball, which is now in my possession. Seamus falls out of the frame. I am a bystander suddenly made central by the appearance of the ball in my hands. A mortified panic sets in as I begin to rise in a graceless, mechanical motion and hoist the ball up toward the hoop. I am jostled as the ball goes in. A whistle. I don't recall if I made the foul shot.

Years after the fact, John LoBreglio explained to me the backstory of Seamus's recruitment at Vassar, which had its origins in a conversation he had with his father after one of our many losses my sophomore year. LoBreglio was a junior. He walked over to his father to hear the postgame analysis. His account of that conversation:

"You guys don't have a point guard."

"Yeah, Dad, I know."

"You need a point guard."

"Yup."

"Someone like Seamus."

"Yeah, that would be great."

"I'm gonna drop by Seamus's house one day this week and have a talk with his parents. See if he'd like to transfer to Vassar."

"Huh?"

"Yeah, that's what I'm gonna do."

LoBreglio, now a professor in England and the author of many scholarly articles on Buddhist practice in nineteenth-century Japan, wrote:

> My dad always says all kinds of stuff. He once told me just after Ted Turner bought the Atlanta Braves that he was going to approach Turner and convince him to let him manage the Braves. At that tender age, I believed him. I started dreaming about sitting in the dugout with the players. And in fairness to him, though most of these schemes have come to naught, he actually pulled off a few. Like Seamus coming to Vassar. Yet at the time, something in me was worried enough that he just might embarrass our family, that I felt compelled to say, "But he doesn't have the grades. They'll never let him in here."
>
> "We'll see, we'll see," said Sal.
>
> A few weeks later I got a call from Sal: "I dropped by and spoke with Seamus's parents about him coming to Vassar."
>
> "Oh God!" I thought. "He actually fuckin' did it."
>
> The reasons I was so appalled and embarrassed are hard to explain without going into a very long background account of growing up in Woodlawn, being an Italian-American minority in a virtually mono-ethnic Irish-American neighborhood of which the Careys were a very prominent Irish-American family; the details of the intense sporting dynamics and rivalries in our neighborhood; my father being simultaneously perhaps the most-loved and the most-hated coach in our neighborhood sports league; my playing ball with Seamus since around fifth or sixth grade; and on and on. You might think that I would've jumped for joy at Seamus coming to Vassar, but I felt an enormous sense of dread and responsibility.
>
> Though I knew him very well as a sporting adversary (basketball *and* baseball) for many years, we were not close friends. Nonetheless, what I knew of him, or thought I knew of him, made me feel that he wouldn't like Vassar. I felt that my Dad, on a really random whim after a particularly bad loss, had gone out and ripped Seamus out of his comfortable environment (he won the NYC championship with CUNY the previous year!) and dropped him somewhere he would be miserable.

The college let Seamus in. His living quarters were in Ferry House.

In the modern era, athletes are sequestered in their own dorms, often in close proximity to the gyms and fields where they practice. Ferry House can be described, in both location and atmosphere, as the opposite extreme: an anomalous piece of Bauhaus architecture, Ferry looked like a floating white shoebox squatting defiantly amid Vassar's many nineteenth-century brick buildings. It functioned as a kind of stylish one-building shantytown—to use a term of protest from that decade—that may as well have had a neon sign above it blinking the word *vegan*! (an ahistorical reference; I am not sure the word was even in circulation in the 1980s, when we would have said *vegetarian,* and long before athletes started extolling plant-based diets—see Chris Paul). The connotation of vegetarianism, at that time, for me, was kind of sallow and low-energy.

Ferry House's unusual physical structure was accompanied by an unusual social structure: there was a kitchen, and the cooking and the cleaning were communal. Perhaps this was a consciously mischievous decision on the part of someone at the college, the cultural equivalent of throwing a kid in the deep end to teach them to swim.

I don't know what personal interactions Seamus had with his housemates upon arriving, but ten days into the year, Seamus deserted. He had tacked a note to LoBreglio's door.

"John. I've gone home. Won't be back. Left Stephanie's tennis racket downstairs with white angel."

I have a memory of LoBreglio when he relayed the news, his face ashen. Stephanie was his girlfriend at the time. I guess she had lent Seamus a racket.

His absence didn't last long. He was convinced to come back "at the urging of an old respected friend of the Carey family," as LoBreglio put it, "and wound up not only sticking it out, but thriving academically." When he returned, he was put in a regular dorm with a meal plan in the cafeteria along with everyone else.

What does a coach do when he inherits a poor team and tries to improve it? He tries to get better players. And he tries to make his players better. The latter is an arduous process. Gallagher arrived with his round and, I thought even then, somewhat innocent face, which contained within it a fiery sort of ambition, as though he had purchased a dilapidated house and was going to do all the work of fixing it up himself. The idea of physical transformation in the weight room had not taken root at that time. I wish—with an occasional flare of passion that is probably unseemly—that all the faith in weights and strength conditioning had existed back in the 1980s when I played college ball and was a long, gangly concoction of arms and legs.

At the time the emphasis in basketball training was on running and conditioning, not strength. Weights were viewed with suspicion, because they might screw up the extremely mystical, unexplainable, and delicate mechanical process by which the ball, having left your fingertips, flies through the air and falls into the hoop.

Gallagher encouraged us in the weight room. But it was optional, whereas the running was unavoidable. *Running* is not a word that does justice to what takes place in basketball practice. Soccer players run and run. Football players sprint. But for basketball there is a special drill whose name explains a lot: *suicides*.

Let's contemplate the title, a dramatic plural of an unpleasant word. If it were singular, it would be, in practice, less morbid. "Now it's time for the suicide," coaches across the land would say. And one awful thing would occur, and then it would be over. But it is not singular. It is plural, like the rings of Saturn or the gates of hell.

Here is a suicide: you run to the foul line, touch it with your hand, then run back to the baseline from which you started, touch that with your hand, then run to the half-court line, touch that, then back to the baseline (touch it, or risk having to do it all over), then to the far foul line, then back to the baseline (touch!), then to the far baseline, then all the way back in a sprint that is accompanied by a countdown. The countdown, called out by the coach, started at an arbitrary moment. He always looked at his watch, but I never believed it was a scientific thing. He would wait until the last, slowest person on the team would get into finishing range and start counting down from ten. Then this last hapless person would reach down deep to try and get to the end before the countdown reached zero. If he did not, the whole team had to run an extra suicide. We did ten of these after every practice, sometimes more, with thirty-second breaks in between.

Sam Adams had made us run the same drill. The difference, besides the diabolical countdown, was that Gallagher had us run more of them.

And yet if that was the only difference, it would mean the big difference was more of the same. More suicides, more discipline, and an extra practice day (Saturday morning at eight!). But that was not the case. Coach Gallagher brought intensity to the program, a need. He needed it to be successful. He needed basketball to be the most important thing in our lives. And we got the strong impression it was the most important thing in *his* life. His previous coaching position had been as an assistant at Manhattanville, a school that regularly trounced us.

Meanwhile, though I only vaguely grasped this, his day job did not change when he came to Vassar. Now, as before, he taught second-grade English somewhere far away, perhaps Long Island or Westchester. He lived far away, too, and had a wife and young daughter. His car was a beat-up gray Toyota. I remember seeing him in the parking lot once, when I had stayed late working on my shot. I came outside and saw a lone car in the parking lot with smoke rising from the exhaust, a small gray Toyota set against the grainy black and white of a parking lot at night. It was a cold, wintry night, and I saw his face in profile under the parking-lot lights. My thought then, seeing him in that little car, an hour-long drive ahead of him, was to marvel at how strange it was that my coach was now a citizen and would have to obey traffic laws just like everyone else. And somewhere beneath that I felt: Wow, he must really like being a coach to come all this way.

Our first year with Gallagher was a moderate success. At 10–14, we won more games than the three previous seasons combined. Against Manhattanville, his old team, we played tough until the final seconds. Down by one point, I grabbed an offensive rebound directly under our basket and spastically flung it off the backboard. A moment later the buzzer sounded.

I was already in the unhealthy habit of looking over at Coach whenever something good or bad happened on the court. After this absurd, unforgivable miss, I looked over helplessly, but I didn't see his face, only his back, slumped but taut, as he walked down the length of the bench with his pigeon-toed stride, away from me, his fists balled. To this day I will sometimes stand under the basket in that same spot and shoot the layup. I think about what I did wrong—I shot with my arms and forgot to use my legs. I rushed. I let Coach down.

I was, and continue to be, a player for whom the point-blank layup is more difficult than the spinning fallaway in traffic. I had played team ball since junior high school, yet my game was primarily formed on summer playgrounds. In order to thrive I needed flow, improvisation, unconsciousness—all the habits coaches try to erase from their players. I couldn't think and play at the same time. When we were walked through the various offensive sets, Gallagher explaining as we went, I acted like an automobile driver who has stopped to ask for directions only to promptly zone out, returning to consciousness only when the litany is over, just in time to say thank you. I wasn't without talent, but one of the difficult-to-communicate things about organized basketball is the invisible ability, separate from physical talent, or even basketball talent, that is required to integrate into the team system. Every year of my career I had at least one breakout game. And every year I had dismal failures. I was in the starting rotation for part of every season and was benched for periods of every season, even my senior year.

The mysterious alchemy of overcoming limits is something Gallagher approached bluntly. You were to be bludgeoned by the force of his personality, the precision of his schemes, the wisdom of his drills. There was something else too—his commitment. I don't know when it first dawned on us, but at a certain point the whole team became aware that our coach was working extremely hard. Every opposing team was scouted at length. The man was driving to games in whatever free time he had. He returned with detailed diagrams of our opponents' plays and their star players' strengths.

His emphasis was on passing and motion, a banal observation for anyone who follows basketball, and yet at a certain point the sheer meticulousness with which a plan is presented to you begins to carry its own moral authority. Were we the most scrupulous students of the Gallagher system? Not really. There was a play called "Power," which was signaled by his raising a fist. He would call it from the sidelines in the spirit of a sneak attack or a secret weapon. We went into a bit of assigned choreography, and the result was that one of our big men (myself included) was supposed to get the ball in the low post.

Big deal! Every basketball coach in the world has some equivalent play. And yet I can still feel the conviction with which he explained its design, the triumphant raising of the fist on the sidelines, where he prowled in his disheveled suits, the unquenchable hope with which he yelled it out, small white fist in the air held in what now strikes me as a kind of Black Panther revolutionary-style salute: *"Power!"*

For all this, I don't think it would be fair to measure Coach Gallagher on his success with the team. And yet that first season we managed a substantial improvement, and his second season, my senior year, we finished with a winning record, ending the season with a streak to get that exalted statistic, something that had either never ever happened at Vassar before or not for a long time, no one was sure. The LoBreglios, father and son, were now gone, but their legacy lived on in the form of Seamus Carey and another recruit, Seamus's little brother, Michael.

There was also a very interesting figure named Karl Butler, who had played with the Irish Olympic team, a prize recruit of Gallagher. Like Seamus before him, Butler was somehow placed in Ferry House, but he was a basketball nomad, kind of homeless, having played at several other programs. Butler was merry wherever his game should take him. The bulgur, barley, kale, spinach, and whatever other wholesome ingredients that prevailed at the Ferry kitchen were part of the adventure of his life.

Butler once showed me photographs he had taken in Dublin, including one of a small boy standing in front of a burning car. I thought it was cool, provocative, and I used it on the cover of a college arts magazine I was editing. I lived in the arty, boozy margin of Vassar life and hated jock culture in general even as I loved basketball; at Vassar you could have it both ways. Gallagher did not see it that way, really, though in a way he understood.

"Fucking poet," he muttered once when I showed up at the van for the two-hour drive to an away game wearing a blazer and a long black scarf. Gallagher was aware of my pretensions and ambitions in the literary field, and though he feigned impatience, I always thought that deep down he approved. He had a winking, conspiratorial humor that he displayed in tiny, measured doses, on the sly, when no one was looking. He murmured that comment about my outfit with a smile. I was one of many stars in the harsh galaxy of Coach Gallagher's basketball cosmology. I was part of something special.

* * *

I wrote a version of this essay seventeen years after my last basketball practice as a college player. That number is now thirty-four years. Given the elapsed time, I thought I should try to follow up with Coach Gallagher.

I contacted him, and we exchanged a series of emails during which we tried to make a phone date. This became much more complicated than it needed to be; mostly, perhaps out of habit, I couldn't quite seem to follow his instructions. A note of exasperation briefly entered into his correspondence, which elicited in me a pang of fear and panic. For a moment it seemed as if we were going to re-create our whole dysfunctional dynamic thirty-five years after it had last played out in basketball practice.

We eventually connected for a long phone call. His career as a college basketball coach had lasted only one year after I left.

He had hoped for a full-time job at Vassar and when, after a couple of years, it didn't materialize, he quit. I shared with him my fleeting awareness of his life outside the team, a remembered glimpse of him sitting in his Toyota in the dark parking lot outside of the Walker Field House in Poughkeepsie, after practice. He elaborated on the image, describing long driving trips he would take en route to some far-off place in Westchester or Long Island to recruit high school players. His decision to leave Vassar occurred when, nodding with fatigue behind the wheel, he nearly went off the road on a wintry night on the Taconic State Parkway on one of those recruiting missions.

"I simply just nodded out along the Taconic Parkway that night," he clarified in an email. "As best I remember it, I was woken, thankfully, by the sound and feel of the car starting to rub up along the little dirt embankment on the side of the road. I realized over the next few days that it was probably time to just focus on teaching and living down in Westchester and getting back into high school coaching there again. Recruiting is so important at the college level, even at the Division III level. If you're coaching you want to be as successful as possible, and players do that for you. At the high school level, particularly at a public school, you take the players who live in your district who come out for the team and go to work with what you have. At the college level I think it's best if you are full time at the school. Even though I truly wanted to coach at a college full time, it all worked out. I enjoyed all the years I kept coaching at the high school level and the high school and elementary teaching I did."

He spoke about it all without any rancor. His last serious coaching job, or the one he referred to as especially gratifying, was as coach of his daughter's AAU team. About what he might've done differently: he said that at the time he thought it wise to work his way up from a small program to a big one, but in hindsight he felt that an aspiring coach should attach themselves to the biggest program they can find because those are the people who "can make the calls for you." I shared with him my regret that I never spent time in the weight room; the concept of using weights to train for basketball was still a decade away. "They thought it would ruin your shot," he said in a tone of fond amusement at the folly of the old ways.

"I am sorry I missed the point-blank layup against Manhattanville to win the game," I wrote in an email. "I still feel bad about it."

"I don't even remember the point-blank layup you missed against Manhattanville to win the game, so don't lose any sleep over it!" he responded.

Mostly what I got from our conversation was a reminder of the curious juxtaposition in his personality of a sense of authority, beneath which lurked an explosive temper, and something else that felt almost boyish, playful, and sweetly modest.

The span of time from when I first reached out to my old coach to when I last communicated with him encompasses nearly eighteen months, during which a few serenpiditous events took place. One was the reappearance of Rick Pitino in the story. Celebrated, and then disgraced and defrocked, one of his two national titles vacated because of accusations of recruiting irregularities—Pitino is a world unto himself—he went off to coach in Greece. But then he was resurrected, so to speak, and given a second chance when hired to coach Iona College by its new president, Seamus Carey.

Another took place just the other day: I drove my son to northwest Connecticut to ski, and on the way home I got very tired. It was dark. This had happened once before, the previous week, when I was too tired to fight through it and pulled over at a rest stop. The boy is ten. I had to explain the idea of a rest stop, and then I put the seat back and napped for ten minutes. When I awoke I saw that he had also napped. He never naps. I think he got into the spirit of the idea of a rest stop. This time I was so tired I missed the rest stop. I was getting extremely sleepy, my head jerking, the car veering. It was alarming. I got off at a random exit and drove to the first place I could pull over. It was a deserted parking lot with a familiar name. When I woke, refreshed, ten minutes later, I realized, as I drove out, that it was the parking lot of Manhattanville College.

I reported this to my old coach. He wrote back:

"You have asked me questions for your book about my falling asleep behind the wheel of the car while doing coaching things for Vassar. Then you fall asleep behind the wheel of your car and wake up in the parking lot of the college of my coaching job previous to Vassar! There's something mysterious going on here."

Maybe that mysterious something is what education is—a kernel of experience and epiphany gathers momentum and begins to accumulate meaning, picking up stray bits of haunted serendipity as it goes.

—2022

Anthony Davis and the Plight of the Modern NBA Big Man

At the college, high school, and grade school levels of basketball, there is always a tall guy sitting like a potted plant at the end of the bench, basketball's version of the special-cases lounge. Such a person is called "a project." A slight aura of pity and forbearance surrounds these players, beneficiaries of affirmative action for tall people. This extends all the way to the professional level. "Big men get paid" is a basketball truism, and the NBA has long been haunted by the specter of marginal talents being paid huge sums mostly because of their size. There have been disappointing guards drafted out of college, but the legendary busts, from Sam Bowie to Greg Oden, tend to be big men. "You can't teach height," another basketball truism, is also a double entendre: you can't teach someone to be tall; the tall are hard to teach.

But why is it that some big men develop and others do not? What is it that must be learned? I was fascinated to read, in Jonathan Abrams's book *Boys among Men: How the Prep-to-Pro Generation Redefined the NBA and Sparked a Basketball Revolution,* that when Kevin Garnett was a tall, slender thirteen-year-old, he would spend all his free time at his local basketball court in Greenville, South Carolina. The police would have to chase him out at night, and he would arrive with a ball before dawn. But if the playground was a refuge, it was also a theater of cruelty where a six-foot-four, three-hundred-pound player nicknamed Bear would dominate him verbally and physically. "I've got your mind in my pocket," he would yell at Garnett after scoring on him. "I own you." Even after Garnett outgrew his tormentor in height, even when he showed clear signs of becoming a star, the dynamic persisted. "Garnett did not verbally retaliate," Abrams writes. "He maintained a straight face and returned daily." Was this masochism or fortitude?

Garnett, now retired, was one of the most ferociously competitive trash-talking players that the league had ever seen. He is a direct antecedent of what are now called *unicorns*—big men who can dribble, pass, protect the rim, and shoot the three—but his most lasting legacy on the court may be his habit of knocking away the jump shots that opponents shoot after a whistle. One sees this all the time in today's NBA—a player shoots after the whistle just to get a stroke in, to see the ball go in the hoop, and an opponent expends considerable energy to rise up and swat it away before the ball can go in. It's a bit of ritualized psychological warfare, as if to deprive the opponent of every possible satisfaction. "I've got your mind in my pocket. I own you."

Anthony Davis never rode the bench in the special-cases lounge. Nevertheless he is a kind of project. In spite of the fact that he was a blue-chip recruit out of high school; played basketball at Kentucky, where he won a national championship and was named most outstanding player of the NCAA tournament; was the number-one pick of the 2012 draft; and then played on the 2012 Olympic team (which won gold, and where he was the youngest player)—in spite of all this, for most of his career, Davis has been discussed in terms of potential. Even when he began to post impressive numbers and made the All-Star team for the first time in 2014 (as the replacement for an injured Kobe Bryant), the talk of the present was always accompanied by speculation about what was to come. As recently as December 2017, five seasons into his career, ESPN's Adrian Wojnarowski wrote, "Davis is still an ascending, transcendent talent, a size and skill set from the future plopped into the present."

Some of this sense of anticipation regarding Davis is owing to the fact that the idea of growth is fundamental to his story. As Vinay Mullick, the former athletic director of Perspectives, the small charter school that Davis attended in Chicago, put it to me, "Sophomore year he was six feet one, very thin, very long. He wasn't thrown onto the national stage until he was practically a twelfth grader. There were times when he didn't think he would get looks. He would tell me, 'I don't know if basketball is going to work out for me.' He had an uncharacteristically long period of innocence. He was six-ten by the time he graduated. You're not going to see that again. The story of growth."

Even though Davis has a height and wingspan unlike almost any other human—Wojnarowski referred to his "condor arms," but why not go all the way and call them pelican wings?—he is somebody who young people can hope to be. He was once a six-foot-one sophomore whose fantastic dreams of basketball glory were dying. And look what happened!

The era of speculating on Davis's upside has recently been replaced by a sense of astonishment at the present. Among the bevy of statistics generated by the Pelicans' Game 4 sweep of the Portland Trail Blazers: Davis has now scored a total of 258 points in his first eight playoff games. "Only Michael Jordan (283) and LeBron James (266) have scored more points in their first eight playoff games over the last 40 years," according to NBA .com. Also, Davis's Game 4 totals of forty-seven points, ten rebounds, and three blocks are the most in a playoff game since Hakeem Olajuwon, who scored forty-nine points in 1987, in a game that went to double overtime.

Davis's impact is just as substantial on defense. He was the most outstanding player when Kentucky won the NCAA championship, based almost entirely on his defense and rebounding. His length and his ability to move his feet were essential to the Pelicans' strategy of containing Portland's explosive guards, Lillard and CJ McCollum. On offense he exerts a gravitational pull wherever he is, inside or outside, and perhaps most of all when rolling to the basket off a pick-and-roll. There is something almost dreamy about the way he plays—things that should be out of reach are suddenly within his grasp.

I once sat with Davis along the baseline of the Smoothie King Center, the Pelicans' arena, after practice. It was a few days after his twenty-first birthday, in March 2014. He gazed out onto the court, where a few of his teammates were still taking shots, while I peppered him with banal questions to which he gave equally pro forma answers. I was sufficiently focused on him that I had no idea a ball was careening toward my face. I learned of it only when, with frog-tongue speed, his hand reached out across the empty seat between us and caught the basketball an inch or so from my cheek. He held it for a split second, then tossed the ball back onto the court. His hand retracted back onto his lap. By the time I turned to thank him, he was again looking away.

Back in 2014, his coaches were working on his moves in what they called "the Malone Zone."

"As in Moses?" I asked.

"As in Karl," they said.

"But Davis doesn't move at all like Karl Malone."

They explained that the space at the elbow, just outside the key, was where Karl Malone had done his work, and that was where they wanted Davis, because once you turned to face the basket, the defense could no longer touch you. The idea was to save Davis from undue banging in the post against sturdier players. Head fakes, drives to the baseline, spins back to the middle, jump hooks, short jumpers—that was the plan. Most of all, Davis was ideal for that staple of the NBA offense, the pick-and-roll. Davis has since moved his game both closer to the basket and farther out—he has become one of the league's best finishers on the pick-and-roll, but he also takes the occasional three and can put the ball on the floor for pull-up jumpers. He is an astonishingly unique player, yet it's a strange irony of the NBA that he is part of a crop of such players, a herd of unicorns— Joel Embiid, Giannis Antetokounmpo, Kristaps Porziņģis, Karl-Anthony Towns, and Nikola Jokić, along with his teammate DeMarcus Cousins.

Last year I called Kentucky coach John Calipari for insight into the new, modern big man in the NBA, because he seems to have coached so many of them—Cousins, Davis, Towns, all of whom work both inside and on the perimeter in ways that would have been unfathomable seven years ago. Calipari was an agreeable, engaged conversationalist who referred to his star big men by their first names with such evident pride, even a kind of adoration, that I started to feel as though I were in the presence of a very high-end florist, walking me through his inventory, alluding lovingly to the gorgeous stalks surrounding him. I could imagine him talking like this in the living room of a gigantic high school student who was a year away from becoming a multimillionaire—someone like Cousins, Davis, and Towns. But his message, to my surprise, was that he was, in a sense, the unicorn deprogrammer.

"No one wants to be center now," he said. "You can't even put C next to their name in the program. I have to say *power forward, wing, strong forward*. They think being known as a center limits you. But you want to be an All-Star? Do you want to get paid? You have to master the game seven feet and in. You have to get tough around the basket and learn to fight with two hands. You have to go get forty [points] and twenty [rebounds]. What did Karl do the other night? Thirty-three and nineteen! Anthony and DeMarcus didn't care about shots. Anthony took the fourth-most shots; DeMarcus probably took the third- or fourth-most shots. Just because you are not shooting doesn't mean anything."

Cousins was picked fifth in the draft, he noted, and Davis was picked first. "Even Skal [Labissière], who we tried to force stuff on that he wasn't capable of getting, we tried to say, 'You have to get tougher around the basket.' Anthony and DeMarcus and Karl all got it. By the end of the year they were like, 'Screw you, you are not bullying me—I am bullying you!'"

I asked him what drills he used in order to work on these skills. Most of what he described involved playing with a reduced-size rim to create more rebounds. One in particular stood out—two guys set up beside a reduced rim, a coach shoots, and whoever doesn't get the rebound has to run. "It's a scrum. It's like a bone that is thrown into a pack of dogs. Are you hungry? For some guys, it starts caving them in. They have got to be able to look at themselves in the mirror and say, 'Man, I have got to change.'" We ended the chat with a riff about longevity. "Big guys last longer," he said. "The guys we had might get a fourth contract. I don't know why, but, historically, if there was anyone playing late in their careers, they were big guys. The six-five guys: they were lucky if they played until they were thirty-three."

I am six feet five and a half, and I played basketball continuously from seventh grade through the four years of Division III college. I never really transcended being a project. The projects never stop searching for redemption. Dedication and hard work are always extolled in sports as the key to excellence, which is true, but it masks the degree to which these activities can be a drug. Garnett bouncing his ball on a dirt road on the way to the court before dawn could be a parable of commitment to the game, or it could be an example of a strange ritual of self-abuse in which he was going to be alone with the ball and the hoop in a place where he had been humiliated in public twelve hours earlier. Perhaps basketball pain was itself the attraction, a means of obliterating another kind of pain. You never hear the phrase *basketball junkie* anymore; it sounds too unhealthy. But there is something compulsive about filling an empty hole over and over, the repetition like some kind of homeopathic cure.

Now I am fifty-two, still an avid player. Being so invested in basketball at my age may seem childish, but there is a certain dignity in being the grumpy, irrationally competitive old guy on the court. Yet even now there will invariably be moments when someone half my age gives me tips— "Don't bring the ball down!"—or makes noises of encouragement that seem almost paternal, as though I am still some foal who, having finally managed to take four steps in a row without falling down, might possibly live up to his potential.

The Anthony Davis that I have witnessed this season seems to be someone who has changed in ways that go beyond his skills on the court. In a November game against the Timberwolves and Karl-Anthony Towns, Davis scored seventeen points before the end of the first half and then threw a tantrum about a foul call and was tossed from the game. DeMarcus Cousins had to run over and wrap his burly arms around Davis to calm him, a role reversal that was rather disturbing. Cousins was notoriously irascible. Davis was usually cool to a fault. Perhaps they had returned to the primal scrum John Calipari described. Davis, Cousins, and Towns had all played for him, after all. As Davis exited, it felt as though the whole arena had just witnessed one of those mysteriously intense outbursts that sometimes occur when an extended family gathers in one place.

On another occasion, after a come-from-behind win against the Oklahoma City Thunder, Davis took a long time coming out of the shower. I wandered over to the visitors' locker room, where the OKC stars Russell Westbrook, Paul George, and Carmelo Anthony were in an extended meeting, all of them draped in white towels like a scene from the Roman Senate. I joined the gaggle of press in the center of the room, all looking down at their phones like frightened birds, waiting for the green light to talk to the players while frantically eavesdropping. The only word I could make out was *shots*.

Back in the Pelicans' locker room, almost all the players were gone, except for Davis. I watched Dante Cunningham, an exceptionally slender forward, stop in front of the cooler by the door on his way out and load his pockets with bottles of Gatorade. He was dressed in black sweatpants and a black hoodie with the hood over his head. Like a credit card, when he turned sideways to make his exit you could hardly see him. Now all that remained were members of the press who were still waiting for the star. Davis at last strode into the room—a man in a hurry. "Let's talk," he said. He took questions, and as he had all season, his whole career, really, he parroted the theme of how the most important thing was winning. On this night, like many others, he had played almost the whole game.

"Did you get tired?" I asked.

He turned to me, looked me straight in the eye, as though it were a question that offended him, and said, "No."

—2018

The Maserati Kid

I turned down the driveway, which descended slightly from the road, the house barely visible through the pines. The feeling was of entering a secret world. Just past the open-air garage, filled with vintage Corvettes and Maseratis, was a basketball court.

It was a sunny August morning in East Hampton. I had come to play in a memorial game for a man who had died in the Twin Towers. The man who had built this house.

I was a friend of a friend, recruited to help fill out the roster. Since the guy's last name started with G, and since my childhood friend Jimmy Gartenberg was killed on that same day, in that same place, I gave a private nod to Jimmy.

The court was a basketball fantasy: glass backboards, three-point lines, beautiful landscaping. A TV crew would be filming, I had been told. The widow had written a book. I would be both participant and prop.

The game got going, grown men hustling. The players were mostly members of my tribe—middle-aged guys who seem normal enough until you see them on a basketball court, satisfying the need.

A boy played too—fourteen or so, braces, spindly arms. It was the boy's father who died on 9/11. He was hitting shots like crazy. Game of his life. At first I thought this was touching. But there is an entitlement to pulling up for a long jump shot.

A woman mingled on the sideline amid the men. She was well put together, in jeans and a white blouse, hands in her back pockets. The widow. A photographer stood on the sidelines, snapping shots with a tele-photo. What was so far away, I wondered, that she needed that zoom lens?

The kid was hustling, driving, taking shots, and making most of them. Voices of encouragement and praise came from the sideline.

Someone told a story about standing on this court with the widow just after 9/11. "I've got this asphalt jungle back here," she said. "What am I going to do with it?" Just then her boy, four years old at the time, came out and started dribbling a basketball.

Apparently his dad had been really good. But a dead baller is like the fish that got away, always much better in memory. I looked at the kid now, wheeling and dealing. I was moved, happy to see him so supported by his dead dad's friends. But *supported* in the context of such outrageous wealth is a complicated word.

The next game, I waited for the kid to drive the lane. I was going to block that kid's shot, smack it over the gorgeous landscaping, show him what happens in the real world. But his dad died on 9/11. Isn't that knowledge enough?

At any rate, I never got the chance. The teams were changed. Now he was on my team. I watched him hoist jumpers. Score.

In the end, after the last game, I slapped the kid five, said, "Good game." I shook the widow's hand.

Leaving, I paused at the garage, its floor polished as glass. The Corvette was a shimmering silver. I wonder, now, Why did I wipe my feet?

—2011

The NBA Kaleidoscope

The era of NBA superstars being empowered to choose the teams that they play for with free agency began when Oscar Robertson's antitrust lawsuit, initiated in 1970, was settled in 1976. The era of superstars also functioning as their own team builders began when LeBron James, then of the Cleveland Cavaliers, staged a live television special in 2010 called *The Decision*, during which he announced, "I'm going to take my talents to South Beach." I missed the live announcement, because I was out at dinner with my wife for our anniversary, celebrating our own "Decision." Afterward, I was driving through a small town in Long Island when a man wearing a blue Knicks jersey burst out onto a porch. "LeBron is a homo!" he screamed into the night. From this, I gathered that James was not coming to the Knicks.

Some things, like the general aversion of superstar athletes to the klieg-light atmosphere of the work environment of James Dolan's Knicks, have not changed since *The Decision*. But the sense of shock that a superstar could not only write his own ticket to the team of his choosing but coordinate a few other tickets has mostly worn off. Or so I thought.

What exactly is at the root of the delight that so many people—obsessive NBA fans and casual followers alike—feel at the sight of the frantic swapping of players and teams that erupts every year at the start of free agency? Perhaps it's the illicit mood of conspiracy and betrayal.

Forty percent of the league's players were free agents in the summer of 2019. There was a strict starting time for when negotiations between teams and free agents were supposed to commence: at 6 p.m., June 30, 2019. And yet within minutes, several high-profile deals worth hundreds of millions of dollars were announced, the equivalent of a couple announcing a marriage a few minutes after claiming to have met for the first time.

Within the first week of free agency, $3 billion worth of contracts had been signed. As the NBA analyst Tom Haberstroh noted, out of the twenty-four players who participated in the 2017 All-Star Game, only eight still played for the same team by the summer of 2019, and three of those eight played for the Golden State Warriors. Part of the pleasure of anticipating these trades, surely, is the idea that while you need a transcendent talent or three to win championships, you also need chemistry. And chemistry can be hard to predict.

These athletes are humans with their own personalities, after all, and many of them have to figure out a way to function on a team without being its best player. Some players, like Carmelo Anthony and Allen Iverson, famously struggled with this transition from first option to role player. And those are the famous ones that you have heard of. To watch even a little bit of the NBA summer league is to feel a chill at the enormous amount of talent that is so close to NBA caliber but will not make the cut. The players who do make it have, among their myriad talents, the ability to adapt to a team situation.

As anyone who has ever played with a chemistry set knows, sometimes you make a big mess and have to start over. The speed with which players and teams turn fickle has reached dizzying heights, driven both by teams and by the players. Two years ago the Clippers pitched Blake Griffin as the face of their franchise, going so far as to stage a mock jersey retirement in a darkened arena as a choir sang, and calling him a "Clipper for Life." Six months later they traded him to the Pistons. Some of the assets that the Clippers acquired in the wake of the Griffin trade were combined with the Italian player Danilo Gallinari and traded to the Thunder in exchange for Paul George, who himself had yelled at an ecstatic Oklahoma audience just a year ago, upon signing a contract, "I'm here to stay!"

Acquiring Paul George was not an end in itself, though; it was the price of admission to the Kawhi Leonard show. Leonard has long been thought of as the league's most taciturn superstar—no social-media presence, no quips, disarmingly minimal and honest answers in postgame interviews, such as the time he was asked what the championship he had just helped win would mean for Toronto fans and for all of Canada, and he replied, "I'm really not sure, I guess you really have to ask somebody on the street." He plays the game at a fast tempo that has the curious quality of seeming to be almost slow. He's not slow. He is deliberate in his movements, calculated like an engineer with his footwork, and powerfully explosive when he makes a move. In a surprising reveal, it turned out that all these traits applied to Leonard's behind-the-scenes negotiating style: he is cunning, he is calm under pressure, and he gets the job done.

The free agency of 2019 seemed chaotic as it initially unfolded but now seems tidy in hindsight: Kevin Durant and Kyrie Irving to the Nets was the overture. Leonard and George to the Clippers was the spectacular crescendo. The Russell Westbrook trade to the Rockets rolled in as a thundering encore.

The NBA kaleidoscope seems most remarkably symmetrical and strange when seen from the Pelicans' perspective. At the end of 2019 the Pelicans were mired in gloom. Going to games at the Smoothie King Center was like visiting a house where the parents are divorced but forced by circumstances to live together for a few more months. The Pelicans star Anthony Davis had asked for a trade midway through the season, specifying the Lakers as his preferred destination. The Pelicans, out of some combination of spite and savvy, refused to grant his wish. Davis was benched. The team claimed that they wanted to prevent their asset from getting hurt; the NBA insisted that Davis, one of the league's marquee players, play, or there would be a fine. The second half of the season saw Davis limited to about twenty minutes a game. He sat out most fourth quarters.

I went to a number of games during this time, in order to soak in the strange atmosphere and get a look at visiting superstars like Nikola Jokić, Ben Simmons, and Giannis Antetokounmpo, who eventually became the league's MVP. Such is the current fashion in basketball footwear that all these stars wore pastel-colored sneakers in shades of pink, green, and blue. Their festive footwear seemed to mirror the happy mood of these players and their teams, all bound for the playoffs while the Pelicans—whose pregame warm-up jerseys looked like pajamas—sank into slumber. And then came the draft lottery and the ludicrous good luck of getting the number-one pick, which turned into Zion Williamson, who is replacing Davis both as the team's standard-bearer and prime ticket seller and as the most anticipated rookie since LeBron James.

There was a brief pause to wonder if Williamson would be enough to make Davis stay, but there was never much chance of that; things had gone from bad to worse in the divorce. Not long after the draft, Davis was granted his wish and traded to the Lakers. So it goes. The Lakers, in the wake of the disappointment of not landing Leonard, scrambled to fill out their roster. Among their signings was DeMarcus Cousins. Two years ago the Pelicans' media guide featured Cousins and Davis side by side on the cover under the new team slogan, "Do It Big." Now they both play for the Lakers, along with Rajon Rondo, who also re-signed with the Lakers and who was the point guard on that Pelicans team with Davis and Cousins.

Rondo is known to be a difficult and recalcitrant but highly cerebral and skilled player. Perhaps sensing a limited market for his services at the end of the most recent season, he granted a very forthcoming interview in which he spoke with old-guy exasperation about the younger generation: "Guys aren't at the age where they can have a man-to-man conversation versus texting you," he said. "Everybody wants to text you: 'How you doing? We cool?' People don't understand how to have a real conversation and talk out problems."

Somewhere in the midst of this most recent turn of the NBA kaleidoscope, I thought of a haunting quotation that I heard a long time ago. It is one of those strange moments of basketball cinema verité, forever findable online, when something unplanned happens and the circuitry of the league flashes briefly into view. The camera is fixed on a seven-foot-tall Turkish player named Semih Erden, who is standing, with tousled hair and a down jacket, in front of a hotel gift shop while being interviewed by a couple of reporters. This is in February 2011. Erden has just learned that he has been traded by the Boston Celtics to the Cleveland Cavaliers. When I looked into the clip more deeply, I learned that Erden was coming back from an injury and had just taken a few days to go home for personal reasons, whatever that might mean. Who knows what events in his life were animating his face at that moment? The camera zooms unsteadily on his face, and he looks genuinely surprised and upset by the news of his trade, almost tremulous. He attempts to compose himself and makes some remarks about how this is part of the business of the game.

Then the video cuts to a shot of Erden walking across the lobby and, by chance, running into Lawrence Frank, then an assistant coach with the Celtics and therefore someone who was at least indirectly involved in the trade. Frank, at five feet seven, is one of the shortest coaches in the NBA. The young seven-footer with shaggy hair bends down, and Frank embraces him in an obviously consoling mode and vigorously pats him on the back. When they stand to face each other, Frank holds Erden's arm. "The one thing about the NBA," says Frank, his right index finger up in the air drawing circles, "it goes round and round. We will see each other again. We gonna miss you, though. You did a very, very good job." "Thank you," says Erden, and he puts a giant paw on the coach's shoulder.

Frank's phrase stayed with me. It's prophetic, though not for Erden, who was soon out of the league and now plays in Turkey. But it applies to a lot of what goes on in the business of "the league," and it applies to Frank, who was Doc Rivers's assistant at the time of the video and would soon take the head coaching job of the Detroit Pistons. He later worked as an assistant coach to Jason Kidd, his star player when he coached the New Jersey Nets, earlier in the decade. Now he is the president of basketball operations for the Los Angeles Clippers, who, of course, have just signed Leonard and George. The Clippers' head coach is Doc Rivers. Rivers won his sole championship in 2008, with perhaps the original superteam—Paul Pierce, Ray Allen, Kevin Garnett, and a young point guard named Rajon Rondo. Another twist of the NBA kaleidoscope, whose new configurations always fascinate.

—2019

The odd, pajama-esque quality of the Pelicans warm-up jersey in the spring of 2019, when Anthony Davis was going through the motions of his last season with the team that drafted him, is a triviality that hardly bears mentioning. Except that the saga of Davis's departure, now pretty much forgotten in the fanfare of his joining LeBron James and winning a championship in their first season together in the COVID-19 Bubble of 2020, had a fashion-related coda that reflects on the relationship between cities and their sports stars, which is the relationship most impacted by the NBA kaleidoscope. Davis, for his last game as a Pelican, came to work in a T-shirt that read, "That's all Folks." The graphics mimicked the old Looney Tunes sign-off. No one seemed to focus on the Porky Pig aspect of this, perhaps because it was too weird, but the phrase itself was seen as a rude kiss-off to the fans of New Orleans. In attempting to quell the tiny tempest about the T-shirt, Davis explained that not only did he not mean anything by it, but he didn't even choose the shirt. A stylist picked it out, he said. And this was the last glimpse of Davis in New Orleans, a peek into the strange world of Davis's life, in which the celebrity has his clothes chosen and laid out for him like a king or a small child—in either case infantilized.

A final coda arrived two years later, in a photograph of empty supermarket shelves. The photograph was taken in the immediate aftermath of Hurricane Ida, in early September 2021—over two years after the T-shirt incident—a period of duress and hardship. Every edible thing has been removed from the store, it seems, including all the salty snacks. Except, on the bottom shelf, in the corner, bunched together like refugees, one sees a plethora of potato chip bags, untouched. On closer inspection, each of these bags features Anthony Davis's face.

Most Definitely

The Westchester Wildfire, a newly formed franchise of the USBL, held open tryouts at their practice facility at the State University of New York at Purchase. Nearly eighty people showed up, in spite of the $150 fee, for the privilege of running up and down on the same court on which the Knicks practice. A fair number were playground all-stars for whom the tryout was a kind of one-day basketball fantasy camp. Myself among them. Before the tryout began the gym was filled with bouncing balls and large men lazily shooting and loosening their bodies while tightening their game face.

Then a whistle blew, the terse shriek that is the basketball equivalent of a judge pounding his gavel, and the tryout began. Right away we were split into three groups. The serious contenders, immediately recognizable by height, demeanor, and reputation, were in one group. Everyone else composed the other two. We did running drills, passing drills, three-man weaves, fast-break drills. Everyone strained and pushed themselves to their limit.

There is an almost masochistic thrill in witnessing the undeniable fact of your physical inadequacy as you try to keep up with players who can run twice as fast as you, jump twice as high as you, and who themselves cannot keep up with the very best players on the floor, who can run twice as fast as them, jump twice as high, and who themselves were long shots to make the team, which would be composed of players who were long shots to make the NBA. To try as hard as you can is an interesting thing; interesting to do the trying and interesting to see other people try. As hard as I could was too slow, too weak, too close to the ground. I watched a guy, not too much taller than six feet, race down the floor and then take off just inside the foul line, sending a crashing dunk through the hoop with two hands. As hard as he could was impressive. Surely this guy will make the team, I thought. He didn't.

The last thing we did during the morning session was break into small groups to play three-on-three. It was here, finally, that I got my footing and began to execute some moves. Every time I scored or blocked a shot I thought, "Did anyone see that?" But I knew it was too late. One guy I played against was rail thin, light skinned, with a spray of freckles across his face. He wore a white headband and his hair was cut like Kobe Bryant's. I posted him up and felt his heart beating. His chest literally thumped against my back. I'd never felt that before. Why was his heart beating like that? Perhaps it was sheer physical effort and adrenaline, but I think it was panic in the face of reality. All of us in our group had failed to distinguish ourselves. We had seen what the competition was like. It was clear we were outclassed. Some illusion had been shattered. It was not a great loss, the sting wasn't too bad, but the moment did require a fleeting acknowledgment that we had allowed ourselves to hope, to dream a little. Or had we been hoping for this very sting, for the tough love of life?

Most of the players were cut before lunch, including me. Dream over. The remaining players came back for an afternoon session. There was a good deal of talent on the floor. Zach Marbury, Stephon's younger brother, was there, as were Brian Reese from North Carolina, Kitwana Rhymer from U Mass, and Lenny Cooke, the high school player who declared for the recent NBA draft and then failed to get drafted.

Cooke, who had at one point vied with LeBron James as the nation's top prospect, might have ended up in the G League, or in Europe, had he come out of high school a decade or two later. But in 2003 he found himself in the strange limbo of leagues like the United States Basketball League, where sub-NBA players operate on a barnstorming circuit, hoping to develop their skills, attract attention, and move up to the NBA.

Hoping, in other words, for the spectacular caterpillar-to-butterfly transformation experienced by John Starks, whom the Westchester Wildfire have named as their first head coach.

Starks kept a low profile during the morning session, haunting the sidelines briefly and then appearing upstairs at a booth overlooking the gym. At one point another familiar face from years past appeared next to him up there—Jeff Van Gundy.

Starks went from bagging groceries in Tulsa to the Continental Basketball Association, and then on to the Knicks, where, in spite of his Oklahoma accent, he embodied a hyperactive energy and enthusiasm that went beyond the Knicks franchise and seemed to speak to the whole city, at least for a little while.

When a TV crew stood in front of Cooke before the tryout began and posed the question, "Lenny, do you still think you have a shot at the NBA?" his answer was inaudible. But I'd like to think it was "Most definitely."

This phrase—*most definitely*—was for a period of time the touchstone of everything John Starks said. He used it as the preface to every statement, the beginning of every answer. It was a linguistic crutch and philosophy of life rolled into one. It was the essence of Starks. At some point someone must have told him to drop it, and apparently he had some speech coaching somewhere along the line. When he spoke at the midday press conference, he was smooth, composed, and didn't use the phrase once.

He sat beside the team's owner, Gary Lieberman, to say how happy he was to be here, where he spent so many years with the Knicks. He was relaxed in blue shorts and a gray Westchester Wildfire polo shirt and looked remarkably unchanged from his days in New York, his round, almost babyish forehead as smooth as ever, the pensive eyes, the little, almost bashful smile. He spoke about how playing for Pat Riley and Jeff Van Gundy has taught him a lot about what it takes to win. When asked about the talent he had seen, he said, "It's too early to tell right now. You can get a sense of a player's athletic ability, and you can see their offense, but you can't really see how well they're going to play defense until you see them in a full-court game."

With Van Gundy in the house, one almost expected to see Patrick Ewing stride in. Starks said he hoped his former teammates would put in appearances. "There's a host of players and former coaches who will come by, and I welcome that, because I learn too."

Asked if he would consider suiting up, he said, "I won't pull a Michael Jordan."

Lieberman, the team owner, a hedge fund manager with a pink hue to his face and small, nail-bitten fingers, roamed the sidelines of the afternoon session and explained the secret method he used for acquiring Starks as a coach. "I was watching the Ewing retirement ceremony, and I saw John interviewed. He said he wanted to coach, so I called him up."

The afternoon workout was intense. There were running drills and then four-on-four fast-break drills. Jerrold McRae of Northwestern and Greg Stevenson of Richmond were standouts, both of them throwing down gigantic dunks in traffic. Craig Austin, from Columbia, last year's Ivy League player of the year, had a calm, distant, almost zenned-out expression the whole time. He has a wandering eye, which is an odd attribute for a guy whose game revolves around a jump shot. Zach Marbury looked more like his brother Stephon than Stephon himself—the round head; the terse, almost militant hand gestures, directing traffic; the faintly fascistic air of a martinet. But he did not have his brother's game.

Then there was the long-faced and extremely skinny seven-foot-two Terry Sellers, in his late twenties, out of Compton, now residing in New Jersey. His thin legs were nicked and scratched. One of the coaches, asked why Sellers didn't have a higher basketball profile, said, "The streets got him," and shook his head sadly. I had a vision of him literally falling into a hole.

In an empty hallway near the lockers, I bumped into Lenny Cooke, six feet, five inches but just eighteen, having an emotional conversation with a small man in a gray suit carrying a briefcase.

"I'll give you two hundred dollars out of every week's paycheck!" said Cooke.

"Listen, I can't help you," said the man.

"I'll give you two hundred dollars out of my paycheck every week, I swear!"

Oh God, I thought, what? Loan shark? I got a glimpse of the small man's brittle dyed black hair: he had loan shark hair.

"I'll give you three hundred dollars every week! Please!"

"Hey, listen, I'm already in for two thousand dollars so far, your travel, your hotel, I can't do any more!" said the man.

I walked away. It was a random snippet that made the distance between the promise and the reality of pro basketball seem very large.

Seeing Starks roaming the sidelines of his old practice facility and knowing he came from an environment like this was an example of sheer Most Definitelyness.

In a way the whole tryout was John Starks impersonation day. Everyone wanted to be like John.

—2003

The All-Star Game Diaries

The NBA All-Star Game day commenced ninety minutes before tip-off with a press conference by a player who wasn't playing, Kobe Bryant. He has a fractured bone in his knee. Bryant has been an All-Star sixteen times; in a quarter of those games, he was named MVP—a tie for the record set by Bob Pettit. This is the first time he has not been able to play. In this sense he was representative of the theme of the whole All-Star weekend: a league in transition. David Stern, the league's commissioner for thirty years, had ceded the role to Adam Silver, his bald, bespectacled deputy and chosen successor, for whom this game was a kind of debutante ball.

Bryant walked into the media room to face the phalanx of press wearing a white button-down shirt, open at the collar, and a suit of some elusive color in the vicinity of beige and yellow. The color projected calmness, neutrality to the point of invisibility, and leisure, as though he had come to the Big Easy in order to take it easy. But Kobe Bryant is not a take-it-easy guy. He is the most famous player in a league of very famous players. To the extent that he is associated with calm, it is usually the kind that manifests itself under pressure.

Bryant fielded questions that ran the full gamut of journalistic approaches: provocative ("Do you think you will ever play again?" "I hope so."), banal ("What do you think about your new shoes?" "I love them."), softball ("How has the league changed most since you arrived in it?" "The global impact. When [Stern] came on, in 1984, I was six, living in Italy. Games all of a sudden started becoming televised."), stupid/obnoxious/

provocative ("Not that I am suggesting anything, but do you have a retirement plan?"), and interesting ("What's up with all these injuries, and what could the new commissioner do about them?")—the last two, in fairness, asked by the same guy.

His response to the retirement question was a brief bit of meandering stream of consciousness that ended, "I don't want the rocking chair before the game. It would drive me crazy. I'll probably just pop up and vanish." The remark provoked the room to laughter, but I thought the line was kind of spooky.

Did "pop up and vanish" simply reflect his wish to be elsewhere in that moment? Or was he fantasizing about a Salingeresque retreat from staged events like this one, where he is required to face an armada of needy journalists with boundary issues, unsure if they want to be his best friend ("Do you like your new shoes?") or if they want to jab a nail into his palm to see what sound he will make, so they can report on it ("Do you think you will ever be an All-Star again or even play again?").

Bryant was unusually subdued; there were no proclamations about his comeback, no declarations about the power of his will to overcome obstacles. Perhaps this was a calculated plan to lower expectations far enough that he could exceed them upon returning. The guy is a creature of Los Angeles, after all. He is addicted to buzzer-beaters. He has an instinct for the third act. But his relative calm may have reflected the mood of a man who has spent his entire adult life being confused with God and is now confronting his mortality.

This is the mythic riddle posed to every physical genius at the end of his run: Can you exist without the thing that has created you? Can you be a dancer without the dance?

And what if the answer is no?

When the interview was over, Henry Abbott, of ESPN, drew attention to four specific words in Bryant's response to the question about injuries: "I think we will have to look, as a league, and maybe reevaluate things we can do," Bryant had said, "whether it's rest period in between [games] or different forms of recovery."

Different forms of recovery is a phrase with many possible meanings. An image of Lance Armstrong in a yellow jersey floated through the room.

The regulation of steroids and other performance-enhancing drugs is one of the most delicate subjects facing the new commissioner. The NBA has urine-based drug testing, but blood tests for human growth hormone have yet to be implemented; the players' union has been resistant. The matter remains unresolved.

The East and West All-Star teams had special uniforms for the games. The colors were a nod to the host city's penchant for vibrancy: the West's uniforms featured a purple fleur-de-lis on red; the East featured a green one on black. But what was most striking were the sleeved jerseys—not like the usual tank tops but like T-shirts.

Among the players of big-time sports who flicker across the screens of the world, NBA players are the most physically revealed. By this I mean they are the only ones who play in shirts without sleeves. Players have been working back toward the mean: baggy shorts, to start with (Michael Jordan), progressing to sleeves (Allen Iverson), under armor (Dwyane Wade), tattoos (everyone). I'm tempted to say that it's all the equivalent of a shrink or a professor wearing a beard, but there is quite a bit of facial hair in the NBA too; the most famous rabbinical beard in America probably belongs to the All-Star from the Houston Rockets, James Harden.

Still, the sleeved shirts are jarring. The motivation for this change, as I understand it, apparently has to do with the average American male's reluctance to wear a tank top. The T-shirt jersey has shown signs of being a big seller. There is also the issue of advertising on the jerseys, which the league has long discussed. There is only so much real estate to be sold on a tank top without obscuring the team logo; sleeves are the equivalent of the landfill on which Battery Park City was built. This issue, minor but not at all minor, is one of the many confronting the new commissioner.

The game, when it got underway, appeared to demonstrate how its host city's nickname, the Big Easy, might translate on a basketball court: so much talent and so much room in which to put it on display. The score at halftime was 89–76, with the West in the lead, which could pass for the final tally in a matchup of defensively minded teams.

The night was a parade of astonishing dunks. Blake Griffin, for example, had scored twenty points by the half, most of them dunks, on ten-for-thirteen shooting. Part of the pleasure of watching Griffin is the way he looks at the rim at more or less eye level for a second or two with that impassive glare of his—repurposed for comic effect in his television ads but at its root deeply menacing, a boxer's glare—and then, as though from out of nowhere, he brings down his arm from behind his body, the ball in hand, in a massive hammer blow. Take that! The movement mimics one of those rubber mallets that gets handed out at carnivals, when you have stepped up to try the strength test. You raise it above your head, arch your back, and bring it down using all your might, with the faint hope of ringing the bell. Griffin makes the bell ring loud and clear. You could summon a town meeting with the sound of a Griffin dunk.

LeBron James also had a number of impressive dunks. His style of dunking relies more on a combination of power and quickness. He converts alley-oops like Griffin, but more often he gets to the rim on drives. His finishes are powerful, but part of the thrill in watching him dunk is the catlike way in which it happens. Unlike Griffin, who stares at the rim as though to terrify it, James almost flirts with it, turning his shoulders away in a coy, I-won't-look-at-you sort of way; he often finishes with reverses, or semi-reverses, his eyes already elsewhere as the ball is going through the net. By that time he is often beyond the rim and so in effect is dunking behind his head. Griffin is a sledgehammer; James is a switchblade. James has joked about trying out for a professional football team—at least I assume they are jokes, a feint in the direction of Michael Jordan's famous baseball sabbatical—but the mood of his dunks is less NFL than Cirque du Soleil.

The most anticipated All-Star story line was the matchup between LeBron James and Kevin Durant. Even in a game filled with beneficent passes and uncontested dunks, there was a tension whenever the two players were matched up. Durant is having another transcendent season, building from one seemingly remarkable peak to another. James, however, remains the standard. I noticed that Durant seemed to play closer in style to a regular game; in one instance he led a fast break down the center of the court but, instead of passing, drove to the basket, not to dunk—though he had a few of those—but to lay it in after creating a bump of contact for which, normally, he might expect a whistle and an old-fashioned three-point play. He seemed kind of hungry.

The game drifted into farce; the West had a lead of eighteen points at one point. Griffin was having a breakout performance. But then the

East came back. The game got tight. With two minutes to go, I predicted overtime, an expression of my wish for it not to end—it was so much fun to watch. But the East pulled away, winning 163–155, on the strength of some remarkable playing by Kyrie Irving, one half of another, less heralded matchup against Stephen Curry. Both are fantastic shooters and can get to the basket, but what really sets them apart and makes them thrilling to watch is their dribbling. Both have blended Allen Iverson's crossover ethic with Chris Paul's herky-jerky acceleration; they don't penetrate defenses so much as burrow under them. Curry, at one point, split a pair of defenders by dribbling between his own legs.

Curry's profile is much higher than Irving's, maybe because he is so spindly, an unlikely NBA star, or because he plays in San Francisco, or because his teams win. Irving plays in Cleveland for an owner, Dan Gilbert, who may be best known for penning a furious letter about LeBron James after the great abdication and sending it into the world in Comic Sans font. Irving's coach, Mike Brown, had been fired once by Gilbert and then brought back, with Gilbert saying he made a mistake. With Cleveland not winning, Irving is paired with the volume shooter Dion Waiters (*volume shooter* is a wonderfully polite euphemism for *ball hog*), and Gilbert cannot do much about the coach unless he announces that his second mistake after firing Brown was rehiring him.

And yet, in the second half, while Blake Griffin and Kevin Durant were putting up gigantic numbers and Carmelo Anthony was setting a record for three-point shots in an All-Star Game, Irving was putting the East on his back. He had seven points and seven assists at the half, which is impressive but gives no indication of what was to come. He finished with thirty-one points and fourteen assists, missing only three of his seventeen shot attempts, and won the MVP trophy. He is twenty-one.

After the game the players' work for the night was not over. There were still the mandatory interviews; each player had his own little desk in a media room, as though he were a newscaster himself, around which journalists and TV cameras crowded.

Griffin was asked, "Do you worry that you will be pigeonholed as a dunker?"

"Yeah, I'm terrified of that," he deadpanned, to laughter.

The last press conference of the night, the bookend to Kobe Bryant, was Kevin Durant. He had scored thirty-eight points—tied for the high score with Griffin—but his team lost. The MVP title went to a player four years his junior. Durant is a five-time All-Star, was the All-Star MVP in 2012, and has the highest All-Star scoring average of any player in history. He is either the best player in the world or the second best. He is certainly the best player in the NBA not to have won a championship. When he sat down at the table to face the bedraggled group of reporters, he seemed agitated and distracted, which is unusual for the modest, affable Durant. He stared vacantly for the first five or six seconds, while his fingers seemed to play an imaginary piano melody on the table.

The questions hovered in the "Do you like your shoes?" zone; I asked him one: "I was really struck with how you drummed your fingers on the table in a way that made me think you had some background in the piano. And I wanted to ask if you have musical training, or maybe New Orleans is starting to sink in after a few days?"

Durant threw his head back and laughed at this, and then he became stone-faced. "I have no musical talents. So I guess I made myself look good with that," he said. "That's a great question, though. I always wanted to play the piano, so now that you said something, I might take up lessons."

When one of the greatest basketball players, who nevertheless is still number two, starts talking about piano lessons, it is not a sign of his desire for a hobby but rather a statement about his capacity for self-improvement. If Bryant was yielding the baton, ever so slightly, of will as an agent of transcendence, I felt Durant was now picking it up.

—2014

Kobe Bryant's remarks on how he would like to "pop up and vanish" after he stops playing are so on the nose as to be uncomfortable. But there is no question that Bryant and his public were starting to come to terms, during that All-Star Game, with his mortality.

There was a similarly transitional vibe to the remarks of Kevin Durant. He was playing for the Oklahoma City Thunder in 2014, with two more full seasons with the team ahead of him. His was the last press conference of the night, and the pressroom had a moonlit, speakeasy vibe. Surely he felt a desire to get back to the hotel and whatever lay before him that night. Yet there was something else going on. He had the slight impatience of someone at the bar as it approaches last call without having gained any of the satisfaction he had come here craving. Durant's journey from innocence to experience is one of the most compelling NBA narratives of the past half-decade. He had been so open in his early years in the league, and here was a little glimpse of the Durant to come: not the happy-go-lucky, aw-shucks kid but the edgier, more contemplative, more exposed adult.

The Two-Thousand-Dollar Popsicle

The guy who owned the house on Calhoun Street that we had sublet had been out of town while we were there, tending to his triplets, but our correspondence had the comradely tone of people who are dealing with little children, and it almost felt as though he and my wife were friends. But two weeks after we left, he popped up with a new tone. There was a problem. It involved the long, white couch in the living room—the cleaners had found an exploded Popsicle underneath the cushion. "Still in the wrapper, with the stick in it," he wrote to my wife.

He sent pictures. The Popsicle was red. It looked like a crime scene.

Replacing the slipcover would cost two thousand dollars. Could we please send a check?

My wife, distressed, relayed this to me on the phone.

I somersaulted into a state of grief. If you have little children and find yourself subletting a place that has a long, white, linen-covered couch, you should throw sheets on it. This is obvious. And yet we did not take these precautions. Why not?

I lamented this oversight for about one second before moving on to the real issue, which was much darker—it was my fault. I have a weakness, indulged only occasionally, for sugar-free Popsicles. I like them in combination with NBA basketball. I had watched the playoffs during that month in his house. I remember the hard-fought series with Chauncey Billups playing for the Nuggets. Somewhere in that smorgasbord of NBA basketball that is the first and second rounds of the playoffs, I had once

(once!) bought a box of these Popsicles. I must have let an unopened one slide down between the cushions. Then, at some impossible-to-determine point, an hour or a week later, while we were innocently going about our lives, a silent bomb exploded and incinerated two thousand dollars while we blithely went about the business of living.

Our life in the sublet place had been mostly happy. The house was located on a prim, pretty street in New Orleans right next to Audubon Park. Sometimes, in the morning, I would stroll out into the heat shirtless, my baby boy on my hip wearing a diaper and nothing more. In the park, with its birds, water, and sweating joggers, we fit right in. I rejoiced in the feel of his skin on mine, and in the smiles his baby fat elicited. But now, hearing of the Popsicle, this indiscreet shirtlessness felt like a rationalization for being a slob.

Part of the horror of the two-thousand-dollar Popsicle was the money. But another part was the fact that in my marriage my wife is the neat, fastidious one worried about germs, and I am the easygoing one who doesn't mind a little dirt. I love her for her neatness, but she finds being the neat one tiring. So now this happens. It was like Moody's and the S&P rushed in to downgrade the Husband Bonds to junk.

"I try and keep this family organized and in one piece," she said, despairing.

"Let me handle this," I said. I had made a mess; I would clean it up. I wrote the guy an email asking him to call me.

He called her instead.

We were in the kiddie shoe store when his name came up on her ringing phone.

I stepped out onto Broadway. She had dropped her phone a week earlier. The glass had cracked. She was now keeping it in a ziplock bag.

"I'd like to discuss a way of setting things straight with your couch that doesn't involve two thousand dollars," I said, pressing the sandwich bag to the side of my face.

His voice sounded terse, clipped, annoyed. He said that we had "treated the marble countertops like a chopping block. But I don't want to deal with that. All I want is the couch the way it was. It was brand-new."

I recalled my wife saying, "You can't use a knife on marble," to which I had responded, "It's stone! What can a knife do?"

"Two thousand dollars is a lot for a slipcover," I said.

"There is a one-day sale today at Restoration Hardware, 10 percent off. So it's eighteen hundred."

"Can it be cleaned?"

"It's a red Popsicle stain," said the guy. "Look, you can just not pay this. I suppose you could just walk away and …" It was hard to hear him through the bag. "It's up to you," he concluded.

"Let's be clear," I said, adopting as majestic a tone as is possible while talking into a sandwich bag. "I'm not going to say, 'To hell with you, I'm gone, you can keep my deposit, but there's nothing else you can get out of me, and if you want to sue me be my guest.' I'm not going to do that. I just want to explore what the options are. Two thousand dollars is a lot of money to fix a Popsicle stain."

I thought of the white linen chairs, which had also suffered. He did not bring these up. I told him I would send him a check.

Inside the store, my wife had picked out the shoes. The boy, a size five six weeks earlier, was now a size seven. It was slow in the store; several sales ladies cooed at him, but in return he offered only a long, cold stare. Then he walked away, pausing only to look back over his shoulder and blow them all a kiss. It caused an uproar of swoons.

My daughter, meanwhile, presented me with her choice: a pair of pink cowboy boots studded with rhinestones.

"No," I said reflexively.

"But Daddy!"

New shoes. Summer shoes. One pair for each kid. The Popsicle, I calculated, could have bought them twenty pairs each.

Afterward, we stood on Broadway, at a loss, literally. My daughter held the pink balloon that she had been given, to her delight, and asked me to tie it to the stroller so it wouldn't fly away. I did this, making it extra tight. After the two-thousand-dollar Popsicle, it was imperative to hold on to whatever assets remained.

We walked to Central Park, and on the way we stopped at a grocery and bought a bottle of lemonade and some sliced melon. These two items were nearly ten dollars. I did the Popsicle math.

I had a rubber ball in my pocket. I had bought it with my daughter the day before. (The Popsicle, I calculated, would buy 1,600 of them.) I bounced the ball as I walked with my little boy on my hip. He made one of his little squeaking noises, some kind of bird sound that connotes interest, and held out his hand. I gave him the ball. He bounced it on the sidewalk. He didn't merely drop it. He threw it! I caught it. This was a delightful development. Teaching my children to play catch had been extremely high on my parental agenda.

We took turns throwing. It was heaven. Except (1) every second or third time I gave him the ball to throw, he would bring the filthy rubber thing directly to his mouth, and (2) the boy's father had just incinerated two thousand dollars in an act of sloth and stupidity. This ball, these shoes, would have to last.

What is it about self-inflicted wounds and their capacity to disorient you? They don't necessarily hurt the most, but they are the most confusing.

The two-thousand-dollar Popsicle made a mockery of nearly every financial consideration of the summer—how much summer camp could we afford? Would we be able to rent a place in the country for a week, or a weekend? What about Whole Foods? Etc. Two thousand was exactly the sort of sum I was protecting. And now it had flown out into the ether with my blessing, because I was being honorable to some stranger upset about his marble countertop. I wondered if taking the high road and agreeing to pay for the stained slipcover was also a form of sloth, a cowardly shrinking away from a conflict at the expense of my family.

The air and light were lovely as we walked along Central Park West, munching on melon slices. At Columbus Avenue my wife and I had a conference, mostly in glances, about the pink balloon. The girl loves balloons. The baby boy does too, which is a problem—he tries to eat them. Her face explained to me that it was a safety issue. Mine replied that the children love balloons. The girl and the boy ate melon abstractedly while their pleasure was weighed against their safety. The decision was easy. My wife untied the knot I had made and let the balloon go.

"It's so hot it can barely go up," my wife remarked.

We watched it rise.

I struggled to remove the phone from my pocket. By now the balloon had gained altitude and was on the verge of drifting out of sight. I was frantic to take a picture of the departing balloon. This felt like the nadir of the Popsicle afternoon, and I wanted to document it. I held the phone above my head and pointed to the sky. A second later the camera turned. Instead of a blue sky with a pink balloon, the screen was filled with an image of my anguished, distraught face squinting upward. The camera had been set to reverse. My face looked Fellini-esque—someone from another time trapped in the modern world where no one can understand them, filled with personality to the point of being grotesque. I didn't take the picture.

My mother was home when we got back, and I told her about the Popsicle.

"A terrible waste," she said, and looked away, stricken, shaking her head. She has bestowed us with occasional gifts—for childcare, things like that. The two-thousand-dollar Popsicle mocked her magnanimity.

My wife bathed the girl, and my mother played with the boy, and I got Restoration Hardware on the phone and on the computer and between the two deduced that the entire nine-foot couch could be had for one thousand dollars more than the slipcover I had agreed to replace. So for two thousand dollars I would get nothing, and for three thousand dollars I could have the couch I had stained in its entirety, having purchased a whole new one for its owner. For one second I was excited.

But I never liked that couch, I thought. It was pleasing to the eye for about ten seconds, and after that it became almost hideous in its lack of personality. Buying a nice couch was a fantasy of ours, but only a fantasy. I would never have agreed to spend three thousand dollars on a couch we really liked, yet now I was on the verge of buying one I thought to be bland and not very comfy.

I pondered how Restoration Hardware had managed to insinuate the innocent-seeming sofa into the increasingly tricky business model by which the thing itself is cheap, but the parts you need for it are extremely pricey. This happens with printers and toner, with razors and razor blade cartridges. Now they had found a way to do it with a couch—very reasonably priced, but if you stain the slipcover, look out.

Meanwhile, the girl had been very upset while getting a bath; she had wanted a big communal bath like the one we took the other day. But she was too dirty, my wife said, and her howls of despair floated down the hall, echoing how I felt. When we all sat down to dinner—my wife, the baby, my daughter, and my mother—she was still teary-eyed. I put a colander on my head and pretended to be a robot. Amazingly, this worked. She stopped crying, and soon she was laughing. I looked at my wife as though to say, "I can be a money-incinerating idiot, but I can also get my daughter to laugh while her cheeks are still wet with tears."

The storm had cleared, as far as my daughter was concerned, or so I thought. A few minutes later, as my wife bounced the baby on her knee and fed him tiny bits of broccoli, my daughter, five, looked at her fourteen-month-old brother and said with crushing matter-of-factness, "I wish I had your life."

A flurry of distressed noises rose from me and my wife. In short order, the girl was sitting in her mother's lap, and I had the baby.

But after dinner, my mother said, "Thank God she said that."

"What do you mean?" I asked.

"Thank God she was finally able to say it. She has been feeling it for so long and acting up, and then finally she was able to find the words to express how she felt."

"You think that was a positive thing?"

"It was wonderful."

The phrase had felt like a dagger in my heart when I first heard it. Now my mother was reframing it as a gift. The depression about the Popsicle lifted a little. I glanced into the living room. There sat a lovely white couch, dignified, faintly nineteenth century in its bearing, like much of my mother's furniture and, for that matter, like my mother. I redoubled my resolve to never let any food enter her living room.

—2012

Here We Go Again
On the 2018 Cavaliers-Warriors
NBA Finals

For the fourth time in four years, the NBA Finals will feature the Cavaliers versus the Warriors, as though each championship series was itself a quarter in a single, long game. An emerging convention of sportswriters covering the NBA has been the habit of referring to each quarter of the game as a *frame*. An account of the Warriors' victory, in the conference finals, over the Houston Rockets, included the line "The defending champs outscored the Rockets 33–15 in what was a pivotal third frame."

A frame is a cinematic reference—a frame of film. Analog-film editors would sit, with a razor, examining each frame, looking for the right place to cut and splice. Fans of the NBA have similar deconstructing tendencies. As soon as a team exits the playoffs, there commences an orgy of speculation about how that team might be broken up, what its financial obligations are, whether each player is worth his contract, which free agent could be pursued at what cost. Everyone is a back-seat general manager looking to make major moves. But, for now, we are at the start of the finals. Each team has the players it has. The chess pieces are all in their starting positions.

On the Cleveland side, there is LeBron James, a spectacular player on so many levels, admired both for his physical gifts (now including the increasingly conspicuous gift of longevity) and for his intellectual acumen for analyzing and remembering the game. But one thing he is not is effortless. There has been a John-Henry-versus-the-steam-drill quality to his game for most of his career, starting with his first stint in Cleveland, when he was always the best player on his team, by far, and continuing, improbably, in Miami, where he joined Chris Bosh, Dwyane Wade, and, later, Ray Allen. All superstars in their own right, but LeBron James was clearly the first among equals. The Miami years were burdened by the weight of the hubris with which the whole adventure was initiated—first *The Decision* and then the press conference unveiling the new trio of James, Bosh, and Wade. *The Decision* seemed ingeniously constructed to annoy a huge contingent of NBA fans. The debut of the Heatles—an eruption of disco glitter and preemptive gloating and flexing—seemed constructed to annoy the gods. They won two championships. Then James returned to the city where fans once set fire to his jersey, and to the team whose owner had written a churlish, bitter, nearly hysterical letter trashing James's departure—the inadvertent effect of which was to make the Comic Sans font as famous as Helvetica.

James, in his fifteenth season, played every second of the game 7 conference finals against the Celtics, most of whose starters were in elementary school when James began his professional career. He is the NBA's version of Atlas. Everything rests on his shoulders.

In this sense the Warriors are his perfect foil. Cleveland is in the Rust Belt. Golden State lives in the cloud, in both the climatological and technological sense of the word. The team's majority owner is a tech billionaire, and its players are conversant in that culture. Draymond Green defended his new teammate Kevin Durant leaving Oklahoma City and signing with the Warriors as no more or less an act of disloyalty than an executive from Apple moving to Google. Durant himself is an active investor in tech start-ups.

I have a long history of enjoying Golden State—the team with Baron Davis and Stephen Jackson that upset the Dallas Mavericks in the first round of the 2007 playoffs made me ecstatic—and I marveled and thrilled with everyone else at the emergence of the Splash Brothers, with Draymond Green as point forward. The whole players-on-string, cut-and-move system introduced by Steve Kerr, one of the most admirable figures in sports, created a beautiful game to watch. I enjoyed their championship in 2015. But after they won their first championship and then rolled to their historic seventy-three-win season, something changed. Perhaps it was the phrase *light-years*.

When I first saw *light-years* popping up on Twitter and elsewhere in the NBA-fan firmament, I had the happy, confused thought that perhaps James Salter's novel of the same name was having—like *The Catcher in the Rye*, *To Kill a Mockingbird*, and *Catch-22* before it—one of those belated moments when a novel is lifted into wide circulation years after its relatively quiet publication. But I was mistaken. The phrase has nothing to do with Salter's portrait of a marriage in crisis in the Hudson Valley. Instead, I found out, the sudden appearance of the phrase *light-years* was due to a remark that Joe Lacob, Golden State's majority owner, made to the *New York Times* about how the team was "light-years ahead of probably every other team in structure, in planning, in how we're going to go about things."

The phrase—now a hashtag—of course had nothing to do with Salter's book, but there was an interesting irony anyway. Salter was a writer who believed in the ideas of greatness and fame, which he felt found their purest expressions in acts of solitary physical grace. Many of his characters were athletes in one way or another—fighter pilots, skiers, or, as in *Solo Faces*, a mountain climber who attains fame for his ascents in the French Alps. *Light Years*, a brilliant novel, is about the dissolution of a marriage.

Salter belongs to the one-person club of former fighter pilots who became literary writers with a hand in the world of Hollywood. (Besides his screenplay for Robert Redford, *Downhill Racer*, he directed Charlotte Rampling in a movie, *Three*.) His memoir, *Burning the Days*, recounts a night of lovemaking, at the St. Regis Hotel, with a beautiful woman, while one of his former colleagues in the air force, Buzz Aldrin, becomes the second man to set foot on the moon. "Pleasure and inconsequence on one hand, immeasurable deeds on the other," he wrote. Not a bad description of watching the Warriors, who are always trying to get to their happy place: the carefree, free-flowing, hot-potato style, which, ideally, culminates in one of those improbable Splash Brother threes—released so fast, arcing so high, swishing through the net in torrents.

Standing both within this system and outside of it is Durant. There has always been something itinerant about Kevin Durant, something cryptic, mythic, and inscrutable. As a child he had to move houses multiple times—"We moved five times. I went to seven different schools," he has said—as his mother struggled. Now he likes to show up places, go places, surprise people.

Durant moves in a way that echoes the movements of both an old man and a young boy. He looks brittle, fragile. He is a world-class athlete, a natural talent, a genetic wonder who also possesses the work ethic of someone who wants—who needs—to live in the bubble of basketball.

There is a detail from Paul Solotaroff's *Rolling Stone* profile of Durant, from 2016, that I find haunting: Durant, who is still a child, more or less fatherless, is asked by his coach to run a drill that involves dribbling up and down the court around pylons; his coach "ducked out to coach a game and told Durant to keep at it while he was gone." The coach is "detained," whatever that means, and comes back hours later. He finds Durant "crying, exhausted—but still doing the drill in his absence."

The Warriors' 2017 finals victory was punctuated by Durant pulling up for a three over an exhausted LeBron James in Game 3. It was a credit to every member of the Warriors that so many stars could bring themselves to work together. I suppose every finals series feels as though profound statements are being made about fate, practice, preparation, self-restraint, self-sacrifice, and team culture.

Can James carry the weight? Can the Warriors find their joy and their range?

Last year at this time, at the start of the third frame, I called the former Cavaliers coach Lenny Wilkens, intrigued by a tidbit of biographical information about prejudice during his days as a player on the St. Louis (now Atlanta) Hawks. I read that the man who lived next door to Wilkens was so appalled to be living next to a black man that every day he would walk backward away from his car, so that he would never have to look at his neighbor.

Something about this absurd choreography made me want to understand, confirm it.

"We had been living in an apartment," Wilkens explained. "Then we bought a house. It was a VA repossessed home in an area called Moline Acres. When we moved in, for-sale signs went up everywhere. I felt they didn't know me. You need to know people in order to make judgments. Eventually, some of the signs came down.

"We had carports, not garages. It was when the season was over that I would be home a lot. Our little girl was just starting to walk. I was out front with her. The guy next door pulled up. And when he saw me, he opened the door, backed out of the door, and walked around. Being young, I thought, I am not going to back down. He would get out on the driver's side, and that is the side that was next to me. So I made a point of being out there. Damn right."

"How do you keep your equilibrium?" I asked.

"My dad died when I was five," he said.

(I used to think the surest way to make a writer was to have their father die or vanish when they were young; maybe that should extend to basketball players.)

"My mother always said I had to make integrity and honesty define my character. And this priest friend in our parish, he would always say, 'Who promised you? Who said life would be a cakewalk?' But he always encouraged me and said if something got in your way, you stop and go around. And then in college I made great friends with some of my professors, all white, mostly Dominican fathers at Providence College. And they encouraged me to make a difference. I decided I was going to try and help my kids.

"Even in this day and age, LeBron James, someone painted something on the face of his house. Why? He's not going to let it discourage him. He's going to keep going forward, to encourage his kids that they can make a difference. When I grew up, my role model was Jackie Robinson. I rooted for the Dodgers. I went to Ebbets Field. I could afford fifty cents for a seat in the bleachers. I watched this guy. He was a man on the field and off the field. A great family man. He was fierce."

I asked about the Warriors.

"These guys, they want to win! They realize that in a team sport, we all have to have each other's back. We have to pass, defend, and the coach has to teach. And they do it extremely well. I am happy and pleased. [Steve]

Kerr played for me, I wanted to keep him, but the Cavaliers at that time wouldn't pay. As a free agent he got a better opportunity. If your team can compete and play together, they could win. You have to put players out on the court together."

—2018

Loitering Backstage
at the NBA

1.

I was taken to the circus at Madison Square Garden when I was about six years old. I can remember what it was like to see the lady standing on the backs of two horses as they raced around, and the spotlight on the trapeze artists, and the clowns piling out of the tiny car. I got one of the little red flashlights they sold there and whirled it in the darkness with everyone else. Kids were whipping the little flashlights into pinwheels of red light throughout the arena, blooming like fireflies. Sitting in the dark at the Ringling Brothers and Barnum and Bailey Circus and participating in this ritual with the little flashlight—everyone was spinning this enchanted object, and I had one too, and I was spinning it too, a miracle of inclusion. It thrilled me and remains an indelible memory of childhood.

Afterward, I was taken backstage. This was also memorable. Clowns walking around in their costume but out of character. The man on stilts walking on his own two feet, carrying the stilts. Animals in their cages. It was the first time I saw, or understood, the backstage world that made the spotlit world possible.

The next time I entered this backstage space at the Garden was as a stringer for United Press International, a wire service then in decline, for whom I covered several of the less desirable Knicks games in the spring of 1988. It was Rick Pitino's first season as Knicks coach. Patrick Ewing and Mark Jackson were the stars of the team. The Garden was configured in its premodern form, before the 1992 renovation, when journalists sat courtside at a narrow table equipped with rotary phones, and music was provided by an organist who sat in something called the Monkey Box, located high above the seats. My job was to call in the score after every quarter and then call in the final score right after the game. After that, I was to gather a few quotes from the players and coaches and write it up, dictating the copy over the phone.

I was fascinated to glimpse Ewing in person, stoic and furiously silent at his locker, his knees enclosed in ice packs; intrigued by Pitino's boyish, fresh-faced eagerness. But the most lasting image from those first forays into the backstage world of the NBA occurred in the visitors' locker room when the Knicks played the Cleveland Cavaliers at the Garden. A mob of reporters and television cameras bristling with microphones and tape recorders surrounded the Cavaliers' young star, Ron Harper, who sat in front of his locker. His face and bare shoulders were bathed in the bright white light of a television camera while he spoke. At first I could only see the top of his shaved head, his bare shoulders and clavicle. The man had his jersey off, it seemed. Nothing unusual about it. One saw the same parts of his body on television and in the arena. Basketball players are the most unclothed of all the athletes in the major sports. When I got closer, I was amazed to see that he was entirely nude. The bright light framed what people could see on TV. But beyond the frame, in some cases just inches from where some of the crowding sports writers were kneeling before him, there was more to see.

2.

These days I watch NBA games in New Orleans. Being in the stands of the Smoothie King Center is different from being in the stands at Madison Square Garden, but backstage these arenas are all similar. And, as with grand museums, one moves through them wondering faintly what it would be like to stay late, past closing, and be a stowaway.

The Pelicans' first home game of the 2018 season, on October 20, was a loss to the Golden State Warriors. Afterward, I went to the Warriors' locker room. Smartphones, social media, and a coed workforce have made locker rooms a more circumspect space than what I saw in the Knicks' locker room in 1988. Stephen Curry, shirtless with a towel around his waist, sat with his knees wrapped in ice packs so large that they looked like pillows. He perched as though on a throne, each foot propped on a chair, in a séance with his phone. Klay Thompson, Kevin Durant, and other Warriors were in various stages of molting back into civilian life, talking among themselves or to clusters of journalists who flitted in a group among the lockers. I approached the veteran David West, who was seemingly in no rush to change, asked him some questions, and then turned to see Shaun Livingston.

For anyone who has been watching NBA basketball for a while, Livingston is an incredible story, a player who has become an essential supporting actor on the league's dynastic team and who has somehow transcended what had seemed sure to be his legacy—an awful injury on live television, his leg buckling the wrong way at the knee. That he was such a long, spindly player made it all the more vivid and terrible, a brittle twig that snapped. Yet for me, the indelible image of Livingston occurred not on the court but in the locker room, a couple of seasons ago, when I happened to walk past the open door of the visitors' locker room just as he was standing at a buffet of food and scooping some into a Styrofoam shell. One often hears about a kind of science-oriented culinary extravagance when it comes to nutrition and NBA stars—Rajon Rondo's season was apparently revived when his personal chef devised a new milkshake recipe involving avocado—but the visiting-team buffet looked, at that moment, to be that of a middling Chinese restaurant, at best. The Styrofoam shell only added to that impression. But Livingston was hungry and scooped the food with a look of blank anticipation that for some reason has stayed with me; he was clearly going to be eating it on a bus or a plane. I saw all this in the time it takes for a door to close.

Players are also required to speak briefly to the media before games, after which they can return to the locker room or stay on the court and work on their game, usually with a coach or two in attendance to rebound. I like this time—when all the preparations are done but the fans have not yet been let in, and a few players stay on the court, shooting or working on certain moves—the best. I stand on the baseline watching the workout with the intensity of a scout. Before Game 3 of the Pelicans–Trail Blazers playoff series, Rondo put up about sixty three-point shots from the same spot, holding his hieroglyphic hand in a definition of a gooseneck follow-through every time, while at the far end of the court, on the other basket, Al-Farouq Aminu, the former Pelican, practiced his three-point shot, with his distinctive pointed-elbow release, the two of them moving in an entirely autonomous rhythm that was somehow metronomic and connected, like oil derricks pumping in the same field.

When the Pelicans are introduced at the start of a game it gets very loud, dark, and pyrotechnic. I stand near the visiting team at this moment. Flamethrowers start erupting from atop the backboards, and each Pelican player comes out to cheers, the loudest saved for last, Anthony Davis. Every arena now has some version of this ritual. While the crowd is cheering and the place is becoming as smoky as a 1970s rock concert, the visiting team's players jog in place, huddle together, or sit quietly alone. They almost seem to be savoring this brief, private interval when they are anonymous and invisible amid the noise and chaos. For some reason the bench players often jump up and hang from the rims at this time, perhaps because it's their last chance to touch the hoop before taking a seat on the bench. Their bodies rise up, dangle from the rim for a few seconds, and then drop down, a visual effect that only adds to the disturbing fog-of-war feeling of this interlude. The next time you are at a game and the home team is being introduced, look at the visitors' bench—the strange private rituals, the leaping up and hanging from the rim. It's furtive.

Before and after games, I wander the hallways in a slow-motion act of loitering. The supremely gracious ushers of the Smoothie King Center, all outfitted in mustard-colored jackets, will politely move me along when I stay too long in one place. The hallways are both intimate scenes where everyone there has gone through security and has a reason to be there and as anonymous as the sidewalk of a crowded city street. People look straight ahead, attending to their own pressing business, except when they don't. You never know from whom you will get a nod. I once crossed paths with Terry Stotts, the Portland coach, just the two of us in the hallway, and he gave me the most courteous nod hello.

To enter a visitors' locker room is to enter the ramshackle chaos of a hotel room soon to be abandoned. There Kevin Durant is wandering around in socks. I remembered the time his sneaker came off in a game I was watching on television. The camera zoomed in on his socked foot as he eased it back into the sneaker. I peered at them now—those socks I had seen on TV.

Part of the thrill of these scenes is a generic excitement of proximity to these basketball gods, but part of it is seeing them transition from the arena to their lives as mortals, citizens, young men living out of a suitcase on a road trip. I was on an errand to seek out the veteran forward David West. I found him seated in front of his locker in a giddy mood, and told him I had enjoyed comments he had made the previous summer on the *Open Run* podcast about why he had twice taken pay cuts of millions of dollars, first with the Spurs and then the Warriors, to chase a title. He repeated to me what he said on the podcast: "Like we learned from the Egyptians, you can't take it with you."

Certain images linger, such as Paul Pierce and Kevin Garnett coming out of the locker room at halftime back when they both played for the Nets, laughing and bumping into each other in the tunnel, delighted at some shared joke, perhaps the joke of the one season they played for the Nets. Or the children who are present in the hallways. The babies. It was such a surprise when I saw Tyreke Evans, who played on the Pelicans a few years ago, come down the hall toward the special doorway that leads to the players' parking lot holding a baby girl in his arms. With his free hand he dangled a pink handkerchief, or some kind of fabric, that seemed to have her transfixed. With Evans I had allowed myself to transgress the mostly unspoken rule that you should only talk to the players about the game. I told him I was very moved by his appearance in Adam Yauch's basketball documentary, *Gunnin' for That #1 Spot*.

He was wearing black jeans and a black sweatshirt with little rhinestones embedded on the front in the shape of a cat. He looked at me like a black cat, quizzical, maybe a bit suspicious.

"You remember that movie?" I asked. And quoted the line by his brother that had moved me: "These young guys, they don't even know how many people they're playing for," Evans's older brother had said, his voice cracking with emotion at the strain of the suspense of it all—Yauch's movie was about college players on the cusp of their first payday.

Evans's face lit up warmly. "Oh, yeah."

"I love that scene," I said. Now a dumb fan.

He was nice, smiled. "Yeah."

And then later on I saw him in the hallway with the little girl in his arms, her hair in pigtails, her dress pink, stepping through a door.

My instincts during these loitering sessions are deeply, willfully strange, such as the time that I saw a young man emerging from the visitors' locker room, occupied that night by the Los Angeles Lakers, clutching a pair of high-top basketball sneakers with purple trim. That this took place on March 1, 2020, and was the last prepandemic game I attended is something I grasped only after I returned to memory, which is spot-lit, like a dream: The game had ended. The hallway outside the lockers was near subway-platform-at-rush-hour levels of crowded. The young man emerged from the Lakers' locker room clutching a pair of high-top sneakers, white and purple, to his chest. These were clearly important sneakers. I raced after the young man, tapped him on the shoulder, asked him about the sneakers.

"They're Jason Kidd's sneakers," he said. Then he turned and rushed away.

Markieff Morris, the newly acquired forward for the Lakers, was down in push-up position, on his hands and the tips of his toes, in the middle of the hallway. Two trainers were hovering over him, instructing him on the push-up they wanted him to make, one of them touching the small of his back, his jersey still damp from having played in that night's game, to make sure he kept the posture they wanted. After this, they had him stand on these little ramps that elevated his heels, and hold dumbbells at shoulder level while he did ten squats, his eyes facing forward into the anonymous throng that moved around him like a stream moved around some temporary impediment. His eyes met mine impassively. He looked at me, through me, and did another squat.

I approached the trainer. "Why is this happening out here?" To which the trainer replied, with zero attitude, because attitude is a kind of un-necessary encumbrance, and efficiency of motion and optimal outcomes are the religion of sports trainers, "Some facilities don't have room for the away team's players to do postgame workouts so we do them in the hall."

One of the most vivid moments of these occasional visits to the arena's backstage over the past few seasons was that of a golf cart slowly mov-ing down the hallway with the owner of the Pelicans and Saints, Tom Benson, in the passenger seat. His wife, Gayle, in a red dress, was driving. It was like a processional. Everyone gave way as they slowly rolled past, both of them wearing a beatific expression, smiling as though they were a one-float parade, which in a sense they were. I watched as a row of ushers in their yellow jackets all stepped back in unison, their backs up against a concrete wall. Each head turned, one after the other, as the golf cart passed. Something about this turning of heads, one after the other, as the cart passed reminded me of Fellini, who used to cast nonactors in his movies if he liked their faces; he would tell them to look in one direction, count to four, and then turn their head and count to four again. Later he would overdub the footage with voice-overs by real actors. We all watched the golf cart slowly go by. It was like a dream, as though Gayle Benson was driving the golf cart not just to the elevator that goes to the executive box but to heaven.

All this against the backdrop of a very public family rift between Tom Benson and his granddaughter, Rita Benson LeBlanc, and her mother, Renee Benson. Rita had been a presence in the administration of both the Saints and Pelicans. Mother and daughter were suing him on the grounds that he was being manipulated by his third wife, Gayle, the woman driving the cart. Benson passed away in March 2018 but not before the spectacle of his testifying to his own coherence and grasp. The judge ruled in his favor, and therefore Rita has been cast out. I read an interview with her not long ago in which she spoke of the tacit connection she always felt with her grandfather, a connection severed first in life and then in death, in the aftermath of which she seemed stunned, grieving, and candidly adrift. Gayle now runs the Pelicans and the Saints.

Oklahoma City came to play the Pelicans in the fall. The Thunder jumped out to a huge lead and then, as they were in the habit of doing that season, blew it. I went to stand with the Oklahoma beat writers in their locker room. Ray Felton was hunched in gray sweats in front of his locker in his own little world, staring at his phone—there is something so aggrieved about Felton, whose resting face, or maybe resting game face, is that of a person whose car has been towed and he has had to travel to fetch it from the pound, where he is now in line to pay the fee. Steven Adams sat with his legs crossed in a thoughtful philosopher mode while in conversation with a stocky guy in sweats. They spoke emphatically. I am pretty sure this was the strength coach or someone on the staff. But these relationships between members of the team and the team's support staff can be as complicated and mysterious as anyone else's. Who knows what these two guys were discussing? In a strangely muted scandal of the previous season, Blake Griffin punched a relatively minor figure on the team's staff in the head while they were at dinner. The result of this altercation was that Griffin broke his hand, the most scandalous self-inflicted hand wound by a power forward since Amar'e Stoudemire punched a glass fire extinguisher case in anger after a Knicks loss in 2012.* What seemed most notable to me was the intensity of the relationship that Griffin had with the assistant equipment manager.

Eventually Adams, the magnificently unflappable New Zealander, came over to talk to the press. The youngest of nineteen children, he has a comedian's sense of timing. When asked what it was like when they had blown their huge lead and fallen behind, he said, "By then they had us bent over a barrel."

After he walked away, one of the writers turned to the reporter from Oklahoma City and said, "Are you going to use 'They had us bent over a barrel'?"

"Not in Oklahoma City," he said.

Back in the Pelicans' locker room, I spoke to Darius Miller. He played at Kentucky with Anthony Davis and then joined the Pelicans alongside him for two years. Then he was cut. He was out of the league. He spent two years playing in China before resigning from the team. Now that he was back in the fold, I asked what it was like to have been sent to purgatory and then return. He put his long El Greco hands over his face and sighed, "It's good to be back."

I went to the pressroom and wrote for a while, stared at the stat sheet, stared at the wall, and went for another walk. Russell Westbrook, now in street clothes, was chilling in the hall talking to people, leaning against the wall in a white sweatshirt and jeans—a pale faded blue—and retro high-tops. He was dressed like a young man in the 1980s, in other words. He was as casual as someone relaxing in the high school locker room after school has let out. Everyone lit up at the sight of him. One of the Pelicans' towel boys came by holding takeout boxes and stopped to offer a cookie. Westbrook took it. "I'm always the last one to go," he said. "I stay late."

---

* There should be a statistic for the self-inflicted wounds of professional athletes—the physical kind. There is no doubt that NBA players are just as prone to mishaps— slipping in the shower, cutting your hand on a boat—as anyone else. There are contracts, insurance policies, and the basic needs of self-respect that result in the exact circumstances of these events often seeming a bit murky.

I stayed later. I didn't want to leave. Instead, I went to the pressroom and sat there, staring at the white paint on the cinder blocks. I didn't want to leave because I felt that the night had something else to offer. But maybe I was affected by the casual lingering of Westbrook, one foot flat against the wall, thumbs hooked into his jeans pockets, looking up and down the hallway with the patient expectation that something would come by that amused him, interested him. A person, a cookie.

I began to wonder, as I often did in these situations, what would happen if I never left. There is the cultural fantasy of sleeping over at the museum; I would do it at an arena. Eventually I stood, alone in the pressroom, and walked out into the deserted hallways of the arena. I walked up the tunnel and was now out in the arena. A few cleaners were moving on the upper decks between the seats in the distance, but otherwise the place seemed completely deserted. I went back to the hallway and took a walk. Soon I found myself at the now-unguarded door of the visitors' locker room. I stepped inside and stood there for a while. The locker room was now empty of Westbrook and Carmelo Anthony and Paul George and the rest of the Thunder, but it was otherwise unchanged, the debris of tape and empty water bottles strewn on the floor like the silhouette of the circus that had been to town and now moved on.

—2018

The Earth Is Round
and Kyrie Irving

One of my favorite basketball anecdotes involves George "Iceman" Gervin sitting in the locker room sometime in the late 1970s after hitting a game-winning shot. Journalists crowd him asking locker-room questions: "How did you do it?" "How did it feel?" "What were you thinking?" After a brief pause Gervin responds, "The world is round."

I have always loved this line for its lordly belligerence ("You bore me," it seems to imply) and because I feel it holds a profound truth about the game. There are lots of sports that involve a round ball, but basketball is the most cosmic and planetary. The ball itself, often seen spinning on the tip of a finger, is the size of a globe. The climax of every play involves a sphere, usually in rotation, entering a circle, its own brief eclipse. The most popular style of play in the NBA these days is referred to as *pace and space*. A player with the ball in their hand is their own solar system of gravity and velocity.

One way to illustrate basketball's cosmic, planetary nature would be to describe the game as played by the point guard Kyrie Irving. He has a center of gravity somewhere just above his knees and the coordination of a jazz drummer. He is an expert low dribbler, and in the middle of his moves, especially when he puts the ball behind his back, he sometimes seems to sit for an infinitesimal moment on an invisible chair. During the clannish, gossip-filled family reunion that is All-Star weekend, I heard the theory that, among all NBA players, Kyrie Irving is the one whose skills are most envied. This is a category I had not previously considered—not MVP but MEP. Irving's moves with the ball are like physics problems that culminate with the ball falling into the hoop. He excels at humiliating the opponent. Maybe that's what is envied.

As a kid, Irving spent hours practicing shooting the ball with his father using fantastic spins so that his shots would elude the outstretched arms of the defender and bounce off the backboard into the hoop. He is the master of the bank shot, not in the sense of Tim Duncan but rather of Minnesota Fats. When great dribblers like Jamal Crawford or Chris Paul or Irving do their thing, the announcers call it *dancing*, but these players are not dancing with the ball, exactly, or with the defender, or even with themselves. Like a pickpocket or a magician, they are dancing with the attention of their opponent. The whole point is to end up alone. Slowness, even stillness, is as important a feature of these moves as speed. When they hooked up James Harden, another excellent dribbler, to a machine to measure his athleticism, it turned out that his athleticism was truly exceptional, in relation to his NBA peers, in just one category: the speed with which he can come to a complete stop and then start again.

Irving's father, Drederick, was a basketball star at Boston University, from which he graduated with a degree in economics. He worked as a bond analyst with Thomson Reuters. At one point he played professionally in Australia, and that is where Kyrie Irving was born. Drederick grew up in the Bronx, a friend and teammate of Rod Strickland, the inventive, aggressive point guard who played in the NBA for sixteen years. "My guys, like Drederick Irving, Kyrie's father, and me, we would have a group of guys from our neighborhood and we would go to each neighborhood to play in the park," Strickland remarked just a few years ago. "I'm scoring nineteen points per game in the league, going from playground to playground, park to park with a group of guys playing ball." In that interview Strickland seems to emphasize how much less coddled and protected professional players were in the past, even as recently as the 1990s. Kyrie Irving, in contrast, was a basketball prodigy. There was no asphalt under his sneakers, no taking on all comers on a playground in the Bronx or anywhere else. He spent a one-and-done season at Duke before declaring for the NBA draft in 2011, where he was the number-one pick.

Irving did something odd recently by declaring his belief that the earth is flat. Irving's remarks came on a podcast, *Road Trippin' with R. J. and Channing*, with his teammates Richard Jefferson and Channing Frye and the host, Allie Clifton. At the thirteen-minute mark, they are all laughing and joking about aliens. Irving has always seemed like a guy with a good handle on irony, and his remarks about aliens seem mostly comical at first. "I wake up sometimes, and I go outside, and I look. And I tell them, 'Beam me up already! I have seen enough to give you a report on how humans really are!'"

After some discussion Jefferson then asks Irving somberly and with the tiniest bit of trepidation, "Kyrie Irving, do you believe there are aliens?"

"Yes. I believe there are extraterrestrial beings that exist in the universe," he responds.

"Yes, I would agree with that," says Jefferson, relieved.

But before he can wrap up and move on, Irving asks him, "Do you believe the earth is round?"

"Yes, I do."

Moments later, the topic turns to the shape of the earth, and Irving declares in an earnest tone, "The earth is flat."

All-Star weekend commenced the next day. It is a time when thousands of people in the sports media congregate to write about not that much. So Irving was asked about it by ESPN. He elaborated, "I've seen a lot of things that my education system has said that was real that turned out to be completely fake. I don't mind going against the grain in terms of my thoughts."

Was Kyrie Irving a fool? Or was he doing a bit of performance art on the subject of the media's capacity to hyperventilate about celebrity— Andy Kaufman with a jump shot and a crossover? The next day LeBron James was asked about it. "Kyrie is my little brother. He's an All-Star point guard, superstar point guard. If he decides the earth is flat, so be it. He's an interesting guy, and he believes it." I spent the All-Star weekend trying to ignore the ensuing kerfuffle—alternative facts had been introduced by an All-Star. Best to forget about it.

It all seemed to go away until two weeks later, when Shaquille O'Neal, speaking on another podcast in an earnest tone—though with Shaq it's impossible to tell—said he has driven all over the country, has never "gone up and down 360 degrees," and has no doubt based on what he has seen that the earth is flat. (Shaq later said he was joking, but still.)

At which point I decided to call the infamous basketball father LaVar Ball. Once you start contemplating outrageous remarks such as "The earth is flat," one's thoughts naturally turn to even more outrageous remarks, such as the ones that LaVar Ball has been making—that his son Lonzo, who played one year at UCLA and just declared for the NBA draft, will be better than Stephen Curry, that he himself is holding out for a package endorsement sneaker deal for all three of his sons for a price of $1 billion, that he could have beaten Michael Jordan in one-on-one when they were both young men in their prime. Then he said that LeBron James's children would have the problem of dealing with expectations in a way that his own sons do not, eliciting a tart response from James: "Keep my kids' name out of your mouth. Keep my family out of your mouth."

LaVar Ball is certainly the father of three extremely talented basketball-playing brothers. He has started his own brand—Big Baller—and he is often shown in videos walking around his home in Chino Hills, California, doing domestic things and making uxorious remarks about family life. His second and third sons are still on Chino Hills's high school team, and they have also committed to UCLA. The youngest, LaMelo, is a sophomore. I watched several of his games on YouTube, which I would be embarrassed to admit if I wasn't among hundreds of thousands of others who have done the same thing. One especially popular video features LaMelo as he brings the ball up court with his laconic, high dribble and points, repeatedly, at half-court. When he gets there, he launches a shot. It goes in—a half-court shot!—and he walks back on defense looking no more ecstatic than a person who has just refilled a parking meter.

I wanted to see if LaVar Ball was ready to declare the earth round, but first I asked him about his parenting philosophy. He makes his sons focus on strength, skills, and conditioning—three is obviously an important number for him. Asked if he talks to his sons about all the media attention that has come in the past few months, he says, "I don't give them no media strategy. Think about what you say before you say it, but don't make no regrets." He said he doesn't keep any trophies in the house, which is connected to his philosophy that good players make all the players around them better—and it's true that Lonzo's and LaMelo's games are filled with court-long flings, often to their brother LiAngelo, as well as nifty pocket-pass dishes at close range.

"Did the boys complain about the 'no trophies' thing?" I asked.

"My boys don't complain about anything," LaVar Ball said. "When all you have to do is go to school, play basketball, what do you have to complain about?"

"How do you feel about Kyrie's remarks about the earth being flat?" I asked.

"If that's how he feels, I don't know," said the most fearless dad in basketball. "I don't worry about what people say, it doesn't affect me. Everyone can have their own opinion, people can say the earth is square."

After Irving made his flat-earth remark, he subsequently seemed to dance around the subject, implying the whole thing was a joke. A physics professor from Duke, Mark Kruse, was interviewed on the matter. "Perhaps he was using it (the Earth is flat) as a metaphor for just generally questioning established models of the universe, which in a sense is great," he said. Or maybe it's the opposite—if you are a basketball prodigy, you live in a bubble, through which, if you are a bright, inquiring kid, everything seems suspect. Maybe the statement isn't a metaphor about questioning received wisdom but an allegory about what happens when all the world is, and always has been, a stage, and somehow unreal.

I was recently reading about how the first astronauts felt when they viewed Earth from space—a sense of the fragility and importance of Earth, a kind of radical humility that has been termed the "overview effect." Writing in his book about the subject, *The Overview Effect*, the historian Frank White quotes the NASA astronaut Sandra Magnus about the experience of seeing Earth from this perspective: "It is all connected, it is all interdependent. You look out the window, and in my case, I saw the thinness of the atmosphere, and it really hit home, and I thought, 'Wow, this is a fragile ball of life that we're living on.'"

—2017

The Nets

The Nets signed two of the three most coveted free agents of this year's class, Kyrie Irving and Kevin Durant. Then they signed James Harden. All of a sudden the team that was a second thought in New York commanded a level of attention and respect. Since 2012, when they moved from the Meadowlands to Brooklyn and an arena that, if not the snazzy Frank Gehry–designed architectural concoction initially planned, is still interesting and modern looking, its rust color blending in with brownstone Brooklyn spreading out on all sides, they have looked like a new team. But the vibe remained a bit hapless and absurd. They were still the team that played in the swamps of New Jersey on some spiritual level. But suddenly, with these signings, it's a new era for the Nets. The old fans are stepping forward to claim that they loved them back when.

"I was once the poet laureate of the Nets," my friend Hal Sirowitz wrote. He included a couplet from their first season in Brooklyn: "Ghosts of brittle Kerry Kittles / Brooklyn Beer and eating Skittles."

Kerry Kittles, the forgotten man of the Nets. I saw him once in the Meadowlands parking lot after a game, in 2002. He was sitting in a dark blue Mercedes in a long gray overcoat, white shirt, suit, and tie. I remember a gray scarf and black leather gloves, but of those two details I am not entirely sure. Someone was in the passenger seat, and two people were in the back. Everyone elegant, like Kittles. It looked as though a banker was having a night out with friends. This was during that awkward era of the NBA dress code. Kittles wore his suits with graceful ease.

Surrounding that little oasis of light inside the dark blue sedan was the mostly vacant Meadowlands parking lot, which spread out all around them in a sea of white rectangles painted on black asphalt. The Nets game had long since ended. The only cars there belonged to Meadowlands staff and, I guess, the odd player still emerging from the showers. I had been at the game as a journalist, had driven my car, which is why I was rolling across the empty parking lot at that hour turning to see Kittles and company, dapper in the dark blue Mercedes.

The Nets won the Eastern Conference for the second straight year in 2002. They made back-to-back trips to the finals, losing to the Lakers each time. I was visiting the Meadowlands in March for an article I was writing on Jason Kidd. Being in his presence, his aura, was a curious experience. I can't think of another player whose movements and speech are as smooth, soothing, even mellifluous—even doing postgame interviews Kidd can seem to be telling a bedtime story—and yet he played with such force. Being around him, in spite of or because of how soft-spoken he was, always accompanied a palpable sense of suppressed violence, of his having a temper. Maybe it had to do with the scandal that preceded his trade from Phoenix to the Nets, when there was an altercation, allegedly, with his wife. But his wife was cheerfully present. Still, one wondered. (Also present was a rookie named Brian Scalabrine, who nearly twenty years later would recount to the *New York Times* the mental games he played to keep himself focused in his role as last man on the bench, and in this way prolong his NBA careeer, telling himself things like, "If I miss this next shot, my kids are going to die.")

The second-to-last time I ever had a drink was at a Nets game that March. It was a strange time in my life—I was carousing a lot but not getting much done and vaguely rationalizing it all with the idea that I needed to keep my spirits high in light of the traumas of events of the recent past that, it had begun to dawn on me, were not so recent by the spring of 2002. By this I mean a breakup with a woman, the sudden death of a friend, and the less sudden but very unpleasant falling out with another friend with whom I worked. All of this happened, or commenced, in the last months of 1999. And then one morning in the spring of 2002, during a week in which I made a couple of trips to see the Nets, night games for which I had my own private pregame festivities, I woke up and decided to take a break from drinking. But that night I went to a dinner party; the wife of my late friend who had died in 1999 had a new boyfriend. They were serious. The boyfriend had moved back from Spain. The dinner was at his place and followed Spanish protocol—we didn't eat until around 10 p.m., by which time four of us had drunk six or eight bottles of wine. The night went from there.

The next morning, I woke and peered at the to-do list taped to the wall—it included the Jason Kidd profile—and realized I was not doing any of the things I was supposed to do. I will stop drinking for two weeks, I declared.

The two weeks were difficult but manageable. I decided to stretch it to two months. It's been nineteen years. And yet every day I think, "It would be nice to have a drink." I don't know what I am doing with this long streak of abstention. I take it seriously, and yet I allow myself ginger ale with bitters (which has some alcohol). At the other extreme, once, having popped a fancy chocolate bonbon into my mouth only to discover that it was filled with strong liquor, I rushed to get a napkin and spat it out as though it were poison. Maybe I have to go to meetings, after all? Or maybe I am just making a fetish out of abstention, keeping it going so I can feel as though I am accomplishing something. Maybe I should just loosen up, take it easy, and have a drink. In moderation, what could go wrong?

None of this has anything to do with Kittles or the Nets, except I associate him, and them, with those nights in the spring of 2002 when I was making trips to the Meadowlands to watch Nets games, and often having some pregame drinks in advance, and then wandering the Meadowlands halls and locker rooms all lit up, and then deciding to take a break for nineteen years.

I didn't drive my own car usually, I should add. The most vivid memory from that stretch of days—even clearer to me than the look on the face of the Nets PR guy who was watching from the stands while I interviewed Kidd after practice, and who called out, as I stood there in sneakers proposing that we play a game of one-on-one, "No one-on-one!"—involved the bus that took fans from Port Authority directly to the Nets game. I remember the dark interior of the bus as it careened off the highway and into the Meadowlands parking lot one night, where the driver, disconcertingly, got lost. Everyone on that bus had taken the trouble to get to the game early, perhaps sensing the possibility of things going wrong on a bus ride to the Nets. And sure enough, the driver began to circle in the vast space between Giants Stadium and the arena, seemingly unable to find his way. The parking lot was no less dark and bereft before the game as it had been after, when I saw the Kittles party in their dark-blue Mercedes. It almost felt like we were all lost at sea. The arena loomed in the distance, a brightly lit basketball Shangri-La. Eventually everyone on the bus was yelling at the driver, directing him, screaming, "Left! Left!" when he started to turn right and "Right! Right!" when he started to turn left, until with the aid of this ship of fools we eventually arrived at our destination.

—2021

Lost in the Game

1. The Language of Pickup Basketball

When my mother went into surgery, I left the hospital. The alternative was sitting in a waiting room staring at a giant screen waiting for her name to pop up. It wasn't a dire situation medically, but I didn't see the point of marinating in my own worry for ninety minutes. I biked north on York Avenue—past Sotheby's and the cul-de-sac where the writer George Plimpton lived, and had his *Paris Review* office, and threw his parties. Plimpton's famous aphorism about sportswriting always offended me, or challenged me: "The smaller the ball, the better the writing."

I headed north until I arrived at Carl Schurz Park—a little slice of green along the East River that is hard to call a park in comparison to Riverside Park or Central Park. But it has a court.

I was surprised to find a slender Asian teenager in high-tops taking tentative shots.

"Can I shoot with you?" I asked.

He nodded. A moment later he was standing by the fence looking at his shoes or his phone as I dribbled and shot with his ball. Was this a matter of shyness or some cultural barrier that made him assume only one person could use the ball at a time? I felt as though I had mugged him.

"Come shoot with me, and I can get your rebounds and you can get mine," I said.

He was maybe thirteen or fourteen years old, impossibly slender, and tall for his age, I thought. Cargo shorts, Jordan high-tops, a black tank top, and a black Nike baseball cap on his head. It was as though he had purchased an outfit for the explicit purpose of shooting hoops in a New York City park.

He came over, and we shot around in silence. I wondered if he spoke English, but it didn't really matter. The language in which we communicated was basketball. He had an awkward shot—he was a teenager in the midst of a growth spurt. As I got loose, I started doing little "shake and bake" moves with the dribble. These are point-guard moves, city moves—head fakes, hesitations, spins, dribbling between the legs, letting the ball hang in the air beneath your hand for an extra moment before crossing it over. All in slow motion.

He responded with tiny movements of his own—a fake, a crossover. The city game combines the gestures of dance with those of a three-card monte dealer. I was sure he was playing out his own private basketball fantasy life. He seemed like a new inductee into the basketball cult who had not yet been briefed on playground etiquette.

I took it upon myself to explain. For example, when one person misses a shot, the rebounder throws him the ball and jogs to the perimeter while the person who missed goes in for a layup. Then they pass it out to the shooter, who will then shoot until they miss. I didn't explain this with words; I just threw a leading pass at him after he missed. Then, after I missed, I jogged toward the basket with my palms up and facing out—the universally understood sign language for "throw me the ball."

He threw me the ball.

It recently occured to me that I was fluent in a foreign language. A language that is so intuitive that I forget other people don't understand. I was playing pickup basketball in Brooklyn Bridge Park, where I was meeting a friend. She showed up, watched the game. "I could see people were following a code of behavior and a set of rules that everyone in the game understood," she said later. "But I had no idea what they were."

If only this were the sort of thing one could put on a curriculum vitae. "Languages: English, pickup basketball."

*   *   *

My basketball life is metabolic, instinctive, and compulsive. To say that for a long time I never really thought about it is only half-right; playing the game was what I did to avoid thought. Like a heavy drinker attuned to the moment in the afternoon when it is acceptable to make the first drink, my afternoons were—and are—always punctuated by a moment when I am suddenly aware that going to play basketball is an option.

Toward the end of that long-ago midday session of shooting around at Carl Schurz Park, I was feeling good and attempted a dunk. As almost always happens, I missed. But the rim rattled, the backboard bobbed up and down, and this turbulence gave our little gathering at the church of hoops a kind of credibility. A moment later he dribbled the ball out near the top of the key, and I stepped toward him as if to guard him. There was no way I was going to even pretend to play one-on-one with this kid. I couldn't resist the gesture, though.

I love playing one-on-one and in situations like this—two people at a court in their own world, maybe each with their own ball. I played organized ball continually from seventh grade through four seasons in college, yet much of my basketball education took place on playground courts, and one-on-one is a foundational aspect of the playground game. I always play my best basketball when I am the best player on the team. When you play one-on-one, there is no ambiguity about who this is.

Also, playing one-on-one with a stranger is a bit weird if you are not used to it. I don't mean the physical intimacy of the contact, though there is that, but rather that there is some vulnerability in the very act of trying, making an effort, in a contest that pits you directly against someone else. You could lose, and you have to deal with that. Conversely, you might win, feel good about it, but then have to try and hide that feeling. Expressing too much joy can be seen as a weakness too. After all, there is no outside authority to make the game or enforce the rules, and this makes you both more vulnerable and more free. There is a kind of autonomy in the physical space of a playground. It's part of the city, in full view of it, yet fenced off and apart. In such a space one can get lost in the game.

I didn't play one-on-one with this kid, but the basketball catharsis I had come for had been achieved. I had gotten lost in the world of shooting. I hadn't thought once about my mother, who came out of her surgery just fine. I would have forgotten about the event entirely but for this basketball interlude, and maybe the fact that this was the same hospital in which, many years earlier, my father had passed away.

When I waved goodbye to the kid, he waved back at me with a passivity that seemed forlorn. I thought of a line in John Edgar Wideman's book *Hoop Roots* that I found curious and true, and return to often, even as I don't really understand it: "We play basketball to meet our fathers."*

2. Fathers

There is an anecdote in Jonathan Abrams's book *Boys among Men: How the Prep-to-Pro Generation Redefined the* NBA *and Sparked a Basketball Revolution* that has always fascinated me.

In 1989 Kevin Garnett was thirteen years of age. He would go to his local playground, sometimes arriving before dawn and not leaving until he was shooed away by the police at night. During the day there was a competitive game, and one player in particular, Bear, was constantly in his face. He was over six feet tall and three hundred pounds and singled out Garnett for abuse. Nevertheless, Garnett returned to this court with a compulsion that sounds almost like an addiction.

I can say from experience that to be humiliated on the basketball court is an expense that has compound interest—you can't entirely leave the humiliation behind, because people have seen it, and you will be tested again to see how you react to the abuse when you return to that court. But

---

* I have written to Wideman, through his representatives, asking him to elaborate on this remark, and he, wisely, has ignored these entreaties. What is the point of an aphorism if you have to explain it? Would Heraclitus expound on what he meant by "the same river twice"? There is also the fact that Wideman lays out a very literal explanation of the remark in the book in which the phrase appears, *Hoop Roots*. Wideman grew up playing basketball in pickup games on the same playground in the Homewood neighborhood of Pittsburgh where his father had played. His father dominated. One of the players he dominated was a guy named Ed Fleming, a serious talent who would go on to play in the NBA. Fleming would then go on to abuse the young John Edgar Wideman on that same court. Wideman describes his first real conversation with Fleming outside of the basketball court, which ends with Fleming saying his first name, John. "He'd always called me Wideman on the court. The surname detached, objectified, like when it's entered in a scorebook. Wideman. A clean slate for each new game."

in another sense you can leave it behind, because, after all, it happened in a world contained almost entirely within the playground and the park.

Today a player of Garnett's height and talent would probably have been spotted long before he was thirteen. He would have been brought indoors, into the complex preprofessional ecosystem of basketball that points toward the NBA (though rarely leads there). Why did Garnett keep coming back?

The first time I bounced a ball without the supervision of a gym teacher at school was around 1977. By no means was it at the same level as the famous spots like Rucker Park or the West Fourth Street courts, but the playground at Riverside and Seventy-Sixth had a good basketball reputation at the time. It was usually crowded enough on weekdays that when you got on the court for a full- or even a half-court game, you had to win or be consigned to waiting another hour. On weekends it was packed. For me, street basketball was a place where I was beaten, humiliated, and insulted. It wasn't personal, but it was. It wasn't racial, but it was, a little. It was about talent but also about physical grace and personal style. It was also about justice and injustice. I embodied the latter because so much height had been squandered on a person who had so little talent. But I kept coming back.

Was I driven by a love of the game? Yes, I suppose, but only if you expand the parameters of "the game" to include the basic act of survival in an inhospitable environment. Or maybe the definition that needs to be expanded is the one for "love." Is an addict driven by a love of the drug?

I first arrived on this court when I was around eleven, and for a while I only peered at the players on the full court. Eventually I played—or tried to. Mostly I stayed on the half-court, but even there it was hard to get picked for a team. I often had to call my own next, which I hated (and still hate) doing because it implicated you in the politics of choosing players. Eventually you would probably have to get into it with someone else who claimed they had next. So I always tried to get onto a team.

The triumphs of street ball—the game-winning shots and so forth—tend to fade from my memory while the defeats and humiliations stay with me.

For example, in my early twenties I got punched in the face by a guy named Red. I don't recall the infraction, just some words back and forth, and then I was on the ground. My response was to get back up and keep mouthing off but not hit back. The game resumed. Later, just as I returned home, my friend Tom Cushman called. He had been on the basketball team with me in high school; he was a musician, a sardonic guy. I wasn't ready to talk to him or anyone else just then.

"Can I call you right back?" I said.

I slammed the phone down in its cradle before he could answer and, in the silence of my bedroom, burst into tears. I sobbed for what felt like a long time. Red was a burly asshole with freckles. I saw him infrequently on the court and had never laid eyes on him anywhere else. I had kept it together, finished the game, walked home. Now this sudden rain shower of tears. I composed myself, wiped my face, and reached for the phone. Only then did I see that I had not put it cleanly back in the cradle; it was ajar. I picked it up. No dial tone.

"Hello?" I said.

"I heard all that," said Tom.

Street ball as a place where you test yourself, as you would against a father. Street ball as a place where the triumphs and defeats are only partly about basketball.

3. Barclays

In April 2008 I got a call from the well-known street photographer, Jeff Mermelstein, who was working on a project about basketball in Brooklyn. We would go around to different playgrounds and gyms, he said, and he would take pictures and I would write something to accompany them. The resulting project, for which I would get paid, would be displayed inside the fantastic future home of the Brooklyn Nets. There was a catch, though. The project's patron was the real estate developer Bruce Ratner, the man who brought the Nets and the Barclays Center to Brooklyn via a massive real estate development for which basketball was a kind of Trojan horse.

To involve myself with Ratner was to be a collaborator against the citizens of Brooklyn, for whom this massive development was an attack on the scale and texture of their neighborhoods—Park Slope, Fort Greene, Cobble Hill. Also Brooklyn Heights, where the Saint Ann's School, from which I graduated high school, is located. The drama of Ratner's Brooklyn development has been unfolding since 2003, and as of 2019, it's still not over. In fact, it's not even primarily Ratner's anymore.

My first thought, therefore, was "no way."

On the other hand, it would be a chance to roam the basketball courts of New York, or at least Brooklyn. When I travel, I always make a point of playing in whatever city I am visiting. In New York, however, I always imagine myself as some version of John Cheever's the Swimmer, going from court to court to court, but I never do it. Instead, the afternoon rolls around, and I rush to the nearest court as though to the nearest bar. So I said yes.

We visited the courts on Tillary Street next to the Brooklyn Bridge, near where NBA stars Bernard and Albert King had grown up in the Fort Greene projects. Then we went to see a tournament in Bedford-Stuyvesant, where the two teams from neighboring housing projects were playing for a tournament championship. One team wore red jerseys, the other yellow. The court was bordered, at one end, by a high brick wall painted deep maroon. The star of one of the teams had once been a major talent, I was told, recruited by Division I colleges. He may have attended one, briefly. But the streets got him. The story came to me in fragments from someone standing next to me on the sidelines.

I watched him, trying to locate the young talent emerge within what he had become, a high-volume shooter who raged and demanded the ball. Some players develop basketball skills within the structure of superior athleticism, and some players are possessed with an intuitive knack for the game—referred to as *court vision*, or *basketball IQ*, or *feel for the game*—around which they train their way toward athleticism. At the highest levels you need both.

This guy had lost his hops, but his basketball skills had not developed to make up for it—you could see he was used to overpowering opponents, but the rise was no longer there. He was already, in his mid-twenties, a lion in winter. When Jeff sent me images from that day, one of them featured this guy on the ground, on his back, sweating, with no one else in the frame. My sense of him that day was that he had been running, jumping, yelling, raging, the whole time, surrounded by a lively crowd pushing in on the sidelines, but the photograph told a different story—the frame is entirely empty except for this guy on his back, the look on his face like that of a soldier who had just been shot. The picture captured a sense of his isolation and even grief that in the rush of real time you could only sense. Sometimes these games mean nothing to the people playing them, and at other times you feel as if epic stories of identity and loss are being played out on the court.

It was a promising start for the project, but the Ratner money ran out, and it was discarded along with the Frank Gehry designs.

For the past few years, I have gone out to the Barclays Center every June to witness the NBA draft. There is so much ecstatic pageantry; it's like a high school prom but with the promise of huge sums in the immediate future. There is also an undertow of grief, some of it stemming from the memory of what was overcome. In the 2019 draft each of the first three picks spoke emotionally of the people who helped them get to this point. Zion Williamson, with tears streaming down his face, spoke of the sacrifice his mother had made to get him to this level. Ja Morant, the number-two pick, said of his father, "He made me who I am today," and wept. R. J. Barrett rested his head on his father's shoulder in such a way that his face was hidden from the camera while his father calmly praised his hard work. It almost seemed like a joke until Barrett's body began visibly shaking with sobs, a thunderstorm that had passed when he lifted his head a few moments later.

As with a prom, some of the night's tension, beyond who is picked when, stems from the knowledge that while this is the end of something, it is also another beginning with no assurance of what is to come. Most players drafted in the first round make real money for several years, but many don't last in the league for much longer than that.

I tend to spend just a few minutes out on the floor of the arena, where the big stage is and the players wait with their families for their name to be called. Most of my night is spent backstage, where the draftees are shuttled down long corridors from room to room for a series of interviews, photo shoots, and press conferences. There are party spaces for receptions that also serve as photo shoots. There's a lot to see and overhear—like in 2018, when Michael Porter Jr.'s tiny little sister said, "I can't believe you are in the NBA" to her brother. But he towered so far above her in his white suit, and was so thronged with people, that he didn't seem to hear.

This year, at the end of a long hallway, I came upon an absurdly small plaque dedicated to Bruce Ratner. It was dated 2012, the year the arena was completed, a comically tiny remnant of the circumstances by which the whole complex was built.

4. Moses and the City Game

Here is an unprovable fact that nevertheless holds up under common-sense scrutiny: New York City has more public basketball courts than any other city in America—more than Los Angeles, more than Chicago. New York City has, I would venture to say, more actual hoops attached to backboards than any other city in the world, and the person most responsible for this fact is Robert Moses.

The legacy of Moses was defined by Robert Caro's magisterial book *The Power Broker: Robert Moses and the Fall of New York*, which continues to send ripples through a general population who, were it not for this book, would almost certainly have never heard of a man named Robert Moses. The effect of the book on me, when I read it, was galvanic. It is both the *War and Peace* of New York history and a Mephistophelean portrait of a man for whom power was a driving force. It is also an X-ray of the many economic and political forces that shaped New York City, most of which operate out of the public's view, or at least mine. Caro's prose has a meticulous, granular specificity and also an incantatory style. It's thrilling when Moses is able to envision, in a single burst of inspiration, entire parks, beaches, highways, and other public works that have had an indelible effect on city life. And it's distressing to see the contempt with which Moses treated the people and neighborhoods that his plans destroyed. When, by the end of the book, Moses finally comes toppling down, it feels a bit as though you are witnessing the demise of a tyrant.

As kids, we take a lot of our built environment for granted, a condition that can last well into adulthood. Caro's book was, for me, the beginning of my consciousness that the city in which I grew up was built, planned, the result of specific choices. Among these many choices—the decision to build all these basketball courts.

According to Alexander Garvin, a professor of urban planning at Yale and author of *The Planning Game: Lessons from Great Cities*, 25 percent of New York City's territory is devoted to public parks. This is the largest percentage of any American city. A huge portion of these parks were created by Robert Moses.

Garvin's book is devoted to the realpolitik of planning as it has played out in a number of different American cities. It is implicitly a field guide to getting things done at the municipal level. Unsurprisingly, he takes a very bright view of Moses, who during his long tenure as chairman of the New York City Parks Department oversaw the creation of 658 playgrounds.

I have tried to understand how it was decided that a New York City playground should have, among its amenities, a basketball court. Most of these decisions were made not long after Moses took over the New York City Parks Department in 1934, a time when the game was not nearly as prominent in the culture as it is now.

I wondered if there was one unsung individual who, in a Parks Department planning meeting of that era, advocated for basketball courts while another individual wanted shuffleboard. Poking around the Parks Department archives from this period, I found nothing that would answer this question. But there was a memo about all the tournaments the Parks Department sponsored in its playgrounds. "All kinds of tournaments and contests are held," it begins and proceeds to list the activities: "Baseball, basketball, volleyball, handball, marble shooting, paddle tennis, checkers and jacks."

Had things played out differently, we might be making movies called *Jacks Dreams* or talking about March Madness in terms of marbles.

Playgrounds and public basketball courts almost always sit side by side, and the similarities are instructive. Both are a bit haunted and even scary when empty, and noisy when full. Both appear to be chaotic scenes of innocent recreation when seen from outside the fence. Inside the fence it is more complicated. In the case of the basketball court, profanity and insults are part of the game. There are always currents of violence in a basketball game, and sometimes street basketball feels as much about the very act of asserting oneself as it is about the game of basketball. My sense is that pickup basketball players in New York are much more decorous and respectful of each other these days than they were in the 1970s–1990s.

"You can be loud without being disrespectful" was an actual phrase I heard uttered on a court in the summer of 2019, and more than the sentiment expressed, the very sentience of the thought would have been unusual when I was younger. The world and the country and the city and the neighborhood—they all change, and so do the courts in their midst.

And yet: the basketball courts of New York are like old-growth forests. Standing on one, it can feel as though the city grew up around the space. They're just there. But forests are dense, vertical spaces; the basketball courts of New York have the reverse optical and emotional effect. In a dense, vertical town they are like asphalt meadows, a dull gray flatness, sometimes painted Parks Department green, that is like an Etch A Sketch on which complex arrangements are traced every day and then erased every night, to begin again the next morning.

It was in Caro's book that I learned, with amazement and pride, that the entirety of Riverside Park had been dreamed up by Robert Moses in one burst of inspiration while standing on a promontory at Seventy-Sixth Street and Riverside Drive. In this very spot a set of stairs now descend to the court where I grew up playing. On which I still play.

5. Backboards

I went down to the basketball courts on Riverside Park on a recent Saturday and found a bunch of obstinate old basketball dinosaurs warming up. Dinosaurs not because of age, though a bunch of us are up there in years, but because we have refused to accept that this once fertile, well-regarded oasis of basketball has more or less dried up. It used to be a minor basketball mecca. Obviously, it was not a world-famous spot like the West Fourth Street courts or Rucker Park, but it was a place where quality players showed up, along with a wide assortment of others. It was crowded in the afternoons and packed on weekends.

We took shots in that pregame ritual in which other people are acknowledged in the most indirect ways (like giving the ball back after a made shot). There were even a few college-age players with some skill who had not gotten the memo that pickup basketball should be sought out elsewhere—at downtown courts near Battery Park City, uptown in Harlem, or out in Brooklyn and the other boroughs.

In 2015 I wrote a piece, "The City Game?" pondering why street basketball in New York seems to be so much less vital and so under-populated with serious players, compared to earlier eras. I came up with many possible culprits—gentrification prominent among them. But the one that seems most conspicuous is the simple fact that many areas of life that once fell under the category of play have become professionalized.

There are afternoons when these courts are almost empty in the afternoon except for a couple of athletic young men, usually black, coaching considerably less athletic young boys, usually white, for an hourly rate that can reach $100.

I thought about this as teams were divided up and the game commenced. I guarded a wiry guy with a jump shot. This meant I had to work on defense, stepping out to guard his shot. My big move, when I have to guard shooters, is to force them left, though I never pay attention to whether they might actually be a leftie or not. On offense I'm thrown into the conundrum of my basketball life. At six feet, five and a half inches, I was much taller than the wiry guy, and it was presumed that I should "go down low." But I never want to. I played small-time college basketball in the 1980s and regarded the post as a prison. On offense it is a place of violence but also of a kind of passivity, a contradiction captured in the basketball phrase *feed the post*. It's as though the big man is an animal who must have the ball meted out to him a bare minimum of times lest he become unhappy, lethargic, or unmotivated to do his work on the defensive end, which is to rebound the ball and immediately hand it over to the guards. In this respect being a big man overlaps with being a drummer—point guards and wing players are the guitarists. They get to move around, freestyle, while you toil in the engine room, keep the beat, absorb the blows. Now I handle the ball, get in a rhythm with my dribble. I shoot from the outside. I face the basket and drive. I can do it, until it all goes wrong and I miss a few shots in a row, at which point I retreat to the old ways.

After the game a longtimer named Joe pointed up to the backboard and said, "I've been trying to get the Parks Department to change this backboard for years."

"Why?" I said, instinctively alarmed by all change. "It looks fine."

He pointed to the wooden frame to which the fenestrated old metal backboard was affixed. It had rotted a bit. The rim itself was sagging and must have been one or two inches too short, though none of the old-timers seemed to mind this. Then he pointed to a faint oval high up on the backboard above the rim.

"Used to be a sticker. Some little girl climbed up there and put it there in 1978," he said.

"I've been coming here since 1977," I said. "And I don't remember a sticker."

"It lost its color years ago."

"What color did it used to be?"

"I think yellow," he said, and we both stared at it.

I suppose I will be grateful when they replace the rim and backboard with one that is of a true height and that doesn't make such a huge clanking sound when the ball goes off the backboard. But I will be a bit sad to know the remnant of that sticker will be gone. I just now found out about it. Now I want to hold on to it. I am tempted to say I learned that from playground basketball too, which is to say I learned the instinct to hold on to things. But the opposite may be true. Pickup basketball in the park is like a river in the sense of Heraclitus's ancient aphorism: you can't step into the same river twice. The river changes, as does the person. But in another sense the playgrounds of New York may as well have been formed by the glaciers that cut the route of the Hudson River, visible from the court in Riverside Park. It feels sometimes as though these courts have been there since the beginning of time.

—2020

The Pleasures of the Old Man Game

The first round of the NBA playoffs is always a smorgasbord of basketball pleasures. The talent level is so high. Everyone is playing hard, and egos are on the line. The sheer abundance of it—multiple games each day, most of them shown on regular cable—is a shock to the casual fans who have not been wired into the NBA League Pass. This year's playoffs promise several dramatic story lines: the prospect of the Cleveland Cavaliers and the Golden State Warriors meeting again in the finals for the third time in as many years; the James Harden–Russell Westbrook MVP race, embodied in the first-round Oklahoma City–Houston series like some kind of prank; Kevin Durant as the nexus of so many fractured subplots that he should win the award for Most Shakespearean Player (MSP). For me, though, there is a special pleasure in a more esoteric strain of this year's playoffs: the players who have mastered the art of the Old Man Game.

Old Man Game is not defined by the age of the player, though its practitioners are often old men by the standards of the NBA. Old Man Game involves a cranky, crafty set of moves built around misdirection, leverage, and angles. Put another way, Old Man Game doesn't involve a lot of jumping. Players with Old Man Game are incredibly gifted athletes, of course, but their gifts are hard to discern. Sometimes they are post players (like Al Jefferson) whose games have an invisible something—what could be unscientifically described as "throwing your ass around" (see Boris "The Big Brioche" Diaw). But they are wings and guards, too, and even point guards. For a long time, my favorite Old Man Game player was Andre Miller, a point guard who spent his summers grilling hamburgers and never touching a basketball. (Summer, in today's league, is the season of self-improvement, hard work, and reinvention. Miller, in the course of seventeen illustrious seasons, used it for vacation. Then he would play himself back into shape during training camp and the preseason. When asked how he got himself down to playing weight, he said, "I starve myself.")

Miller always managed to get to spots on the court where you didn't expect him to be and then get the ball somewhere that it ought to be. His movements were herky-jerky, low to the ground, clever. (Is it because basketball so emphasizes height and the ecstasies of vertical leaps that a player's low-to-the-ground exploits—the dribbling of guards Kyrie Irving and John Wall, for instance—produce so much pleasure?) Miller was a late-season acquisition for the San Antonio Spurs last season. "His basketball IQ is off the charts," Spurs coach Gregg Popovich said at the time.

It makes sense that one of the great Old Man Game players ended up with the Spurs, who have had a strong element of Old Man Game in their DNA since the old soul Tim Duncan joined the famously grumpy Popovich in 1997. Duncan, who retired after last season, was the most inconspicuously gifted athlete of the past twenty years. His most visible, showy act of athleticism may have been a moment late in Game 7 of the finals against Miami in 2013, when he missed a running hook shot and then the follow-up tip and then, after running back on defense and getting into defensive stance, slapped the floor with the palm of his hand so hard that I actually grabbed my own hand in pain. It would have been an emotional gesture from any other player; from Duncan it was the equivalent of a minute-long primal scream.

Then there is Manu Ginóbili, a player whose game is so sui generis that I hesitate to attach the OMG tag. Yet it's been there, unmistakably, ever since his rookie season. Ginóbili, who has played for the Spurs since 2002, is the NBA player whose game is most redolent of silent-movie comedians. In an ESPN profile last year, Zach Lowe included a great description from the Argentine player Pepe Sánchez, who grew up with Ginóbili. "He would go to the basket, get crushed, stand up to shoot free throws, and get crushed all over again," Sánchez said. "He was so tiny. He was fragile."

Ginóbili, at thirty-nine, plays the Old Man Game out of necessity, but the subversive, resilient part of the Old Man Game—the confusion of motion and misdirection, the ability to see angles no one else can see, the brazenness to chance the unwise pass—was built into him even as a kid.

The marquee OMG matchup of the first round of the playoffs is between the Spurs and the Memphis Grizzlies. Ginóbili's counterpart on the Grizzlies is Vince Carter, who, at forty, is the oldest player in the league. Carter's Old Man Game is pleasurable on its own merits—his three-point bombs, his lumbering body language. But the pleasure is made greater by the fact that he once practiced the ultimate young man's game: an epic, high-flying insanity epitomized in a terrifying fist pump that almost killed Kevin Garnett. I saw him play in his early years with the Toronto Raptors, and what was most striking about his game back then was his lightness on his feet. Now, though his playing weight is surely twenty pounds more than when he was young, he still has that lightness—and now and then he'll unleash a dunk, as he did early in Game 1 this week against the Spurs.

Along with Carter, the Memphis OMG is led by the baby-faced thirty-five-year-old Zach Randolph, who has played like an old man since he arrived in the league, in 2001. Randolph is incredibly strong, with a barrel chest and huge, soft hands. He generates more joy with the use of the pivot foot than any other player in the league does. (One measure of Old Man Game is the degree of aesthetic pleasure a player is able to generate without jumping, leaving the ground, or going anywhere at all.) Some years ago, the journalist Henry Abbott described Randolph's game: "Randolph most commonly catches the ball with his back to the basket. Feet spread far apart, he then pivots, deploying his skinny legs like a geometry student with a compass. (His pivot foot is the point, his outside leg is that pencil, describing a circumference within which defenders like [Antonio] McDyess are not welcome.) Turn, turn, nudge, bump, turn … having etched his circle, he is then free to unleash, essentially, whatever he wants. Great footwork, long arms, a love of contact and all those lefty scoring moves are tools enough to tear down a dynasty."

Another member of the Grizzlies, the center Marc Gasol, exhibits another iteration of the Old Man Game. Gasol is a creature of habit—I once watched him take pregame shots from the same spot, seventeen feet out, with absolutely identical body motion, most conspicuously a jutting of his chin toward the basket—and yet he is a player who radically changed his game this season. After Gasol broke his foot last year, his coach, Dave Fizdale, encouraged him to start taking more three-point shots, which he now does regularly with the same meticulous discipline. It's because of the somewhat robotic nature of Gasol's game that his moments of goofiness are so pleasurable—on Monday night, just after a whistle was blown, he headed the ball into the basket.

A player with Old Man Game, again, is not necessarily an old player. But Old Man Game is fascinating, in part, because it reflects the NBA's version of the American anxiety about aging and death. When Dwyane Wade missed an open-court dunk in the first game of the Boston-Chicago series, Sherman Alexie wrote a poem (OK, it was an email) that read: "Wade's missed dunk was … a five second film about death."

Tony Parker, the once sprightly point guard for the Spurs and a core member of four championship teams, is now featured under such headlines as "How Long Can Tony Parker Keep the Vultures at Bay?" In Game 2 of the series against Memphis, the TV announcer Reggie Miller, intending to praise Parker's level of play, remarked, "He has one foot on the court and one foot…" Instead of the natural conclusion of that sentence—"in the grave"—he veered toward something to the effect of "one foot on the sidelines in a suit talking about the game, with us!" It was an illuminating comment that seemed to channel the ambivalences of a competitive athlete's life after sports. Does Reggie feel as if he is calling games from a crypt?

The Old Man Game is something we are likely to see more of in seasons to come. Everyone around the league is obsessed with the grind of the schedule and the toll it takes on the star players, who engage in far more strength training than did players in previous generations. The jumpers jump higher; the fast players play faster. At the same time, people are acutely aware of the ravages that these jumps and dunks take on players' bodies: teams like the Spurs are making a conscious effort to discourage dunking as part of a larger effort to increase their players' longevity. In the NBA, as in the broader culture, there is a desire to extend youth as long as possible.

A few years ago, in the locker room after a New Orleans Pelicans game, I wandered away from the cluster of journalists surrounding Anthony Davis and talked to Al-Farouq Aminu. In the course of our conversation, the tall, soft-spoken young player kept using a phrase that brought the realities of improving and conserving an athlete's body into focus: "Your body is your business." Aminu told me that on some nights after home games he would finish early enough to go to the movies with his girlfriend. A high draft pick, he was on the verge of falling out of the league back then; only a solid season playing with the Dallas Mavericks at the NBA's lowest pay rate turned things around. (Now he's on the Portland Trail Blazers.) I didn't think to ask whether he ordered his popcorn with butter. I am guessing he didn't, though who knows, maybe it was a youthful folly that he has since given up for the sake of his game.

—2017

The Warriors' Torrential Victory

It is over. The floor is strewn with confetti and small children. NBA-championship celebrations used to be backroom affairs. The players didn't linger to commiserate; they escaped into the champagne-drenched oasis of the locker room. That's where Michael Jordan clutched his trophy and cried, thinking of his dead father. This time, Cleveland's players exit stage left. It's an orderly procession. LeBron James and the other Cavaliers are shown walking toward their locker room in a dark tunnel that seems to be lit only with a black light; parts of his sneakers glow, but everything else is in shadow. Out in the bright arena, everyone stands up and goes nowhere—except for the kids, who mobilize.

Some of them are free-range, pinballing around the crowded floor or doing a dance—like Riley Curry, age four, who at one point uses the championship trophy as a mirror in which to adjust her hat. Others are held in their fathers' arms. To a baby, every father is a giant, but this is extreme. There is Draymond Green's son, with a pacifier, and JaVale McGee's daughter, wearing a gold headband over her few wisps of hair, like a flapper, as though they remade *Bugsy Malone* with infants. Ryan Curry, age one, rides in her father's arms like his pudgy-cheeked dancing partner, jerked this way and that, her face aglow with her newfound altitude and overwhelmed by the maelstrom around her. (A squadron of nannies, I assume, are gathered in some darkened hallway nearby, waiting to be deployed.)

Then the players' parents are present. "Look at me!" Kevin Durant's mom commands at one point, when a microphone and camera are in her son's face, directing his attention to her eyes by grabbing his pharaonic beard in a way that suddenly makes me reconsider that signature facial hair—it had seemed such a statement of manhood and independence—as nothing more than a handle. Then the players are all brought together, shorn of parents and children. The whole team is wearing matching black championship T-shirts and gray championship caps.

Doris Burke, an elegant master of ceremonies, has the microphone.* Durant, the series Most Valuable Player, is interviewed first. Then comes Curry. Television viewers are treated to that strange reverb that occurs when a live mike is sending a signal both to the TV audience and into the arena. It's the universal sound of ceremonial events, of retirements and graduations. The championship trophy embodies both. It is a certificate of achievement ("They can never take that away from me" has become a kind of talismanic utterance of players who win their first); it's also a signal that school's out for the summer, that this particular group will never be together again, not like this. As Heraclitus said, sort of, you can never step into the same NBA team twice.

Water has been a prevailing metaphor for this season's Warriors, and not just because their logo includes a bridge. There is the spectacle of seeing the basketball sent on long, high arcs at a great distance from the basket and then, with the trajectory of a water cannon putting out a fire, dropping down into the bottom of the net. There is Stephen Curry and Klay Thompson's nickname, the Splash Brothers, a term born in a tweet

---

* There are the play-by-play men—and now women—and there are the "color commentators," which is Burke's role. Every color commentator lends their own particular atmosphere and sense of drama to the process by which the intricacies of the game are elaborated. Burke's signature, in my opinion, is to foreground the role of will. She is always emphasizing in her tone of voice the role of willpower, discipline, force of personality, work ethic, persistence. Like Howard Cosell and Ernest Hemingway, she has a style so distinct it can almost be parodied. I can picture her calling a broadcast of an afternoon with Sisyphus. "What you have to understand about this man is that he is not going to give up. When that rock rolls back to the bottom of the hill, he is going to put his shoulder to it and push. He is not going to be denied."

on December 21, 2012; its creator would later remark, about this accomplishment, "It's something no one can take away."*

There is the aquatic flow of the Warriors' offense, in which the surface motion creates an unseen riptide that pulls defenses away from the open man. And, most of all, the feeling that the Warriors, even in their worst moments, even when their game is off and they seem vulnerable, are like a massive tonnage of water contained in a vessel—the other team's defense—that is bound to give way. And when it does, a torrent of scoring will follow. Even Cleveland's commanding double-digit lead in Game 4 felt precarious until the last minute. With their victory in Game 5, the Warriors tied for the best playoff record ever, 16–1.

After Curry, Thompson is summoned. Burke calls his name. There is no response. The moment has the cadence of a teacher taking attendance. Burke, and the camera, scans the crowd during a deliciously comic pause that lasts twelve glorious seconds before she again says, "Klay Thompson!" in a tone usually reserved for people calling into an empty room in which some little kid is hiding. Midway through this pause the camera finds him, Golden Gate's very own Bartleby the Scrivener, who, incredibly, seems to be shaking his head. No, he seems to indicate, he would prefer not to. He is way in the back, behind Kevon Looney, who didn't play, and JaVale McGee, who didn't play, and David West, who did. In the foreground a shiny phone is held up by a pair of female hands, taking a picture of someone else. Thompson stands there as though hoping the moment will pass. He finally comes forward, not so much struggling through the crowd as being pushed through it by his peers. He takes his turn.

The previous day, Kerr said, of Thompson's defense, "He's like a yellow Lab who chases the ball all day."

Now Thompson submits to Burke's questions:

---

* What a spectacle it has been to have Mark Jackson as a principal television commentator on the team that he helped build and coach and that then fired him at the end of that first Splash Brothers season, after which it rose to greater heights under his successor, Steve Kerr. It's an awkwardness that Jackson has continuously redeemed with his proclamation, made in his first year as announcer, that Curry and Thompson were the best-shooting backcourt of all time. At the time it sounded far-fetched. But when he repeats it now, it has the ring of accepted fact.

"When KD [Kevin Durant] was added, you said there would be no adjustment," she says.

"We went 16–1. Wasn't much of an adjustment," he replies. "Easy to adjust when you are winning."

There is something about Thompson's game that feels like the unseen core of the whole system of Warriors ball. Somewhere in the midst of the whole series, I wondered if, speaking as a Knicks fan, I would be happy with a trade of Carmelo Anthony for Klay Thompson. The answer was yes, in a heartbeat. They are both incredible shooters. And yet the ball always tends to stick to Anthony, while Thompson acts as if it were a scalding object, a hot potato he has to get out of his hands—he has a strange quality of scoring prolifically while hardly ever actually seeming to have the ball. On any given night he might score more points than anybody else has ever scored, and defend more tenaciously than anyone else has ever defended, but he does it all while hardly seeming to be present. "His gaze is unflappable," a friend wrote to me. "Almost soulless." He is in some way the soul of the Warriors team.

I once worked in a bagel factory that had, beneath the ovens, a big porcelain sink into which a pipe poured water twenty-four hours a day. The water, whose purpose was to cool the oven motors, splashed into the sink and gurgled down the drain. The sink was situated next to the stone staircase that led from the office, freezers, and flour silos to the store upstairs, and I would pause beside it sometimes to watch the water splash down and vanish and be replenished all at once. Of no direct relevance except that a bagel is a round with a hole in the middle, and the always emptying, always replenishing sink was hypnotic—I would sometimes stop while rushing up or down the stone stairs and just stare into it, hypnotized. Every moment was a repetition—the water continued to pour down, splash onto the porcelain, and spiral down the metal drain—and yet every moment was different from the last. Within the monotony was a kind of suspense and also a refuge. When I picture myself amid the chaos of the bagel factory, transfixed by that pipe and the sink and the water, I can't help but think of an anecdote James Naismith recounted about the very origins of the game, when he passed a boy throwing a ball into a basket and a few hours later found him engaged in the same activity. When Naismith asked the boy why he was still shooting the ball, the reply was that he wanted to see if he could get the ball to go in again. One *again* is usually followed by another, the question's resolution leading to its replenishment, an elegant, continuous circle.

—2017

French Math at the NBA Draft

The NBA draft is the scene of family happiness that feels both intensely cathartic and also overdetermined. The players sit at round tables before an enormous stage; behind them are rows of press tables, and behind that two separate TV sets with live commentary. The proceedings are witnessed by half an arena of fans, most of them wearing jerseys of the Knicks, Boston, Philly, Lakers, OKC, and on, including two separate Shawn Kemp Seattle SuperSonics jerseys. The atmosphere in the stands is a peculiar mixture of slavish devotion and a yearning to lament. Chants of "Fire Phil" ripple through the arena now and then, driven by a bearded young man in a Knicks jersey who stomps around with a piece of cardboard on which these two words are written.

Adam Silver appears at the podium. Names are called. Thin young men rise to hug their weeping mothers, kiss their smiling sisters, slap hands with fathers and brothers and friends. They are handed a cap with the name of the team that drafted them on it as they make their way up to the stage, and a minor pleasure of the evening was seeing this cap get pulled down over huge Afros, which got smushed.

It's like a graduation, though it's not entirely clear what is being graduated from. Not high school. There is an age minimum of nineteen for NBA players, even though the one-and-done era is getting awkward and is probably nearing its end. The first seven draft picks of this year's draft were all freshmen, a record. And it's not a college graduation—there were only two seniors drafted in the first two rounds.

Up on the podium there is a handshake with a commissioner, or a soul shake, depending on last-second hand communications. Then a smile for the cameras. There is no diploma other than the contract that will soon be signed. A huge video monitor is filled with highlights of the young man onstage doing his thing. Then the draftee steps off one stage and onto a television set for a live interview with NBA Fantasy Insiders Dennis Scott and Rick Kamla. This produces some nice moments, such as when Josh Jackson, a large, athletic player whose highlight reel of cacophonous dunks is playing on the screen, is asked, "Where do you get that competitive spirit?"

"My mom," he says, adding that he would play her one-on-one, and she would regularly win and make him cry.

From there the players move on to a haunted house of media obligations that wind their way through the concrete hallways of the Barclays Center like the stations of the cross—the social media room, the interview room, the Tissot watch presentation room, and, finally, the live room, a farmer's market of media obligations. The players must stop and talk at each stall. In the hallways they are harassed or approached or ignored by the free-floating mob of journalists and functionaries and also random kids who are, I presume, related to someone who knows someone somewhere who is important somehow.

The Frenchman Frank Ntilikina, a resident of Strasbourg, in Alsace, on the border with Germany, is drafted number eight by the Knicks. I go down to the interview room to see him up close. He wears a dark red suit and red bow tie with a crisp white shirt. All basketball players look slenderer in person than on TV, doubly true of these young guys in the draft, but Ntilikina is nearly avian. The child of Rwandan parents, he is a six-foot-five point guard who was born in Belgium and moved to France at an early age.

He is asked for his thoughts on Phil Jackson and replies, "The triangle is a system that brings him a lot of championships. I think I can definitely fit with this system."

He is asked about his suit. He has been working with a tailor on his suit for about three months, he says.

I ask him a question that begins, "I'm wondering about your childhood in France." I point out that New York is famous for producing point guards who hone their skills in competitive pickup basketball games.

"I'm wondering if any such thing exists in Strasbourg and if you could say anything about when you fell in love with the sport when you were a kid?"

"I fell in love with the sport when I played with my brother in the park. I was every day going to the park trying to play."

"Which park?"

"Close to my house. It's called 'la Citadelle.'"

He says he was four years old when he fell in love with the game when his brother "brought [him] to just have some fun outside."

Then he is out in the concrete hallway surrounded by a gaggle of press like a statesman emerging from a high-level meeting. They are all French—correspondents from *Le Figaro, Le Monde*, and others. They are full of gossip. He is leaving in a few hours for a 2 a.m. charter flight back to Paris because the professional team for which he plays, Strasbourg SIG, is in the last game of the league finals the following night. It's a charter flight that, one of them claims to know, cost $90,000. A camerawoman named Gaelle mentions that Ntilikina's childhood coach, Abdel, was among the party at his table and was happier than she had ever seen him. I am intrigued that Ntilikina had flown his childhood coach over from France to join his family on this occasion. He is the youngest player in the draft.

I asked her how she knew him. She explains that he had been her coach when she attended basketball camp at age eleven. I pause over this fact—she is rather small, but who knows? Maybe she was a basketball prodigy at eleven?

Meeting him is suddenly a top priority. Gaelle, amazingly, has his number. There is a series of texts and confused, murky phone calls. I go to an arranged spot and realize I am scanning the crowd for a person whose only defining characteristic is that he is, as Gaelle put it, "glowing with joy."

Twenty minutes later I am standing before Abdel Loucif out in the food court next to Café Habana. He is still glowing with joy. He wears a gray suit and a shirt with no tie. His frizzy hair is combed back, his forehead broad and gleaming. He doesn't speak all that much English, and I speak almost no French. But it is wonderful to talk to him because his basketball lexicon is infused with unusual ingredients that I cannot readily identify, but this makes me happy too.

Abdel first coached Frank when he was thirteen, he said. "He worked a lot. When he missed a lot of shots, he got to the playground after practice and worked alone."

"Which playground?" I asked.

"The Citadelle! At the Citadelle he played very free, but in practice he was very rigorous. My philosophy when working with young players is to give them a sense of pleasure in working. Frank's values, I saw it in his eyes from the first day. We begin the first practices, and you tell him to go to this line, and he goes. And when he plays in a game, he immediately uses what you taught him. But he uses it in a way that makes it his own.

"Not a lot of young players have this ability to combine what you tell them with the ability to improvise. Not a lot of young players can do that."

It turns out that Abdel came to basketball from an unusual angle. He grew up in Schirmeck, a small town near Strasbourg, and studied mathematics and physics at the Strasbourg university. From the ages of twenty-three to thirty-two, he was a math teacher. Only then did he begin teaching and coaching young girls in basketball. For ten years he did both and added, "I helped many girls that I was training when they had difficulties in mathematics or physical sciences."

A bunch of young kids in Knicks jerseys walk by, and I ask one of them to take our picture, and while the kid sizes up the frame—"Portrait or landscape?" he asks, earnestly—I can't help but blurt out, "This guy right here coached Frank Ntilikina when he was a kid!"

They besiege Abdel with questions about how Frank is going to help the Knicks, which Abdel interprets to be questions about how Frank will improve himself. He starts mimicking weight lifting until I explain that their interest is not Frank but the Knicks. The kids are suddenly seized with a sense of duty to explain the basketball horror in which they have spent their whole life—I don't think they were even born during the glory days of Latrell Sprewell, never mind Patrick Ewing. They take turns saying how awful and hopeless the Knicks are and how Phil should be fired.

Sometimes I think being a Knicks fan is just the process of fermenting bitterness until it turns into joy.

Abdel continues to exude a magnificent mixture of gravity and elation.

"The NBA was for him a great dream," Abdel says when I ask him more about Frank at thirteen. "When his name was called tonight, I was so happy. I remember when he began to play, and we speak a lot of times of NBA and some players, like Durant, one of his favorite players. And now he is here."

Afterward, as we prepare to part, it occurs to me to ask what kind of math he specialized in as a teacher. In what might be the most auspicious Knicks news of the night, he responded, "Geometry."

"You're kidding! That is so great!" I shout. "The triangle!" And Abdel throws his head back and laughs. The Café Habana is lowering its gates, the hour is getting late, and we shout and laugh and pat shoulders. I am at last enveloped in the irrational joy of sports fandom, when you think other people's triumphs are your own.

—2017

Zion's Burst

I don't think I have ever experienced such an abrupt transition of mood—within myself and throughout an arena full of people—as I did in the fourth quarter of Zion Williamson's first regular-season game in the NBA. It was a home game. A Wednesday night in late January 2020. This was Williamson's takeoff, at long last. I had come to this game to be present at the dawn, the better to fathom the trajectory of this player whose reputation was intrinsically linked to flight. Yet something was wrong.

It wasn't just that he played poorly, and briefly, during the first three quarters of the game. He appeared in four-minute stretches that neverthe-less seemed to exhaust him. This was understandable, explainable—he was a nineteen-year-old playing his first regular-season game after coming off knee surgery and an extended period of rehabilitation. No amount of practice can match the intensity of a live game. And yet even factoring in these measured expectations, one could not help but note how ungainly his movements were, how he seemed to be dragging his leg. I kept get-ting text messages, while at the game, from people watching on TV, their concern mounting with every minute he was on the court failing to do incredible things: "Why isn't he in game shape?" "My neurologist wife says there is no question that he is in pain from the way he moves!"

For the first three quarters, the Spurs were in command of the game, but even as the arena crowd reacted to what was happening on the court, the narrative of the game was eclipsed by the narrative of the player. It was a narrative of a career that had just begun. That was the assumption, the hope, the wish. But there was also the fear that maybe this was not the start. Maybe it was the middle. Maybe this was the end! Not an entirely rational thought, but much about Williamson seems to defy the rational. Through the first three quarters, he scored five points and had four rebounds, one assist, and four turnovers in twelve minutes. Not bad for a debut, but not bad, or even pretty good, would not suffice. Some irrational appetite for the amazing had been unleashed by Zion and also upon him.

For the past six or so years, I had been making forays into the NBA world as a kind of credentialed amateur, wandering the back hallways and locker rooms, scanning for some valuable object that I assumed I would recognize when I found it. Williamson's arrival in New Orleans as the most-hyped draft pick since LeBron James required no interpretation. I took a seat in the front row of the parade in order to see what there was to see. The first encounter was draft night 2019 at the Barclays Center. After he was drafted with the first pick, there was a press conference. He fielded everything with a sweet, energetic demeanor, humble and elated in his cream-colored suit. Then I asked a question: "New Orleans is famous for its brass bands. What is your favorite brass instrument?"

It turned out to be more of a gotcha question than I intended. Offbeat, I thought, but manageable. Instead, it provoked Williamson to widen his eyes and reach for a water bottle.

"I really don't know?" he said at last, in a way that was gracious and charming.

I attended Media Day, the traditional commencement of training camp, on September 30, 2019, at the Pelicans' practice facility in Metairie. For the first time ever, there were no spaces in the parking lot, such was the crush of out-of-town press. I attended Zion's first preseason home game against the Utah Jazz on October 11, which capped off a stellar preseason performance. This was followed by the news that he would need surgery on his knee.

I attended his re-unveiling at a practice the following January, for which journalists from all over the country had again flown in, if in slightly smaller numbers than on Media Day, as though to confirm with their own eyes that he was ambulatory and wearing shorts. We were led into the gym and saw the man lofting little jump shots a couple of courts away. The viewing lasted fifteen minutes. This number now seems fraught—"In the future, everyone will be famous for fifteen minutes," Andy Warhol famously opined. A tendril of anxiety had begun to bloom—what if Zion's fifteen minutes had already occurred?

The signature event of all of these encounters, the most vivid and strange, took place at the beginning, at Media Day, at the practice facility. Amid the loosely festive chaos of the day, with players and media members moving around the practice facility in a dazed, excited, first-day-of-school sort of mood, I pulled aside an assistant coach and inquired about the players in training camp without guaranteed contracts. The NBA teams are now allowed to have up to twenty-two players in training camp, of whom only seventeen are guaranteed contracts, two of which are called "two-way contracts." This means the player is paid below NBA scale and can be shuttled between the developmental G League and the NBA for a certain number of games.

"What's it like for guys like that?" I asked.

"You're here, but you're not here," said the coach. He said it with the solemn deadpan of Chauncey Gardiner in *Being There* pronouncing, "In the spring there will be growth."

"You're here, but you're not here" was a kind of amulet I had carried through the season. Applicable to just about anything, really, including as a description of Zion Williamson's first season in New Orleans.

The predominant feeling around Zion has always been tantalization. He became famous for viral clips of dunks when he was a junior in high school. When he got to Duke, it became apparent that his freakish physical gifts were combined with a subtle feel for the game. He could find cutters with no-look passes in transition and seemed to relish playing defense, or at least blocking shots. But part of the pleasure of watching him was how implausible it all was—this large, burly young man—six feet six, 280 pounds—who bounces into the air as if he has jumped on a trampoline. It's the pleasure of watching a dancer who is light on his feet. A pleasure that is always enhanced when the dancer himself is not all that light. Zion's elevation is so powerful, so incredible, that he has time to do all sorts of things while up there—cup the ball, or bring his arm straight back, or put the ball through his legs, or twirl around, or some combination of the above. But it's not quite right to say he is light on his feet. It's more that when he is airborne it's like he is in water, weightless. When he is on the ground, you feel his weight.

There is a subset of viral clips that involve his displays of physical power other than dunks—such as his baseline block, against Virginia, or the still photo of him clutching a basketball during a game in such a way that it seems as if the ball dimpled under the pressure of his grip. A fully inflated basketball might become oblong if you sit on it, but it should not dimple under pressure from a hand.

Yet tantalization, by its nature, includes anxiety. Williamson's Duke season was abbreviated when he blew out a sneaker—again, the matter of force—and sprained his knee. At the Las Vegas Summer League he played with a ferocity that was stunning; in one play he takes the ball out of the hands of the Knicks' Kevin Knox, a lottery pick the previous year, as though he were a grown man taking the ball away from a child, and dunks it emphatically. In that brief sequence he reminds me of a young Mike Tyson—"Everyone has a plan until they get punched in the mouth"—because of the force but also because of the brevity of the glimpses. He played only nine minutes before being taken out of the game, after which the Pelicans, out of an abundance of caution, kept him out for the rest of the Summer League. He played four preseason games and posted remarkable stats—23.3 points, 6.5 rebounds, 2.3 assists, and 1.5 steals per game while shooting 71.4 percent from the field—but then came the news of the knee injury, the operation. A torn meniscus, though not good news, is not a major injury for NBA players.

A six- to eight-week timeline for his return was extended to eleven weeks. On the morning of his debut, a contingent of media were let into the Pelicans' practice facility. They had flown in from around the country for the occasion. We were ushered in, a small group, and stood on the sideline of the court, on the other side of which was another court, where Williamson stood at the farthest possible basket, strolling through rebounding and shooting drills. We all peered in his direction, wondering. Was he being gingerly with the knee? Was he just cooling down from an intense workout? Was this all theater? All of the above?

In the foreground, on the court right in front of us, was the trio of Josh Hart, Brandon Ingram, and Lonzo Ball—the Orphans from Los Angeles. They were doing three-point shooting drills. They had all been through a difficult experience together the previous year in Los Angeles—first- and second-year players enduring the passive-aggressive comments and tweets of Magic Johnson and LeBron James, who were impatient for them to grow into players who could win now. A tumultuous year of trade speculation, as Anthony Davis excavated himself from the Pelicans and tried to force a trade to the Lakers. Now he was there, in Los Angeles, and they were here, in New Orleans. They were engaged in some lighthearted competition, taking turns shooting until they missed. The balls hit the rim for a while. Then they started to swish. I remembered the attitude they all had on Media Day at the start of the season, as though New Orleans was a refuge but also an exile, as though they were foreign legionnaires posted to some remote spot where they could lick their wounds and recover. Lonzo Ball made passing reference to Los Angeles being "a global media market," as opposed to New Orleans. But these comments were made to a throng of journalists and camera crews, who were there for Zion Williamson.

Eventually the veterans—Jrue Holiday, Derrick Favors—were sent over to speak to the journalists. We never got near Zion.

I arrived early for the game against the Spurs and stood on the baseline watching players warm up with assistant coaches. This is my favorite part of attending games as a journalist—the time before the doors to the arena have even opened, when you can observe NBA players performing rituals of repetition that transcend the mechanical and begin to seem almost spiritual, ritualistic—*practice* as not a verb but a noun, the way people speak of yoga. It's an opportunity to see the nuances of gesture and movement that are hard to glimpse in the middle of a game but that become pronounced with repetition. The way, for example, Marc Gasol would catch a ball for a seventeen-foot jump shot and, in the moment before lifting the ball to shoot, jut out his chin in a slight but pronounced gesture of defiance, like what I imagine a conquistador might do in the moment before commencing a joust. It's an almost imperceptible movement, but once you see Gasol do it, you see it, or traces of it, every time.

On that Wednesday I watched Jrue Holiday practice a move that reminded me of the famous Michael Jordan push-off in the 1998 finals, combined with a James Harden–esque step-back, over and over. Then came Zion. He ran through some elemental game-situation movements. But there were no pyrotechnics, no tossed-off yet spectacular dunks. Nevertheless, I stood transfixed, phone raised, the camera rolling on slow motion. On one movement—a pass and cut to the basket—he did elevate for a soft dunk. It didn't seem special. Only later, when I watched the video unfurl in slow motion, did I see how his movement as he ran toward the basket seemed ungainly, tentative, but how, as soon as he began to couch into his jumping motion, that changed. Up in the air he went, and once airborne he seemed totally in his element. It was as though, in midair, he was a fish at last in water. And he was up there for quite a while. The facial expression of the assistant coach, Michael Ruffin, when he turned to see Zion aloft, seemed to capture the spirit of the whole night.

A former NBA player, Ruffin was playing the role of Williamson's defender on the play. He is facing the ball handler as Williamson cuts backdoor to the basket, and by the time he turns his head to follow the ball, Zion is off the ground. They had just rehearsed this exact sequence several times; there was no mystery about what was going to happen. When Ruffin turns around, Zion is still on the ground. Everything is going according to plan. Then comes Zion's burst. He rises and then, illogically, he rises some more. Ruffin's expression changes to that of someone watching a cat walk out on the ledge of a building—surprise, concern, and anxiety. The moment goes on long enough for Ruffin's face to take on several permutations, the last one being relief.

Relief was the feeling that overcame me as Williamson erupted in the fourth quarter against the Spurs. He scored seventeen straight points. He did it in the most unusual way—four consecutive three-point shots in a span of three minutes. One more than he made in his entire year at Duke. He also caught a lob and dished in transition to a cutting E'Twaun Moore and, perhaps most impressively, had a shot blocked by Spurs big man Jakob Poeltl and—shades of Tyson and Williamson's attack on Kevin Knox—elevated to grab the suddenly loose ball, gathered it, and then bounced up for a put-back, all before Poeltl had time to react. He took the team from a deficit to a lead in three minutes. He defied expectations again and again and again, and then again, with those three-point shots. And with each basket there were cheers, raucous, elated. I was there as a journalist. I wasn't supposed to be cheering. In place of overt cheering, I let out a series of groans. They escaped me, louder with every bucket. They were not groans of elation but of incredulity and, even more than that, relief. The profound relief of someone who has been trying to get a key to turn in a lock in which it has worked before but now will not work.

Watching Zion perform this magic was like the moment the key turns, the door opens, and beyond it lies the future.

And then they took him out of the game. The team became mortal again. The Spurs, behind strong performances from LaMarcus Aldridge and DeMar DeRozan, regained the upper hand and won.

"I'm not the brightest NBA coach, but I know that if the team medical staff says take him out, I am going to take him out," Alvin Gentry, the Pelicans coach, said after the game. But everyone knew that the story was just beginning for Zion Williamson. Everyone left the building with that tantalizing feeling that it was a story that would finally get to be told. "It was everything I dreamed of," Williamson said after the game. "Except the losing part."

—2020

Pandemic Playgrounds

When the NBA shut down in March because of the coronavirus pandemic, I began driving around New Orleans, where I teach English at Tulane, photographing the city's basketball courts at night. I set off around midnight through the deserted streets, at first to familiar places and then to spots more obscure. I didn't bring a ball; in those early days it felt illicit to even be outside, every surface a threat. Eventually I found myself at the Carver playground next to River Road, the outdoor court I play at most often. I wasn't supposed to be there, it was clear—the gate was locked, and yellow tape was strung across the chain-link fence as though it was a crime scene. But someone had cut a hole in the fence nearby.

That my first expeditions into the pandemic landscape should involve basketball seemed appropriate, since basketball, specifically the NBA, had been more or less at the fault line separating the old normal from the new. The moment is etched vividly in my memory: the night of Wednesday, March 11, I turned on the television to watch the Pelicans play an away game against the Sacramento Kings. The Kings were on the floor warming up, but not the Pelicans.

This was the Pelicans' Heinz Ketchup season. Not in the sense of "I know ketchup and it's not a vegetable," Senator John Heinz's famous retort to Ronald Reagan–era nutrition standards for school lunches. But in the sense of "anticipation." The Pelicans had been making us wait, first for Zion Williamson's debut, and then, once he began appearing in games, for him to be allowed to stay on the court long enough to impact games. He would start to play well and then get yanked. He had been absent for the crunch-time minutes on several occasions. The feeling of the Pelicans season to date had been one of coitus interruptus—tantalizing glimpses of a prodigious talent interspersed by long stretches of injury, absence, frustration. But after his return in January the Pelicans' season, and Williamson's season in particular, had taken a turn for the better.

And so on March 11 I turned on the TV in the distinctly retro mode of a dad who wanted some downtime from family life and everything else. Just a fan curious to see if the Pelicans, with an activated Williamson finally getting enough minutes to play himself into shape, could build on their recent success. What I encountered was the usual pregame scenario of teams warming up in layup lines, minus one of the teams.

The TV announcers were struggling to explain the situation. The first game of that night's doubleheader, featuring the Jazz against the Oklahoma City Thunder, had already been called off. The NBA, along with other sports leagues, had announced plans to begin playing in empty arenas. Meanwhile, as the announcers spoke, game time was rapidly approaching, and only one of the teams was out on the court. While the Kings did layups, the Pelicans were absent, for unknown reasons. Here, but not here.

It turned out they were in the locker room processing the news that Rudy Gobert of the Utah Jazz had tested positive for the virus and that one of the referees for that night's game in Sacramento had worked the Utah-Toronto game two nights earlier. I don't know how word got to the locker room, if it was Aaron Nelson, the team's chief medical officer, or the general manager, David Griffin, or maybe one of the players. Whatever it was, the Pelicans did not come out to play.

Eventually the public address announcer, Scott Moak, explained to the assembled crowd that the game had been called off. The camera panned across the stands, where thousands of people who had just sat down now began to grasp that they would have to leave. Once this sank in, after a few seconds, many of them began to boo. I saw a young girl burst into tears. "When everyone booed, it was a sobering moment," Moak would later recall. "Booing at the decision to keep everyone safe?"

A close read of those hours reveals a day in which numerous sports leagues started making plans to play games without fans. The Jazz-OKC game was postponed at 8:40 p.m. EST. Twenty-five minutes later, President Donald Trump declared a European travel ban. Minutes later, Tom

Hanks and his wife announced that they had tested positive for the virus. At 9:31 p.m. EST the NBA announced that the season was suspended. Yet an hour later, the Kings were warming up on the court; the game was like some Mars rover that keeps diligently collecting data long after the mission is abandoned. Within twenty-four hours pretty much all sense of normalcy in America was upended. What the NBA began on the 11th college basketball completed the following day when the NCAA tourney was canceled.

I watched it unfold in ungoverned real time. In those first confused minutes after the game was canceled, which in some ways were the first minutes of a new era, cameras panned to Lonzo Ball of the Pelicans, who had ambled onto the court with members of the Pelicans staff. He stood a few feet from the basket and flicked up a shot, which missed. The assistant rebounded. He was surrounded, on the baseline, by quite a few other people—ball boys, court wipers, and so forth—who suddenly had something to do. Ball flicked up another shot, which bounced in. Then another, and another. The shots gradually became more assured, nothing but net. The camera cut away, but the image was indelible: confronted with the strangeness of the situation, he retreated to the familiar gestures of repetition, routine, the consolation of seeing a ball go through the hoop, of letting go of something and then getting it back.

Those little flicked shots from six feet away were, in a sense, the last shots of the NBA season that were witnessed, live, by fans. I felt strangely proud of the NBA and of basketball. These nationally televised cancellations Wednesday night set the stage for the avalanche of cancellations in which all of society's regularly scheduled programming was swept away. The next day the NCAA canceled its tournament. High school sports followed. And shortly thereafter, all the rec centers, adult leagues, and playgrounds of America began to shut down.

At least in theory. A week later I stood at the locked entrance to Carver Park with its crisscross of yellow tape giving it the feeling of a crime scene—or Gulliver, tied down by the Lilliputians—and regarded the nearby hole in the fence. I had just become acquainted with the Italian word *furbizia*, in a front-page story in the *New York Times*, which described it as "the

Italian word for the sort of cunning or cleverness typically channeled into getting around bureaucracy and inconvenient laws."

This was the Italian era of the virus in America, when everyone watched compilation videos of Italians coping with the strange reality of lockdown by singing to each other and playing music from their balconies. My wife and I laughed at compilation videos of exasperated Italian mayors berating and exhorting their constituents to be safe and stay inside for the common good ("What is it with these incontinent dogs!"). We were trying to acclimate to the new reality by listening to the Italians tell us, in their actions and in some cases in direct address, not to make the mistake they had made in thinking that the pandemic was a problem that existed far away, while making the mistake of thinking that this was all a surreal and exotic phenomenon that existed far away.

Furbizia rang in my head as I stared at the hole. Then I ducked through. I stood at center court like someone in an abandoned cathedral, an effect that was made more palpable by the fact that Carver Park, like many of the courts in New Orleans, is covered by a metal roof. I walked to the far basket and saw that the rim had been covered with plywood. I walked back to the near basket, where a pile of wood sat off to the side. Someone had climbed up and removed the impediment. I stood beneath this liberated hoop staring up at the orange rim in the darkness until a freight train passing right beside me honked. The sound was thunderous at close range. I jumped and looked toward the conductor, half expecting to see someone glaring at me for trespassing. I felt caught, exposed. But I saw no one, and I'll never know if that honk was a chastisement or if it was just another of the periodic blasts that drift mournfully over the uptown neighborhood throughout the nights.

"There's no concept of social distancing while playing basketball," Governor Andrew Cuomo remarked in those first days of the shutdown. But playing basketball is a difficult habit to break. Perhaps in response to the kind of *furbizia* I had witnessed at Carver Park, the rims were removed altogether a few days later, as they were in all the parks in New Orleans, and in municipalities all over America. New Orleans removed 130 rims from backboards. My native New York City removed 2,100.

For a time I consoled myself with jumping rope and pretending to enjoy jogging. Then, at home, I started using an app called HomeCourt, which tracks your movements as you perform ball-handling and agility drills. A voice exhorts you to go faster, keep up the good work.

One day I walked away from the phone mid-drill and noticed that in my absence the voice kept offering the same encouragement, responding to a person who wasn't there. I thought of the Raymond Carver story "A Small, Good Thing," in which a couple who has lost their son in a tragic accident gets increasingly irate phone messages from a baker from whom they had commissioned a birthday cake that they never picked up.

I stopped using HomeCourt and began going to my local, rimless playground at Laurel Street, where I had existential workouts dribbling the ball up and down the court and taking shots aimed at the orange square painted onto the white metal backboard. The sound was that of a hollow gong. For whom the ball tolls.

In uptown New Orleans there was no widespread cheering for medical workers and first responders at 7 p.m., as had occurred nightly in New York. One man marched down Laurel Street with a ladle and a big pot on which he beat a distinctly New Orleans second-line rhythm. I would clap briefly and then resume my gonging shots, trying to work them into his rhythm.

Does playing basketball by yourself count as playing basketball? For a while I enjoyed just getting into a physical rhythm, running and dribbling, pulling up from deep, but something important was missing, beyond just a rim for the ball to go through.

When summer came, we could not make our usual pilgrimage to New York City, where summer playground basketball was on tap through the afternoons and evenings. Instead, we rented a place in Kent, Connecticut. By chance, a court was down the street. It had not only rims but a meadow spreading out to the base of a mountain that rose behind the backboard. For the first time in three months, I could take shots on a rim.

I am always aware of the moment in the afternoon when the courts—in whatever city I am in—will begin to populate, and playing pickup basketball becomes a possibility. There have been stretches of my life when I consult the clock with the same anxiety and anticipation as a middle schooler waiting for class to end.

On many evenings I would head to the court in the early evening, grateful to get into a rhythm of dribbling and shooting at an actual basketball hoop. Sometimes I would keep it relatively brief, but now and then I would stay out until the sky turned purple behind the mountain. A few times I stayed until it was dark. It may have been more than a few, as my wife made several less-than-amused remarks about being a basketball widow. Moving into that summer house was, for me, the equivalent of a committed drinker moving next to an especially congenial bar.

One day in June I took shots with the son of a friend who lives in the area. We rebounded for each other but otherwise kept our distance. A week later I took shots with his father, who was sufficiently paranoid about the virus that he insisted we each use our own ball; rebounding became a game unto itself, though not terribly enjoyable. In early July the father consented to using one ball. And a week after that, when I drove to the basket, he raised his arm, a Kabuki gesture of defense. We never progressed to actually guarding one another, but we were hardly observing social distance either.

Meanwhile, in New York City they put the rims back. I went down for a day trip in mid-July and walked onto my regular court at Seventy-Sixth Street in Riverside Park at dusk to see not just rims but brand-new plexiglass backboards, rims bright orange and unbent, nets. There had been an upgrade underway at that playground for some time, and I assumed this was the finale. But I later saw these plexiglass backboards on other courts in the city, as though the courts themselves were now in aesthetic alignment with the many translucent glass towers going up around the city.

That first day back, I was wearing a mask and took some shots with another guy who was also wearing a mask. Most of the people at the other baskets, playing games, were not wearing masks. Those who had arrived with a mask would, after just a few minutes of playing, inevitably be wearing something closer to a chin strap.

"Have you been coming out here a while?" I asked the guy I was shooting with. He was a lanky kid with fluid spins and hesitation moves that identified him as another basketball addict.

"This is my second day."

"When do you think you will be ready?" I asked.

"Soon," he said. It took a moment to realize he did not take my question as I intended—when do you think you will be willing to risk playing with other people?—but rather as a question about his conditioning.

At some point I saw a masked man jog by pushing an elderly woman in a wheelchair. He had managed to affix a giant rainbow-colored Hula-Hoop to the wheelchair that created a circumference of six feet around them both, with a tennis ball at each compass point. The masked woman, who I decided instantly was his mother, was frail. Her back hunched, her head bowed slightly on a slender neck, she nevertheless kept her face lifted so she could keep her eyes on the road ahead. I tried to infer, in this brief moment, whether the look in her eyes was one of excitement or terror, if this was a rare thrill, a chance to get out and see the world, or if she was enduring yet another cockamamie idea of her son that she had failed to talk him out of, and was scared out of her mind about the reckless speed at which her son, himself in a mask and old enough to have a head full of gray hair, was pushing her along in this mad contraption. I smiled a little and cried a little. Then I continued to shoot.

Back at the field-of-dreams court in Kent, my shooting sessions were almost always solitary. But now and then I would arrive to find a crew of young guys out there, shooting around, playing games. There were about six of them, and it was clear that they, too, were basketball cultists. I could hear it in their patter, see it in their moves. They had spent hours working on their crossover, their step-back. Some of them had pretty good jump shots. That they were all Asian, and on the short side, just made their passion for the game more evident. It made me privately proud that this sport I had been dragooned into as a kid, because I was tall, had become a kind of global asset, like a stock I had bought low and held. I remembered visiting Michael Kinsley in his *Slate* office on the Microsoft campus in Redmond, Washington, in 2000. He gave me a tour that included the outdoor basketball court, filled with Chinese software engineers involved in a clamorous game of full court. "The Chinese love basketball," he remarked. Although it didn't quite occur to me then, this was probably the first time the notion of basketball as a tech stock that goes up and up, that is scalable on a global level, occurred to me.

When I spoke to Alex Wu, one of the guys running the HomeCourt app, whose use exploded during the pandemic, he mentioned that the app's founders had worked together at another start-up in Hong Kong and would go play basketball a few times a week on the court below their office.

The guys playing in Redmond, circa 2000, were comical in their enthusiasm. The guys in Kent, twenty years later, were an altogether different matter: they trash-talked each other; they had moves, skills. They were not just dabbling; this wasn't just exercise. I tried not to look at their games so as to avoid temptation.

At first they shot at their hoop, and I shot at mine. Other than a nod hello, there was no interaction. But after a couple of weeks, I started hearing some patter that seemed directed at me. As I was doing deep stretches, I heard, "Oh, it's the yoga stuff." Except they didn't say *stuff*.

Later I heard something about Boban. It took me a moment to realize they were calling me Boban Marjanović, the seven-foot-three center for the Dallas Mavericks with the elfin ears and shaggy hair.

I like Boban as a person and a player. In February 2019, when he was playing with the Philadelphia 76ers in New Orleans, I watched Boban crash down onto the court clutching his knee. Everyone on the 76ers' bench jumped to their feet, somber and concerned. Something about the scale and nature of his body makes many of his movements seem like German expressionist theater, epic. He had been having a great game, which lent an extra poignancy to the injury.

Two teammates pulled him to his feet and helped him off the court. They were each tall men, but Boban towered over them. They led him off the court and toward the tunnel to the locker room, which is where I was standing. His long arms stretched over their shoulders, the giant red sneaker of his injured leg held gingerly in the air. He hopped along with their support, but once inside the dark tunnel, he let go of his teammates and began hopping unassisted down the hallway toward the locker room on one foot. Boban's journey, hopping in his red shoes down the relative darkness and solitude of the tunnel, looked like something out of a fairy tale. His enormity, the red sneakers, his pointed ears, it felt allegorical somehow, mythic.

Like many extremely tall players—Tacko Fall, Gheorghe Mureșan—Boban has been turned into a kind of benign pet, a fetish, someone whose humanity and kindness are endlessly crowed about as though charm, like body warmth, is not expected to travel to such extremities. I feel warmly toward Boban. I like Boban. But I don't want to be called Boban. For two decades I have been called Dirk, as in Nowitzki, when hitting shots while playing playground basketball. Boban felt like a downgrade. Their remarks were the sort of trash talk that would normally have been a prelude to playing a game. Now the game had to be virtual.

On my next visit to the court in Kent, I was alone. And yet I found myself working out particularly hard, a kind of dialogue unfurling in my head. "Boban?" it began. "I'll give you some Boban buckets."

This feeling of retort is something basketball brings out in its players. It's probably the one thing that connects the lowest-level players to Michael Jordan. As *The Last Dance*, a major event in the pandemic's early weeks, illustrated, Jordan's need to play in response to a slight was such that he would go so far as to invent them, when necessary. (His most animated moment in the whole ten hours may have been when listening to Gary Payton claim, twenty years after the fact, that he had slowed Jordan down in the finals. Like the dog at the end of Giuseppe Tomasi di Lampedusa's *The Leopard*, falling through the air and regaining its form, Jordan seemed briefly to return to peak form in his expression of bemusement and contempt, the way his ire seemed to energize him.)

After my imaginary session of abusing my Asian friends in the post, I went to the perimeter and said, "But then you might get Tobias Harris!" Harris was Boban's All-Star-caliber teammate in Philadelphia and his good friend. I started jacking threes, then driving the hoop. "You might get Tobias Harris raining buckets on you!"

I didn't actually enunciate these words. And I don't often think about, let alone pretend to be, Boban Marjanović or Tobias Harris. But I had been insulted, somehow, and was now getting my chance at payback. Pickup basketball isn't just a childish activity. It is a portal to a world of childish feelings of dread and humiliation, and also the sense of triumphing over them, or at least learning not to be paralyzed by them. It was this belligerent friction that had been missing during all the basketball I had played during the pandemic. This inner monologue was, I thought, as close to playing in a real game as I was willing to get in the summer of 2020.

The Kent idyll came to an end in mid-August. Instead of heading straight back to New Orleans, we were able to spend a couple of weeks staying at a friend's empty apartment in Manhattan and rendezvous with my mother on park benches. My childhood basketball court was nearby. I went to see it on the first day.

Over the years I have witnessed a noticeable decline in the number of people playing pickup basketball in my most frequented New York playgrounds. Video games, gentrification, and the general professionalization of childhood sports were the culprits—in 2015 I'd argued this in the *New Yorker* in "The City Game?"—but the sense that the people you were most likely to find on any given afternoon were in their thirties, forties, or older was irrefutable. Or so I thought.

On my first visit the courts were packed. The players were mostly young but not completely. Mostly there were no masks. Part of the court's revamp was a new fitness area in the corner, parallel bars, a chin-up station, and so forth. I got in the habit of jogging down with a Zabar's bag in which there were a basketball, a jump rope, and a stretchy elastic band, thinking, "But why do you have to jog to the basketball court to do your workout if you're not going to play basketball? Isn't this a form of self-torture? Aren't you just waiting for the moment that you capitulate?"

I held on, though, taking out my ball only when there was an opportunity to shoot around alone. Then I came back to New Orleans. I made the concession to my local CrossFit gym, a barn with industrial fans all over the place. I joined CrossFit nearly a decade ago for the purpose of keeping myself intact enough to play basketball; without the weights, I felt, my body would crumble to dust.

On my way home I passed the Carver playground. What I saw was so strange I pulled over and got out of the car to get a better look. The court, which on most evenings would have just a smattering of players, was not merely crowded, it was teeming. I got out of my car and walked closer. Big, adult players were at it. Some of them seemed to be very good. A guy was sitting on the playground jungle gym next to a woman and a stroller with a little baby in it.

"Is this some sort of league or camp?" I said. "Some organization?"

He said no, just people hooping. Actually, I don't know what he said. It was loud, and he seemed not that excited to see me. I took a few more steps toward the court and watched the game. All this basketball talent, all of it black.

I had been living in New Orleans for twelve years, and when I arrived, the pickup basketball culture seemed so anemic that I spent the first eight or so years playing in indoor courts at Tulane and the JCC. These were frigid oases in which to collect one's thoughts in the heat; sometimes the games were very good; there was a fairly diverse group who played there, all in all. But I felt sad, when I finally started to play outdoors, that I hadn't done it sooner. Playing ball on playgrounds made me feel closer to the city. It felt as if I had been missing out on a whole dimension of urban life that I was at last getting a taste of. Some of this was the degree to which I was interacting with young black guys that I otherwise didn't speak to that often. It was not so much how they did or didn't talk to me; it was the proximity with which I observed them talking to each other. The physical talent was there, but so was the goofiness of their youth, and also a kind of polite softness, even gentleness, in their manner. If this was too superficial to count as real engagement or an opportunity for empathy, it nevertheless expanded my sense of the city.

Watching the crowded scene at Carver Park, I felt the adrenaline of fear; it would have been ridiculous to walk onto the court in normal times, except I could do it, I had done it many times before, walk up and ask who had next, wait my turn. My height solved some degree of the problem but just some. What you learned on the playground was how to insert the physical fact of yourself, make your presence known. Everyone always disdains all the arguing in playground basketball, the free-floating animosity, but sometimes this was the best part, when you stand there yelling "Respect the call!" or "I had next!" over and over. I felt this pull now. Basketball was almost an excuse for the occasion for conflict. But the pandemic, the pandemic was not over, and everyone around me was at least twenty years younger than me.

I watched this basketball bacchanal unfolding under the Carver Park shed, standing in my baggy basketball shorts and fake Latrell Sprewell jersey like some large, white Mars Blackmon, staring. I always wear basketball clothes to CrossFit as if to say, this is just a means to an end. I saw a big guy spin through a crowded lane and send up a floater that dropped in. The scene was frightening on many levels, only some of which had to do with the pandemic.

At some point over the summer, I started mulling over a work of fiction I would write based on John Cheever's "The Swimmer," in which the protagonist would spend his life moving itinerantly from one basketball court to another. He would start in his own city, branch out to others in his state, travel the country, the world—a pickup basketball smorgasbord, a do-or-die situation each time he walked onto a new court. Cheever's story, as I remembered it, centered on a guy who lives in an affluent suburb in which everyone has a pool. One Sunday afternoon while drinking off his hangover at a neighbor's midday pool party, he looks around and has the epiphany that he can get home by cutting across a series of backyards, jumping in a pool in each one. Swim his way home. The story's mood was allegorical, a bit sad. But also attractive in that glimmering, silvery Cheever way.

I belong to that generation—and I think there are several—who fell under the Cheever spell in the years after what I now understand was his great revival the publication of his collected stories. The big red book with the C. I liked the stories, but it was the elegant prose, and the slightly haughty tone and milieu—a world of gentry fallen, down but not entirely out—that was part of the attraction. Then, a decade after I first read in him in the early 1980s in my high school American studies class (the teacher, at the culmination, played Warren Zevon's "Lawyers, Guns and Money" as a final word on American culture), I was shocked, along with many others, to read Cheever's journals. The headlines involve his bisexuality, his rutting in public bathrooms, his contempt for the people, the men, he was rutting with. But also shocking was how thin the veneer of his hauteur was, how anxious he was about it. It changed things, in a way deepened him as a writer. Some people said it was his best work. It certainly made for some interesting juxtapositions: I always loved his short story "Reunion," about a son's meeting with his father for the first time in years. But the reunion is never consummated; the father somehow forestalls any actual conversation by constantly switching restaurants until it's time for him to leave. It begins, vividly, in Grand Central Station; the son's longing for his father seemed poignant to me and seemed to echo the majestic interior of that space. In the journals Cheever writes of the men's room in Grand Central Station, "One could, with a touch, break the laws of the city and the natural world, expose the useless burdens of guilt and remorse, and make some claim for man's wayward and cataclysmic nature. And for a moment the natural world seems a dark burden of expensive shoes, and garters that bind, tiresome parties and dull loves, commuting trains, coy advertisements, and hard liquor." Then he takes his son swimming.

I eventually decided that it was, at least in part, the outrageous act of repression and fakery in Cheever's fiction that was part of his appeal.

The "Swimmer" adaptation lingered in my thoughts—would I call it "The Baller"?—long enough that I decided that I ought to reread the original for the purpose of orientation. Also, it had been made into a cheesy film starring Burt Lancaster, and an image of a melodramatic and shirtless Lancaster looking distraught was intruding into my thoughts and killing the mood.

I reread "The Swimmer," and it was, for the most part, as I remembered it, but more caustic and much darker. Toward the end of his marathon day of swimming, the sky has darkened to night. The narrator seems to be losing his grip in ways that resonated pleasantly with the exhaustion I would feel at the end of long sessions of playing basketball, an exhaustion that I was, in a way, playing toward. Eventually the narrator breaks down in tears. "It was probably the first time in his adult life that he had cried.... He had swum too long, he had been immersed too long, and his nose and his throat were sore from the water," Cheever writes. The whole story felt a bit creaky and overdetermined in its foreboding but fundamentally familiar, at least until I got to the end: the narrator arrives home to discover that it is locked. At first he is confused, wonders why the "stupid cook or the stupid maid" would have done such a thing as lock the house, and then recalls that it has been some time since they employed a cook or maid. "He shouted, pounded on the door, tried to force it with his shoulder, and then, looking in the empty windows, saw that the place was empty."

I felt a chill when I read those lines, partly as a natural effect of the story—that the swimmer lost everything, most of all his family. I had decided that the story reflected on me in some way, a grown man spending hours on the court, while conveniently forgetting the indictment of this behavior, and the plausible consequences of being a person who, like someone disappearing into a bar, or just a bottle, refuses to deal. Like walking into a bar or jumping in a pool, playing basketball presents you with an immediate reality that requires your attention. While you are in one place, you don't have to be in another, even if that other place is your actual life.

In that balmy, late-summer dusk (because September in New Orleans is still late summer), I stood at Carver Park debating the ethics of joining this game. In one, tiny way, it brought Zion Williamson to mind. I, too, experienced a prolonged episode during which I was close to the game of basketball but not allowed to join in. Even after he returned in January, his minutes were so restricted that he was often on the bench in the fourth quarter, chewing his lips in frustration. During the months he was on the injured list, he usually came to games wearing a dark jacket and baggy trousers. The same ones. His rumpled shoddiness confused me. Stars of the NBA have become such fashion plates. They saunter through their arrival at the arena as though on a catwalk. Why didn't Zion look spiffier? Then I remembered that for all the fanfare, he was a nineteen-year-old kid who had been looking forward to something that had been taken away. He seemed a bit depressed. His wrinkled clothes made him look deflated, and once, when I saw him standing outside the locker-room entrance holding two phones up in front of him, one in each hand, I thought he looked old. Part of the Zion magic is that he seems so heavy and leaden on the ground. Only when he takes flight does he enter a state of grace—made all the more intense by how unlikely his size and shape can somehow rise that high and linger there for so long. But these thoughts only came later. The pandemic wasn't over, but it felt a little over. If the impetus for playing pickup basketball was, in part, to be fearless and take chances, then why not be fearless now, here? How was the risk of getting the virus in any way different from the risk of getting hurt, in the course of the game or otherwise, when you played pickup basketball?

But when you speak of taking risks, the key is the agency implicit in *taking*. The virus was too arbitrary, its ubiquity the result of too much cynicism, to allow for that sense of pleasure and ownership. I stood there in the cotton-candy dusk, staring at the throng on the court with wide eyes, the questions running through my head. Then I walked away.

—2020

The Jokić Files

Jokić's Nose

Nikola Jokić is an NBA basketball player from Sombor, Serbia, whose nose turns the color of a ripe plum after a few minutes of exerting himself on the court. He has a heavy brow that sits low over piercing blue eyes. He often seems to be breathing heavily through his open mouth. His usual expression, when on the court, doesn't suggest exhaustion so much as a kind of muted confusion and mortification, almost a feeling of embarrassment, as though he is not entirely sure what is happening on the court and what he is supposed to be doing. Although nearly seven feet tall, his body was, in the early years of his career, flabby. There was none of the muscle definition one associates with professional athletes. The overall effect was that of a large, chubby kid who was in some way overmatched by his situation. Over years of dedicated work on his body, the flab has abated but the expression remains the same, as does the nose. Organized basketball, let alone professional basketball, is in many ways so strictly choreographed that it is silly to compare it to the chaos of a playground, yet the same subterranean currents of menace and intimidation run through both.

When I first saw Jokić's inflamed-looking nose, I had a visceral sense of a kid on the playground who has been bullied. Not literally punched in the nose but teased to the point where he had gone off to a corner to grieve and recover and was now returning to the fray with only the red nose as evidence of his private ordeal. But this is a projection. I am the kid in this description.

Jokić's Arms

Jokić seems to get scratched on his upper arms more than any other player in the NBA. By the end of each game his upper arms are covered in claw marks, some deep enough to draw blood. "I lead the league in scratches," he told ESPN in 2019, the first year he made the playoffs, and his first year as an All-Star. "I'm always bleeding—I'm used to it."

I asked Miško Ražnatović, the Serbian basketball scout who first discovered Jokić, why this might be. He responded in his customary upper-case email style, "I HAVE NO REAL EXPLANATION, BESIDES THE FACT THAT HIS SKIN IS VERY SENSITIVE."

He often holds the ball over his head with one hand in a manner that suggests a seal balancing a ball on its nose. From this position he will shoot the ball or, more often, pass it. Ben Golliver of the *Washington Post* calls him Mr. Hypotenuse, because his passes often come from above. Sometimes he whips the ball like a pitcher in baseball, though without the windup. Sometimes he cradles the ball like a water polo player. Sometimes the passes are lofted like gentle soap bubbles in a direction no one expected. The effect is like that of a pickpocket. At times he seems to have adopted the movement of Kareem's skyhook and repurposed it for passing. His arms, in other words, are often doing unusual things.

Jokić often seems to redirect the ball with a glancing touch. The effect is faintly reminiscent of Dennis Rodman's habit of tipping the ball to himself, except that Rodman was a famously quick jumper who got rebounds, while Jokić famously never leaves the ground. When, after years of diligent training with the Nuggets' strength coach Felipe Eichenberger, he began to dunk, the event was always noted with excitement because of its rarity.

Jokić moves slowly but continuously, like a deep-sea creature. He moves with an amphibian's dreamy grace, a kind of lumbering lightness, except for every now and then when the snap of a wrist sends the ball flying in an unexpected direction into the waiting hands of an open teammate. Perhaps he gets scratched because even though he never seems to leave the ground—or because of this fact—his arms are often extended above his shoulders, bent at the elbow in the chicken-wing position, ready at all times to extend.

In the summer of 2014, before his first NBA season, he made a pilgrimage to work out at the Peak Performance Project (P3) sports clinic in Santa Barbara, California. I had several conversations with P3's founder, Marcus Elliott, about this seminal visit, which lasted for five weeks.

"The first day I met him he said, 'My basketball good. My body not so good,'" Elliott said. "He grabbed his little belly."

One doesn't need highly sophisticated computer equipment to observe that Jokić can't jump, but his time at P3 provided a highly detailed set of data to underpin the less observable fact that his feet and his fingertips are connected to an unusual degree.

My first conversations with Elliott took place after the start of the pandemic when he had moved his family to the Alps. My sense of him on a secluded mountaintop, in the clear Alpine air, added to the already prevalent sense I had, when talking to him about his lab, of a nearly spiritual quest to get at a simple truth by using complex data. The simple truth of Jokić was that it doesn't matter how far your feet get off the ground. What matters is how quickly you can get to the ball. Jokić had one of the lowest vertical jumps ever measured at P3.

Elliott spoke of P3's 10.6 drill, which measures how fast an athlete can get their hand to a spot 10.6 feet off the ground. This is about where a basketball would be as it bounces off the rim. "The idea is that getting there quickly is more important than how far off the ground you get with your feet. Nikola was in the top ten of all time."

Jokić's Smile

Jokić's nonchalance in his movements is mirrored in his facial expressions, which can seem, at times, goofy, sweet, or strangely detached, a deadpan approaching Buster Keaton's. Clips of him interacting with children suggest he has a knack for making them laugh, play acting, being playful. In one, he insists to a group of kids who want him to dunk that he can't do it. They refuse to believe this. At last he tries, and the ball gets wedged between the backboard and the rim. The clip ends there, like a scene from Charlie Chaplin or Keaton, but in color. The viewer cannot help but imagine what comes next: the gentle giant pretends to jump up and free the ball, but cannot. This penchant for drollery extends to his postgame media appearances. A clip from early on in his career fascinated me: he is asked about a remarkable pass he made to his teammate Kenneth Faried.

"Kenneth jumps really high," Jokić said. "All you have to do is throw the ball up high." The desire to minimize, to avoid not only self-aggrandizement but any hyperbole of the self, doesn't even feel like a wish or a desire, with Jokić. It feels like a reflexive act of self-preservation.

The interviewer, unsatisfied with this answer, rephrases the question—there must be more to it than that, how did he do it?

"Just throw the ball up," says Jokić.

The interviewer tries again. For a moment the scene takes on the uncomfortable feeling of a teacher in elementary school trying to nudge their not-terribly-bright student toward an epiphany. Jokić is like the student who will not be nudged. "Throw the ball up," Jokić repeats in a tone of voice within which one can detect, like the flavor of almond lurking within marzipan, a hint of irony.

At some point in his unlikely ascent, photographs began circulating of Jokić as a nearly obese teenager with dark-rimmed eyes. He looked troubled and even sad. Then there was the photograph of an even younger Jokić looking pudgy in a nice shirt, as though dressed for a special occasion. He turns to the camera and offers a sweetly mischievous smile. These images are important parts of the Jokić legend. They lend him an underdog aura, as though all his jerseys feature an invisible Chico's Bail Bonds logo on the back. For me, Jokić offers the incredible example of someone who looks intimidated but is not intimidated. "Strong Faces" was a refrain among Gregg Popovich and his coaching staff as the 2020 American Olympic team was on their way to a gold medal. Jokić has the impassive, disinterested expression of a sweetheart who would rather get a pastry than a bucket, and I don't mean this purely as a remark about weight—he has the leisurely, *mit Schlag* sense of tempo and pleasure I associate with the former countries of the Austro-Hungarian Empire.

On another occasion, when he was crowded by reporters in the locker room after recording his first triple double, he was asked if it was his coach, Michael Malone, who gave him the game ball.

"Yes," says Jokić. "Then I hugged him."

A benign and placid smile creeps over his face as some of the reporters laugh. "Yeah," he continues. "I was naked and I hugged him." The room erupts in laughter, and he feigns confusion, as though naked hugging happens all the time in NBA locker rooms. "It's the truth!" he says.

Jokić has a broad, bland smile containing within it the hint of some inward-directed joke, which reminds me of Stan Laurel. Then there is my old high school and college classmate Michael Diamond. Something about Jokić—his physical appearance, his at times twitchy mannerisms, his sense of humor—reminds me of Mike D as a young man. Once you picture Jokić dressed in a leather porkpie hat and sunglasses, with a giant car medallion hanging from his neck on a gold chain à la Mike D in the "Fight for Your Right to Party" video, you can not unsee it.

It is a bit overdetermined that Jokić's nickname is "The Joker." It is inappropriate precisely because it is too on the nose. He is a basketball player who in every way is confounding and surprising. This is true of his most subtle movements on the court and also of the larger trajectory of what can now be described, with a straight face, as the Jokić myth. But then, Jokić is a master of misdirection. Perhaps it is appropriate that I am talking about all these comedians when he is, in fact, a magician. His greatest trick has been to turn a fat, ungainly, confused-looking teenager whose nose turns dark red after running up and down the court a few times into one of the greatest basketball players in the world.

Jokić's Hands and Feet

I have always thought that the phrase *good hands* in basketball understates the difficulty of the very tall. Imagine playing a piano concerto while sitting properly in front of the piano. Then imagine attempting the same piece while sitting as far away from the piano as possible, your arms completely outstretched. Everything you do with your hands is more difficult while in this unbalanced state of extension.

Miško Ražnatović, in response to my question about Jokić's hands, wrote: "I EXPLAINED MANY TIMES TO THE PEOPLE, THAT HE HAS BIGGEST TALENT IN FINGERS THAT I HAVE EVER SEEN. ALSO, I SAID TO THE PEOPLE, THAT NOBODY CAN LEARN YOU THIS—YOU JUST GOT IT BY NATURE OR YOU DON'T GET IT. AND HE GOT IT REALLY ON OUTSTANDING WAY. I STILL REMEMBER COUPLE OF SITUATION WHERE HE PLAYED FOR MEGA AND WHAT KIND OF THE SOLUTION

HE FOUND. OTHERS CAN NOT DO THIS, BECAUSE THEY JUST CAN NOT PERFORM WITH FINGERS, HANDS."

Part of Jokić's athletic genius is his sheer coordination. His facility extends to ping-pong, volleyball, soccer, and billiards, according to Jokić's godfather, the Serbian basketball coach Nebojsa Vagic. "The sport he really likes playing," Vagic told the *Denver Post*'s Mike Singer, "especially with me and his brothers, we call that tennis with your foot. It's a net not even a meter high.... He always wants to play that. He's really addicted to that."

We are used to thinking about hand-eye coordination in athletes, or foot-eye coordination. Jokić has excellent hand-foot coordination. Another of Marcus Elliott's discoveries at P3 involved the connection between Jokić's hands and feet. "The first thing he does is weigh his body. He free-falls just a little bit, and then he extends," Elliott said. "It takes such precise timing to apply force to the ground and have it apply to your hands. To have great footwork, everything has to be well connected. We call them kinematic movers. Guys that create a lot more power but are gentle on their feet."

Jokić is in the habit, in the intervals of NBA games when he is not running, of cupping his hands together and blowing into them in the manner of someone who is cold. A lot of players do this, or have some similar tic with their hands. I had thought it might be for moisture purposes. Even though basketball players are drenched in their own sweat and that of others after just a few moments on the court, they seem to be on an eternal quest to moisten their hands. I can recall Steve Nash at the foul line sometime in the 2000s, during his run of back-to-back MVP seasons, his long hair drenched as though he just stepped out of the shower, slapping hands with every single one of his teammates as he was about to receive the ball from the ref and then, like a puppy, profusely licking both his hands before taking his shot. A video of this sequence circulated at the time with commentary about hygiene. Its main importance, for me, is as a prime example of the NBA players' eternal quest for hand moisture.

A number of people who train or in some way work directly with NBA players have suggested to me that it is dryness, not moisture, that Jokić is seeking. Once I had this notion in mind, I noticed that he would sometimes wipe his hands on his jersey as he ran down the court. It is also possible that he is trying to warm his hands. Or cool them.

Jokić maintains no presence on social media. When he is asked about his individual accomplishments, he always claims to only be interested in the team accomplishments, a dynamic that has accelerated as he became an All-Star, then All-NBA, and then MVP. Perhaps he is constantly blowing on his cupped hands as a way of shielding his face. When I shared this theory with Mike Singer, who has covered the Nuggets for the *Denver Post* since 2018, he replied, "I think moisture. He could not care less about hiding his face."

I recently reviewed the photographs I took of Jokić over the years. I have a slow-motion video of Jokić catching the ball on the baseline and starting to dribble while turning his back to the basket. He backs down an assistant coach over the course of several hard dribbles before turning and rising with his elbow cocked high above his head to release his awkward-looking shot.

In real time it happened in a few hectic seconds. In slow motion there seem to be a thousand distinct movements: a sense of force and weight in his upper body and waist when he turns his back to the basket, and all the while a skittering quickness to his feet down below. The overall effect is undulatory, as if, again, Jokić was a large sea creature capable of sudden movement.

The most recent of these observation sessions took place at the Smoothie King Center on January 30, 2019. Looking through the pictures, I found one of Jokić standing at the foul line dressed head to toe in the navy blue of the Nuggets warm-ups, with tangerine-colored sneakers, blowing into his cupped hands with the concentrated manner of someone who has just watched another person use a blade of grass to make their hands into a musical instrument and now wants to do it himself.

Jokić's Bunnies

Jokić with the ball, in the post or otherwise close to the basket, is prone to pump faking, and pirouetting back and forth on his pivot foot like a confused ballerina until the defender is off balance, at which point he will loft the ball into the air. In some ways, his body movement when taking a three-point shot is similar to his body movement when shooting directly in front of the basket—in both cases the ball is high above his head in the hypotenuse position; his large hands release it like a cream

puff; more often than not, it follows the high arc of a moonball, traveling twenty-two feet—or two feet. In some ways it is the shots he takes
at the rim that seem more remarkable when they plop through the
net. For one thing, he is usually taking these shots against an opposing
center, among them the league's most formidable defenders. (A famous
anecdote has Rudy Gobert waving away his teammates when they come
to help with Jokić, yelling, "I got him." Jokić chimes in, "Brother, I have
forty-seven.")

These shots taken at or very near the basket have always terrified me;
they are where my own greatest humiliations have taken place. A tall person shooting at close range is supposed to make the basket. Old basketball
heads will often refer to such shots as *bunnies*. Hubie Brown, while calling
a recent playoff game, watched a big man miss one of these close-range
shots and exclaimed, "You can't miss these bunnies!"

The remark caused me a moment of PTSD. Coaches get so exasperated
by these unforced errors. And what could be less forgivable than a large
man missing a shot on the basket when he is right there? But these shots
are all risk and very little reward. A big man is no more likely to be con-
gratulated on making them than he would be on having tied his sneakers.
It is disorienting to shoot so close to the rim unless you can dunk the ball
or have an angle that allows for use of the backboard. Then there is the
fact that without the orienting distance from the hoop, it's hard to know
where you are. Yet Jokić has that Bill Bradley–esque awareness of where
he and everyone else are, and he often finishes close to the basket with
tiny arcing rainbows that plop into the net. Sometimes he goes straight
up, and sometimes the shot comes at the end of a long session of flailing
his arms around in conductor-like movements, a slow-motion dervish
of spinning, pivoting, stepping through. In these moments his lack of
jumping becomes not a liability but a virtue—an uncanny ability to keep
his pivot foot in one place.

There are echoes of Kevin McHale in this strangely counterintuitive
movement in which a very tall man brings his arm beneath the arms of
his defenders; it looks like Kareem Abdul-Jabbar's skyhook performed
underhanded, at an altitude below the shoulder, which is to say it looks
like Wilt Chamberlain's big dipper.

Players who look like Jokić are often used as a kind of movable stanchion, deployed strategically around the court to set screens. Jokić is very good at this. Much of the Nuggets' offense in the half-court involves Jokić setting picks over and over again, getting the ball, immediately handing it off, getting it back.

To the act of setting picks, an essential but fairly mundane basketball gesture, he brings an almost canine expressiveness: his feet skitter to find their wide base, his shoulders hunch down, and, finally, his arms cross in front of him, his hands placed protectively over his crotch, as he lowers down into a slight squat. There is a feeling of dread and resignation in the gesture, as though he is resigned to being smashed into by another defender while his teammate springs free. The anxiety of the crash-test dummy before the moment of impact. When the ball is handed to him, he always seems eager to get rid of it, as if his hands and the ball were opposite magnetic poles.

There is, to paraphrase J. D. Salinger in his story "De Daumier-Smith's Blue Period," an "After you, Alphonse" comedy to the Nuggets' offense as it revolves around Jokić. They give him the ball, he gives it back, and so on, as if every player wants Jokić to have the ball and Jokić would prefer not to, a tension that creates a hothouse environment for one of basketball's most aesthetically pleasing plays, the give-and-go.

The basketball writer Seth Partnow came up with the term *heliocentrism* to describe the way certain players dominate offenses. Derived from the Copernican concept of the heliocentric model of the universe—which proposed what was, in the sixteenth century, the novel idea that it was the planets that rotated around the sun and not vice versa—the basketball version of heliocentrism focuses on how one player can impact an entire offense and by extension an entire defense, which has to focus on that one player.

Most players who achieve this impact do so by having the ball in their hands. Jokić's innovation is to have an enormous impact on the Nuggets' offense while touching the ball far less frequently than heliocentric peers such as Luka Dončić and Trae Young and, previously, Oscar Robertson.

The usual emotional relationship between the player and the ball is a jealous one. The player wants to possess it completely and lives in horror at the possibility of turning it over or, worse, having it be stolen. They will dive for it, scrap for it. The slam dunk's catharsis is, in a sense, the closest you can come to letting go of something on your own terms.

Jokić, in contrast, exhibits no longing for possession. Quite the contrary, he seems to most enjoy redirecting the ball's trajectory, often with just a wispy touch. What this looks like in practice has an echo of the old move one used to see in which a player such as Julius Erving, George McGinnis, Michael Jordan, and more recently Kawhi Leonard would hold the ball in one hand, wave it around as though to taunt the defense. In this scenario the hand has complete control of the ball. With Jokić it hardly has to enter his grasp before he has tossed it somewhere else. His willingness to give it up inspires his teammates, in turn, to cut to the basket.

A defense could sag off a less talented offensive player, but Jokić's three-point shooting percentage has reached nearly 40 percent. In the paint, he lofts floaters, hook shots, and, as I have said, strange little tippy-toe bloop shots that rainbow up and into the basket at a rate of 56 percent. You can't leave him unguarded, and it is difficult to guard him one-on-one. But it's his passing that is most disorienting to defenses.

Heliocentrism plays out in all sorts of ways when the object being orbited around is Nikola Jokić. While reading *Black Lamb and Grey Falcon*, Rebecca West's classic examination of Yugoslavia past and present, written in the years just before the outbreak of World War II, I kept finding a resonance in passages that had no connection to Jokić and basketball beyond my desire to find one. When she writes of walking into a Yugoslavian street scene with its chestnut trees and toast-colored buildings and how the vista suggested the influence of the Hapsburgs and their taste for sweets and no exercise, I thought about Nikola Jokić. As I read through the brilliant thousand-page tome, I had to coach myself to let go of the hope that it would mention Sombor, the home and birthplace of Nikola Jokić, now used in the phrase *Sombor Shuffle* to describe Jokić's highly unusual habit of launching shots with his right hand while jumping, in a manner of speaking, off his right foot.

Jokić's Gait

When he is not running, Jokić walks with an ambling, almost duck-like gait. His head rolls back and forth on his shoulders. His walk, and his speech, possesses a comedic rhythm I have been trying to place since I first became interested in him. At first I thought it was Chaplin-esque, but Chaplin's gestures are too dainty and precise; the tramp is not a giant. Jokić moves like a man in a bathrobe and slippers.

There is, in his demeanor, the way his head rolls back and forth, a hint of Rodney Dangerfield, but Dangerfield's shtick was to seem anxious and aggrieved while Jokić exists in a mostly placid mood which might be interrupted by the contemplation of a meal for himself or for his horses. Jokić's great passion, other than basketball, is harness racing. He likes to be around horses and owns several. "I like the smell of them," Jokić once said. "The best feeling ever is when you feed them. The sound of them eating in the stable is the best sound you can ever hear. It's just something that I think just a horseman can feel."

Jokić's Snacks

For a long time, whenever I took notes about Nikola Jokić on my phone, autocorrect would almost unfailingly change his name to *jock itch*. But then, around the time Jokić began to be mentioned as a possible candidate for the MVP Award, the algorithm began replacing his name with Djokovic. Is it possible, I wondered, that the algorithm had noticed that the name Jokić was being used more frequently in the context of athletic accomplishment, admiration, and even awe and was now replacing it with the name of Novak Djokovic, the number-one tennis player in the world, who also happens to be from Serbia?

Or perhaps it had detected my conversations with Veljko Vujačić, a professor of sociology at Oberlin and author of *Nationalism, Myth, and the State in Russia and Serbia*, whom I had called looking for stray insights into Jokić?

Vujačić, a cousin of former NBA player Sasha Vujačić, had swatted away the notion that there was some novelty in the idea of an MVP from Serbia. Never mind the preponderance of talent from the former Yugoslavia in the league now—Luka Dončić, Bojan Bogdanović, and Goran Dragić, among others—basketball, he said, had been a big deal in Yugoslavia since the country's strong showing in the 1968 Olympics; the famous Dream Team of Michael Jordan, Magic Johnson, and Larry Bird was formed, in part, he said, in response to the success of Yugoslavia's national team on the world stage. Being a sociologist, he located the cause of this success partly in the general tallness of the population and partly in the fact that "Communist states placed a premium on collective sports. Teamwork and cooperation were the priority, not so much individualism but group success."

He traced the Yugoslavian basketball boom to Krešimir Ćosić, who played basketball for Brigham Young University in the late 1960s. "He modernized the style of play. He was a center who played all the positions. A number of guys in Belgrade started playing on playgrounds, improvising like you see in the American inner cities, making the game faster and more dynamic."

I found a video of Ćosić and was surprised—and also not surprised—to see a tall guy throwing one-armed outlet passes the length of the court and finishing post moves with unorthodox releases that combined Kyrie Irving's spin with something resembling Pete Maravich or the Harlem Globetrotters, an association heightened by the use—in the video—of a red, white, and blue ball like the ones used by the Globetrotters and the old American Basketball Association. In fact, one way to explain both the delight and the cognitive dissonance of watching Jokić's style of play is that he looks like he plays for the Washington Generals while playing like a member of the Harlem Globetrotters.

"The success of Novak Djokovic was a much bigger surprise," Vujačić said. "Completely unexpected. He would be the greatest athlete of all time for Serbia and Yugoslavia."

Vujačić, native of Belgrade, seemed most excited when I relayed the fact that Jokić had for many years been devoted to a Serbian dish called burek—"a cheap, greasy breakfast" is how he described it. "They sell it by weight and cut it in front of you from a round baking dish. [With burek,] a pastry baked in the oven with tons of oil, the filling is usually white cheese or meat. If you are an average person you eat half a pound of it. If you are really hungry you eat three hundred grams, and that keeps you full till the afternoon."

Burek's Mexican-American corollary is the quesarito.

Jokić was chosen as the forty-first pick of the 2014 draft, which he elected not to attend. He got the news of his selection from his older brother, Nemanja, who called him from New York. He had been sleeping. Had he chosen to stay awake, in Sombor, Serbia, and watch the draft in real time, he would have seen, at the exact moment his name was called, a commercial for Taco Bell. The product being advertised was something called a *quesarito*. The story line of the commercial is a kind of Freudian comedy enacted with Mexican food: a man and a woman sit at opposite ends of a park bench. In her hand is a round, floppy quesadilla. In his hand, held like an ice cream cone, is a small, pale baton-shaped object, a burrito. He looks at her and a daydream of their future together plays out in scenes: wedding, children, old age. She, in turn, only has eyes for what is in his hand. She takes her quesadilla and wraps it around his burrito. The screen fills with a close-up of what this mating looks like, a kind of cardiological horror film with greasy meat and oozing cheese. In the middle of all this, Jokić's name appears in a sidebar on the screen.

Jokić's Doubters

As the end of the 2020–21 season approached, the impossible-to-imagine idea of Nikola Jokić as MVP began to gain currency. But there was resistance to the idea of Jokić as the MVP.

On a Zoom call with Jaylen Rose and Kendrick Perkins, two savvy and experienced former players who now work as commentators for ESPN, I asked why this was.

"The topic I want to address is Nikola Jokić," I began, saying the name slowly, as though breaking bad news. A slight pall came over Rose's face; Perkins maintained his poker face. "It seems to me the whole NBA community has had to go through stages of grief before coming to terms with the idea that Nikola Jokić might win the MVP," I continued. "Why do you think this is? And what is most unusual about Jokić's game out on the floor?"

Rose spoke in his customary declarative mode, like someone giving a deposition. "I believe that the NBA community and the media definitely accept the Joker because he legitimately has game and he's unselfish," he began. "It's just that he plays for Denver. And he is also in a league that has LeBron, Kawhi, KD [Kevin Durant], and a lot of other big-name players. To go to your second point, his game is unorthodox. If you are looking for 'highlights,' unless it's a pass or a dime he has dropped, his game is unorthodox. They are the only team in the league that will give the ball to the center who is also their primary ball handler and have him bring it up to initiate the offense. Then they will throw it to him at the top of the key, they will throw it to him at the elbow, they will throw it to him in the post."

Jokić, he said, was not "an explosive athlete above the rim. It's almost like you are asking people to pay attention. To think, to watch, to look." The effort he seemed to be making to generate a mood of enthusiasm about Jokić mostly testified to its absence. The point at which he finally warmed up was when he told a fat joke. "Previously, when he wasn't in the kind of shape he's in now, we used to call him a stretch-mark five."

Perkins began in a similarly philosophical mode, saying he thought Jokić would win the MVP, and that his earlier skepticism—he had expressed his support for Chris Paul—was because Jokić had been crowned "too soon." There were too many other players "still in the conversation." He evoked Steve Nash winning it over Kobe in a year when Kobe averaged thirty-five points per game and went to the playoffs with less talent than Nash's Suns.

"I am not saying Jokić is not deserving," he said. "I am just saying let the season finish out before we crown someone. When I think about Jokić," he continued, "Popovich called him the modern-day Larry Bird. When he first said that I thought, Pop is trippin'! But you have to watch his game. We are talking about an NBA that plays at an up-tempo pace, that is a guard- and wing-driven league. When you play the Denver Nuggets, all that fast pace goes out the window. He controls the game so much he makes you play at his pace: slow!" He went on to list all the things Jokić does well—but he was not radiating joy.

The point at which he finally warmed up was when he told a fat joke. "People are used to having guys that are ripped up like Giannis and LeBron. He has a wack body, OK? And people are not attracted to wack bodies. I had one. Could never get a six-pack. You always had a four-pack, and then the pudge at the bottom."

What is at issue here? The issue of Jokić's body, and what this body has been able to accomplish: twenty-six PPS, eleven rebounds, eight assists in the 2020–21 season. He is the only player other than Wilt Chamberlain with multiple twenty-five-point triple doubles while shooting 80 percent from the field. His 2020–21 PER of 31.28 was the highest in the NBA and tenth highest of all time. (In 2021–22, when he won the MVP a second time, his PER was 32.85, the highest in the history of the NBA.) The names ahead of him include Giannis Antetokounmpo, Wilt Chamberlain, Michael Jordan, LeBron James, and Stephen Curry, all of whom have won multiple MVPs. With the possible exception of Curry, so slight and undersized, with fragile ankles when he came into the league, these are athletic specimens out of classical Greek sculpture. A kind of NBA Hall of Emperors. To ponder the bodies of this group of players is to be presented with a kind of SAT question: which one does not belong? But a discussion of Jokić's unorthodox body and playing style is a stand-in for a more more difficult discussion about his unorthodox aura.

Jokić's Brothers

Jokić has two older brothers, Nemanja and Strahinja. They moved with him to America and live with him and his girlfriend—now wife—functioning as chaperones, personal cooks, cheerleaders, and, most of all, bodyguards. They are large, tattooed men who seem to have anger issues. "They'll try to come out on the court and fight every other game," Jokić's teammate Michael Porter Jr. said in an interview. "They're like mobsters."

Then, at the end of the Nuggets season, Jokić was ejected for a flagrant foul in Game 4 of the Suns series in the 2021 playoffs. He had swiped down hard, so to speak, on Cameron Payne, trying to foul him and stop a fast break. Not unusual in itself, but the gesture contained the frustration of losing, and Payne fell to the ground. Devin Booker charged Jokić. What followed was a highly uncharacteristic confrontation, chest to chest, that pained me—Jokić's face was no longer goofy and amiable but instead had narrowed to a beaky point of anger as he muttered threats to Devin Booker in a face-to-face confrontation. As disturbing as this was, it was even more disturbing when the camera cut to the two enraged brothers, Nemanja and Strahinja, in the stands, just a few rows off the court, their necks bulging and faces red as they shouted and gesticulated violently while security guards stood with their hands up, almost beseeching them to calm down. They seemed to be on the verge of charging the court. There was something touching and even cathartic in the brothers' rage on behalf of their kid brother, Nikola, their desire to intervene. But it was also disturbing—it forced me to acknowledge that in my enthusiasm for Jokić I had made him into a goofy, benign teddy bear and the brothers into a kind of Id stored on an external hard drive. But these were his brothers. Their shouting and scene making was, it turned out, a trait inherited from their father, who behaved in just such a bellicose way when he came to their basketball games in Serbia.

A Lee Jenkins's *Sports Illustrated* profile of Jokić in 2017 summons the image of Nikola as a small child being terrorized by his much older brothers, Strahinga in particular, who would toss him "from one bed to another in the family's small apartment, often during heated games on a plastic mini hoop. 'He once held down my arms and threw knives all around my head,' Nikola adds, punishment for refusing to climb a tree during a picnic. 'That was a little crazy.'"

In that same article, Jenkins outlines a 2004 tableau in which Nemanja, the middle Jokić, is playing college basketball in Detroit and living at the lakeside mansion of his friend and countryman Darko Miličić, a brooding figure mostly remembered as the Detroit Pistons' catastrophic second selection, after LeBron, in a draft that also featured Carmelo Anthony, Chris Bosh, and Dwayne Wade. The atmosphere at the mansion was one of decadence and opportunity squandered. Nemanja is quoted as saying he is adamant that Nikola should not make the same mistakes.

But the juxtaposition between Jokić the superstar and his brothers, who played ball but never at a high level, is not one of partying versus diligence and hard work. The Jokić brothers are poster boys for a kind of masculinity that some people might describe as toxic. Most sports fans are not only familiar with this outward-facing toughness, they enjoy it. A similar sensibility celebrates mobsters. The brothers are, in their attitudes and presentation, the antithesis of soft—softness being the most contemptuous of insults to give a basketball player. Jokić exists entirely outside this paradigm. It's not just that his body is, or seems, soft (always a four pack, never a six pack); it's his attitude, his vibe, his willingness to joke around and show joy, his enjoyment of nature, his obsession with horses, his comfort with his own cuddly eccentricity. He is the superman of soft. Although Jokić is often compared to Larry Bird, in this sense he shares more with Magic Johnson.

Jokić's Shack

The Nuggets versus the Pelicans game on March 26, 2021, was an opportunity to see Zion Williamson and Nikola Jokić, two of the most idiosyncratic and talented players in the NBA, match up. Williamson seems at home in the air and ungainly on the ground. Jokić never seems to leave the ground. Williamson never seems to return.

It was a close game. The Pelicans were still in the playoff hunt at the time, and the small, COVID-restricted crowd was animated. Among them sat me and Alexander, age nine. I had been taking him to these games ever since they opened to fans, buying nosebleed seats for the price of a movie ticket. The kid, in previous years, had tolerated or mildly enjoyed the spectacle of these games without paying much attention to the narratives around the team or its players. He was not particularly keen about sports in general. But for whatever reason, maybe his getting older or something to do with the previous COVID year or with Zion Williamson, I found myself sitting next to a rabid Pelicans fan the night of the Nuggets game. Every Pelicans basket brought huge cheers from him. When he spotted someone in a Nuggets jersey nearby, he yelled out, "Go wear your Nuggets jersey in your living room!"

"That's right, baby," came the voice of a woman seated nearby.

I had always approached these games with some distance. Being a fan of the NBA is an agnostic experience now; there is so much to appreciate across the league. Then there was the legacy of being a Knicks fan, which teaches a certain emotional remove, lest you get burned again. And, finally, my role as an occasional journalist at these games. Normally I would have come as a member of the press, to get a closer look at Jokić. Now I have signed up for a Zoom call after the game. My son's intense fandom got much more complicated when a whole row of college-age Nuggets fans showed up and began to loudly cheer for their team. They were wearing Tulane T-shirts. My son kept booing loudly whenever the Nuggets did something good and cheering madly when the Pelicans scored, in both cases glaring at these guys. I kept telling him to focus on the game.

Attendance was restricted to under five thousand fans. But they were loud. Zion would rise up on his jet pack, bounce off a defender, and finish with a basket, an old-fashioned three-point play. Jokić seemed much less remarkable. As different as they are as players, there are also similarities— both are big guys who score efficiently in the paint, and both have been entrusted to bring the ball up court, a point forward and point center. Jokić scored thirty-seven points, with nine assists and six rebounds. Williamson had a career-high night with thirty-nine points.

Jokić took over on the game's last plays. Leading by one point with a minute and eight seconds to go, he caught the ball at the right elbow, near the free-throw line. Right away he looks this way and that in his casual, befuddled way, as if wanting to ask someone for directions. He glances over his right shoulder, leans that way, and Steven Adams leans ever so slightly with him. Then Jokić spins in the opposite direction and drives toward the baseline. Now he is lumbering toward the basket. He does a Euro step at a speed most people would use to *demonstrate* a Euro step and scores with what I guess is a finger roll, though it looks like one of those artless little underhand tosses one might use to throw a beanbag at a hole at a state fair. A player who likes to play tennis with his feet, and is good at it, can reliably make such a shot. For everyone else, proper form is advised.

And that's it. That is the game. The Nuggets win. On the way out my son calmly asks if I can arrange to have the row of Nuggets fans expelled from Tulane.

Later, I tune in to the Jokić postgame Zoom call. His face fills the screen, bordered on top by his crew cut and on the bottom by the black medical mask that is now positioned as a chin strap. Most of the screen is filled with his eyes, nose, lips. As on all Zoom calls, the sense of remoteness is paired with an unusual proximity and access to a person's facial expressions. Jokić makes his remarks about his just-traded teammate, Gary Harris, at the top. He offers a sober-minded assessment of the other two players who were traded, how they may have better luck getting playing time with Orlando. He wishes them well. He answers questions about the just-completed game. He makes faces.

The old debate within me stirs: Which old-time comedian does he remind me of? I recorded the press conference. The eyebrows, the lips, the chewing of the lips, the scratching of the nose, the way the forehead crinkles when the eyebrows are raised. I return to my Stan Laurel idea. He looks like Stan Laurel. The comedic deadpan of someone who doesn't really understand. A sensitive person. But something else is going on, and the fact that it's a Zoom, and I have it recorded on my phone, allows for greater scrutiny.

He is asked why the Nuggets took so few free throws. He is asked about the next game in Denver, which will be the first one in front of fans this season. "What have you missed?"

"My family," he answers. Also the fans. "The last couple of years they have been our sixth player, and hopefully they are going to continue to do that and help us win some games." A textbook answer delivered impassively, as though a textbook could speak. Is this the deadpan expression of a comedian? Or simply an exhausted athlete at the end of a road trip?

"Mike Singer" comes the disembodied voice of a Nuggets PR staffer, indicating who will be given the floor to ask the next question. Singer, of the *Denver Post*, has covered the team longer than any of the other ten or so press members on that Zoom call, who include someone from Serbia and someone from Peru. His question is about how Aaron Gordon, not yet with the team, is going to fit with Jokić as "an off-ball, cutting-type guy." Jokić surmises he will fit well.

But in the interval between questions, around the time the disembodied voice says "Mike Singer," Jokić starts doing funny things with his lips. He had them pressed tightly together, but now he parts them and brings them together rapidly, as though he were mouthing, "Pap pap pap pap pap pap." Then he makes them vanish, chews on them, sticks out first his top lip and then his bottom lip. He raises his eyebrows. For much of Singer's question, all six or seven seconds of it, the lower lip protrudes. And then it occurs to me that the comedian Jokić most resembles is Bill Murray. Specifically, the character Murray played in *Caddyshack*.

"We will see," Jokić says in answer to the question. "We will see. The fact that he is athletic, catching the lobs, he can play off of me. We will see. It's not going to happen overnight. We are going to work on it. We will see."

Because I have this on my phone as a video, I have been able to watch it many times, and the Bill Murray association feels solid. Jokić makes funny faces that render his sports talk absurd while somehow remaining sincere about his interest and engagement with the sports talk, which is the classic Bill Murray position. Sincerity and absurdity intermingled and indistinguishable. Jokić winning the MVP is the equivalent of Bill Murray's character going out and winning the Masters. Winning the entire PGA Tour.

Amazingly, the tenor of his facial expressions, the wildly expressive deadpan ambiguity of it, doesn't really change once he begins to answer the question. "We will see," he says, and then the press conference is over. The chin strap again becomes a mask covering his face, and the screen fills with his frame rising from the seat. Then he is gone, and for a long time the camera rolls on the empty chair.

—2022

Bol Bol on an Escalator

One morning in July, at the airport in Newark, I saw Bol Bol on an escalator. I had been walking behind my fourteen-year-old daughter, observing the wristband that had just been affixed to her wrist that said "Unaccompanied Minor." She was on her way to summer camp. She walked ahead of me confidently while carrying a laundry bag covered in pink and black dots with the words "My Stuff" written in fat yellow letters. We stepped onto an escalator, going up. "I can't believe I am bringing this bag," she said. "I got it when I was, like, ten."

I was enjoying the singularity of my purpose—get my daughter to the gate, see her onto the plane, and wait, per instructions, for fifteen minutes after the plane took off. The purpose of this waiting, I understood, was so that in the off chance something went wrong, and the plane had to return to the gate, the unaccompanied minor could be handed back to the adult who brought her. On another, less rational level, I felt this mandatory witnessing would help assure that the plane didn't explode in flames. I thought of the Space Shuttle *Challenger*, whose launch in 1986 I watched live, in a room full of college friends. I had stepped away at the key moment when the camera hovered on the faces of the proud parents of the astronauts and then caught their flinch of horror when the shuttle exploded.

"What happened?" I asked when I came back into the room to see a sky full of smoke. It was explained to me, with emphasis on the parents' reaction. I had to imagine it, which in turn means I have remembered it.

It was in this state of mind—anxious yet serene—that I got onto an escalator, going up, and saw a tall young man up above. Long-sleeved T-shirt, sweatpants, feet in white socks and slides, a backpack, headphones. A late-adolescent American man, of an especially tall and lanky variety. He turned to glance down, in our direction. It was Bol Bol. Or I thought it was Bol Bol.

There should have been no ambiguity. Bol Bol is seven feet, two inches tall and very slender. He is the color of black coffee. His hair was, when I last saw him on TV, in short dreads, the same as the man on the escalator. Then there is Bol Bol's face. It is highly distinctive—ambiguous in mood and even, in a way, gender, which is to say that I have always felt his face has a womanly quality. I don't mean feminine, exactly. It is some combination of sensitivity, beauty, and sadness. The overall effect of the face is most distilled in his eyes.

Because he was wearing a mask, his eyes were all that was available. Had he not been wearing a mask, I would have been more certain that it was, or was not, Bol Bol. Had I been with my son Alexander, age ten, and a budding basketball enthusiast, I might have called out, "Bol Bol!" and immediately had confirmation that it was or wasn't him based on his reaction. If it was him, I would have asked to take a picture of my son with him. I did this once with Steven Adams, the fierce center from New Zealand, just a few months earlier, when I spotted him sitting in the back of a white pickup truck outside the CVS on Prytania Street in New Orleans, tussling with his dog, a young German shepherd. He gladly got down from the truck to chat with us, but at the exact moment I tried to take the picture of him and my son, my phone died. I was tapping a black screen.

It was nevertheless an extremely gratifying experience to have Alexander meet and stand next to one of the players that he had seen on TV and also from the nosebleed seats at Smoothie King Center. The sheer size of the man registered in person. It helped with my predicament, which by then had been going on for a couple of years, in which my son would now and then ask me if I was better than this or that NBA player. I had been increasingly forceful in my explanation that no, not only was I not better than the player in question, but any athlete in the NBA was on an entirely different level than me, that there was a continent of talent between me and NBA-caliber players, and so on. I had made this point over and over, and he had asked less and less frequently, having first given up on the marquee stars—James Harden, Kevin Durant, and the like—and then gone down the bench. The Adams encounter more or less quashed these questions, but Bol Bol would further this education in reality. But then, one of the things that confused me about the man on the escalator was that while the man on the escalator was tall, he did not look seven feet, two inches tall. But, I thought, never underestimate the power of the slouch.

Since I was with my daughter, who doesn't much care about NBA basketball and who at her age was especially sensitive to her father acting strangely or drawing unnecessary attention to himself, which, in fairness, I do now and then, I left the matter alone. Or, rather, I refrained from calling out. Had I been sure it was Bol Bol, the matter might have ended there. But I wasn't sure. The man on the escalator had Bol Bol's eyes, I felt. And his feet were in socks and slides, as had been the case the one time I had met and spoken with Bol Bol.

Basketball has always been the province of the tall. But tallness is not enough, or rather it has been joined in recent years by other, related metrics. The NBA's defensive schemes have come to emphasize length, wingspan. The goal is to field a team whose arms make a defensive thicket through which it is impossible to thread the ball. Bol Bol is very long. He combines this length with a graceful quickness. Watching him play, you can't quite believe your eyes. He looks as if he is unraveling when he runs. Yet he does not unravel and often performs remarkably intricate moves with a nimbleness and fluttering of feet that suggest deer hooves scampering. In his brief NBA career to date—his first year lost mostly to injury, his second and third spent mostly out of the rotation, with the Denver Nuggets—he has accumulated a highlight reel that includes instances of him blocking a shot, collecting the ball, dribbling it the length of the floor, including behind his back once or twice, and then, his feet moving with a gazelle-like quickness and lightness, coming to a stop just behind the three-point line, where he rises and drains a three. Or leading a fast break and threading a bounce pass to a cutting Mason Plumlee, who finishes with a dunk. Or corralling the ball on defense, going coast to coast, and finishing with a drive to the basket. He rises up over a defender at what seems an impossible distance from the rim, extends his incredibly long arm, and dunks the ball.

I am not alone in my interest in Bol Bol. These highlights gather millions of views online. Someone in the analytics community should calculate an advanced metric that measures tweets and YouTube views per minute played. The acronym would be HHR, for Human Highlight Reel; it would sit neatly beside the other advanced metric acronyms such as PER, RAPTOR, CARMELO—a metric that Bol Bol would surely dominate. The attitude toward Bol Bol in these clips that garner millions of views is always giddy, as though he were the product of a mad scientist—Bol Bol as basketball Frankenstein, which is, I am aware, not a happy analogy, given how Frankenstein felt about himself. Furthermore, though the stars of the league drive fan engagement—a word that encompasses tweets, Instagram posts, YouTube views, and the whole tangle of the NBA's hive mind as it manifests on glowing screens—there has always been an element in these giddy eruptions that feels like a carnival crowd ogling a freak. Almost all of these highlight moments come in garbage time. The closest analogue to the excitement he generates—which in fairness to Bol Bol is not just an internet phenomenon but a palpable enthusiasm bordering on elation in the arena when it looks like he will get minutes—is probably the seven-foot, six-inch Tacko Fall of the Boston Celtics.

Bol Bol is part of a current crop of extremely long and tall—and painfully skinny and twiglike—basketball players who are highly skilled and dexterous. Chet Holmgren (seven feet one) and Victor Wembanyama (seven feet two) are touted as potential number-one draft picks in 2022 and 2023. Then there is the nineteen-year-old Serbian Aleksej Pokuševski, who just completed a promising rookie season for the Oklahoma City Thunder. This is Team Giacometti distinguished from their slender basketball peers by the sinuous, almost unhealthy fragility of their extremely long limbs and their ability to handle the ball like a guard and shoot from distance.

Bol Bol arrived on the national scene in high school, already seven feet tall, with basketball skills and a famous name. He played at the University of Oregon for a short while before getting injured. The trajectory toward the NBA became more complicated when, having been predicted as a top-five draft pick when he came out of high school, his stock fell precipitously in the run-up to the 2019 draft.

The valuation of young basketball players is an industry, hugely funded, highly scientific, and at the cutting edge of data analysis. It's also faintly medieval and superstitious, a scene of negotiation and haggling as chaotic as a medieval bazaar on the Silk Road. Reputations rise and fall because of injuries, because of skepticism about motivation, and maybe because of the complicated legacy of families. The NBA has become more and more dynastic: Curry, Grant, Hardaway, Sabonis, Nance, Brunson, Anthony, Rivers, the list of second-generation players goes on and on. More than any of these dynastic players, one cannot discuss Bol Bol without discussing his father.

Manute Bol was such an unfamiliar, iconically strange figure when he played in the NBA. He was an anomaly in shape, size (seven feet, seven inches), attitude, and affect. He was one of the league's first Africans, along with Dikembe Mutombo and Hakeem Olajuwon. He was one of the tallest NBA players ever. Having spent most of his ten-year career specializing in blocking shots, he then developed a three-point shot. He was one of the first extremely tall players to take, and make, that shot. He was also one of the first NBA players from a foreign country to make activism—on behalf of his native South Sudan—a central part of his identity as a professional athlete.

Manute Bol remains a vivid physical presence, for me and many people, despite, and maybe because of, his early death from a rare skin disease. His difference went beyond the physical. A stranger to the culture and fanfare of professional sports, he seemed to regard it with a kind of bemused detachment. It wasn't that he didn't take the game seriously, but Bol's standards of masculinity had been shaped by experiences in his native South Sudan, a world away from Nike commercials. As Carlo Rotella wrote in the *Washington Post* when Bol died at age forty-seven, in 2010, Manute Bol "had never been invested with the conventional athlete's aura."

Rotella describes Manute Bol's appearance on a ghastly sounding and short-lived TV show, *Celebrity Boxing*, where he was paired against William "The Refrigerator" Perry:

Perry had entirely gone to pot since retiring from football.... The aura of good-natured Herculean potency that had once surrounded him was long gone.

Bol, by contrast ... looked just as tall and thin as ever. He had an odd fighting stance, but his long history of scrapping with beefy opponents who tried to push him around had given him a general idea of what to do. He stood off and poked long lefts at Perry, occasionally throwing a right with some force, catching him with a couple of shots to the head.

The crowd grew restless because it wasn't seeing the flailing that makes incompetent fighters fun to watch, and the referee warned both men that neither would get paid unless they fought harder. Bol, who had agreed to appear on the show only if the name and address of one of his Sudan-aiding charities appeared on the screen, threw a few more punches and took an easy victory by decision.

Perry's feeble blows had not touched Bol, and, somehow, neither had the awfulness of the show. Just by carrying himself as he always had, holding some part of himself aloof from the lucrative childishness and triviality around him, he had managed to pass through "Celebrity Boxing" without humiliation.

Bol Bol is connected to his father by his name, and by basketball, of course, and also through their physical similarities, which are acute, though Manute was five inches taller. There is a photograph of Bol Bol swimming in a motel pool that I am obsessed with, for example—he is entirely underwater, and his long, undulating shape looks, at first glance, less like a man in a pool than a shadow of a man. Or the shadow of some sea creature. An eel. But it's not a shadow, or an eel. It turned out that it is not even a picture of Bol Bol. Someone misidentified it as such on Twitter. Only when I researched the photograph did I learn it was a picture of Manute Bol. What is so striking about the picture is the way the figure in the pool, aglow with the analog atmosphere of a motel pool in the predigital age, looks like a silhouette—there but not there.

The two Bols are connected in the way that children who lose their father or mother at a young age have a bond with that parent, a bond forged in the negative space of absence. I lost my father at about the same age Bol Bol lost his father, which was age ten. This is part of why my attention has always been drawn to Bol Bol, and why I was looking at the man on the escalator so intently.

It was an unusually brief escalator ride, thirty seconds at most, and yet there must have been something about me, or my stare, that got his attention, because he glanced back several times.

I am six feet five (and a half). I was wearing basketball shorts and sneakers, which is true of about half the male population of America at this point, especially postpandemic. Nevertheless, from Bol's point of view, I might have looked like a member of that tribe—scouts, coaches, former players, journalists, avid fans—who compose the country of basketball. Perhaps he expected, with mixed dread and anticipation, that I would provide that hit of worshipful recognition which, however boring and unpleasant in the particulars, is a kind of placenta that encases the life experience of nearly every young prospect onto whom fantasies of fame and riches can be projected. Or, he might have wondered, was I just looking at him intently because he looked strange? A moment after he looked away from us, he turned back. I would say his eyes betrayed a sense of alarm when they met mine, but Bol Bol's eyes are very expressive. Unlike his father, he is an American and carries himself more or less like an American athlete, complete with the dead-eye, impassive gaze that by design has a hint of defiance, as if to say to every player, coach, fan, "You doubted me?" Yet Bol Bol's eyes often seem to be holding some secret emotion within them. In this case the emotion might have simply been, "Why is that guy on the escalator staring at me like that?" When the man on the escalator looked back a second time, our eyes met. I stared into his eyes, wondering if the memory of his father was part of the stuff he carried.

Airports are places of possibility. One of my earliest memories was of my father being called over to a table in a lounge somewhere at the then newly built JFK, where he was asked to witness a document—a wedding license or a will. Everyone at the table wore a jacket and a tie as a matter of course. I remember feeling proud that my father was so evidently a figure of importance and good standing that he would be singled out for this honorary role.

Flashing forward several lifetimes, I once lost my daughter in an airport when she was three years old. She sprinted away from me in the opposite direction from our gate. I ambled after her as she scampered down the concourse, little feet on the granite floor. I wasn't in a rush. Where could she go? She turned off the concourse and entered the waiting area of an unattended gate. A few moments later I arrived and scanned what now seemed to be a lacuna in the airport's architecture, a room of its own. I saw rows of empty seats fixed in place, and here and there, along the wall, doors bolted shut. Portals to nowhere, or anywhere. I scanned the room and saw no little girl. Suddenly I was in a horror movie, or a Didion book: "Life changes in an instant."

The horror lasted for a minute, and then I turned around and saw her running back up the concourse, halfway to the gate and her mother. She was fine. But, for a moment, anything seemed possible. Airports are weightless that way.

The few occasions in my life when someone asked me if I once played "in the league" were in airports. The most memorable of these moments took place when I was traveling with my family and wearing, for reasons I cannot recall, a two-piece suit and high-top sneakers. Perhaps it was that we were returning from Italy and I wanted to keep the atmosphere a bit longer, and so was wearing the suit I bought in Rome. I was also wearing a long scarf. The most relevant detail must have been my beautiful, raucous children rushing around the baggage-claim area, my pretty wife, my bemused nonchalance, along with my height. Some young guy appraised all of this and, with a touching kind of reverence, asked me, politely and absurdly, "Were you in the league?"

Height is confusing when encountered in real life. Six feet five, if you stand up straight, might seem tall in a subway car or crowded room. In an airport, where anything can happen, you might see a six-foot, five-inch person and wonder if they were or had been a professional basketball player. But six feet five is the statistically average height of an NBA player.

On the escalator in the Newark airport, I stared at the dark-skinned man above us, his dreads, his pants, his backpack, and his eyes. Also, his feet, in flip-flops, or slides, to be more accurate.

Bol Bol has European feet. The one time I spoke to him, in the visitors' locker room of the Smoothie King Center, he was in street clothes. His feet were in white socks in slides. Within the sock you could see the strange architecture of his big toe, which hung over the ledge of the slide. He had been injured, had had foot surgery, and was recovering. He stood in the middle of the room, not far from the buffet by the door, and I greeted him. "How are you?" I asked.

He responded with something along the lines of "I am fine, thank you," as though we were in a language class and were practicing dialogue, a feeling that was amplified by his smile. But when I asked him how his rehabilitation was going, it was as though I had strayed from the assigned exercise.

"I can't talk about that," he said, almost apologetically, as though he had been given instructions that he did not want to disobey, which I later learned was most certainly the case. A major breach of etiquette, since the status of injured players and their recovery is a highly guarded secret. One with enormous financial implications, given the amount of legalized gambling that now encases sports.

A faint atmosphere of underachievement and even truancy has been attached to Bol Bol throughout his brief career. He was predicted to be a top-five selection in the NBA draft but, in the end, fell to number 44. After showing flashes with the Nuggets when they convened in the NBA Bubble, he didn't play much in the playoffs when they made an astonishing run to the conference finals behind the play of another player whose body shape and style sit far outside the norms of NBA play, Nikola Jokić, who would go on to win the league's MVP Award. One could say of Jokić, too, that he has "never been invested with the conventional athlete's aura."

In Bol Bol's second year he played a few meaningful minutes but then dropped out of the Nuggets' rotation. If you are not in the rotation, you are supposed to play hard in practice and stand up and wave a towel at appropriate moments while sitting on the bench. You are supposed to maintain focus, keep despair (or just boredom) at bay, stay ready for your opportunity. Bol Bol didn't do these things. He appeared only in garbage minutes at the ends of games already won or lost. "No one knows what's going on with Bol," said a journalist in Denver who covers the team. "They think he's not a hard worker. I have heard he refuses to learn the plays and frankly doesn't care." The team is open to trading him, he said, but not to another team in the Western Conference. "They think he has too much talent."

In the end, they did trade Bol, midway through his third season. His coach, Michael Malone, had been out with COVID, and an assistant, Popeye Jones, took over the head coaching duties. Jones played Bol meaningful minutes in a game against Houston; he had a career-high eleven points in that game, after which Jones, the interim coach, said to Bol, "'I knew your father. Rest in peace to him, a good man.' I said, 'Anything I can do to help your career.' I think he is a really, really good person."

Those two *reallys* suggest, to me, the tone of someone who is having trouble convincing another person of the value of Bol Bol—not as a person but as a professional. That unconvinced person was surely Michael Malone. Malone was obviously impatient with, if not disgusted by, Bol's seeming lassitude or disinterest. Is it too outrageous for me to claim that Bol Bol sometimes seemed depressed? Malone seems to value self-motivation and toughness and despise self-pity.

On Malone's first day back from COVID quarantine, Bol was traded. Another move made by the Nuggets at more or less the same time was the signing of the once fearsome DeMarcus Cousins, the bruising center and onetime All-Star who had played for Malone in Sacramento, where he had been one of the coach's favorites. Cousins, who has his own baggage, physically and emotionally, is nevertheless the antithesis of Bol in body and in attitude: ferocious, strong, irate. If Bol Bol registered as contact and conflict averse, Cousins thrived on both.

In the larger scheme of the NBA, with its breathless anticipation of the next big trade, the transition between a former All-Star trying to regain his footing in the league and the willowy, distracted youngster trying to find a place in it was of no great consequence in the world of basketball—but it nevertheless had a darkly poetic quality that reminded me of the end of Kafka's story "A Hunger Artist," when the emaciated man is finally removed, dead, from his cage, and replaced by a leopard.

The man on the escalator glanced behind him just before he got off the escalator, and there saw a young girl, my daughter, clutching her pink laundry bag with the words "My Stuff," and beside her a man who was probably her father. It struck me that Bol Bol is closer in age, and personal development, to my fourteen-year-old daughter than he was to me or to most of the other professionals he would deal with as an NBA player, such as his coach, Mike Malone, who has willfully retained his tough-guy New York City accent in Denver, an accent he surely inherited from his father, Brendan Malone, a longtime New York Knicks assistant coach. Sometimes I feel as though I am projecting father-son drama onto the NBA, and then you simply pay attention.

I searched his eyes. Bol Bol has intense eyes. I think I project a kind of sensitivity and sadness onto Bol Bol's face, just as I projected a meaning onto the Giacometti shape of his body, which seems fragile. But these projections are grounded in real moments, such as his visible disappointment at the NBA draft. And it comes from knowing about his father, Manute Bol, the original Giacometti in the NBA. Knowing about his father's career and life, and his father's early death. Watching the indelible clip of Bol Bol as a young boy of five or six sitting beside his father, Manute, folded onto the couch behind him. Manute's face is oddly cherubic, his knees as high as his son's head, beaming with delight as his son responds to the interviewer's question, "Is he a great dad?"

"Yes."

"Why?"

"Because I love him."

The father interjects, "I love you too."

I always felt about Bol Bol that he carried the burden of his father's life and also his death, the way all sons carry such things.

"I've been thinking about my dad these last few days, while I've been making my college decision," Bol Bol wrote in an article in the *Players' Tribune* announcing his intention to play at Oregon. "I wonder what he would have done if he was alive right now."

I believe these words even as I sense a performative obligation—the tying up of a loose thread.

When we got to the top of the escalator, I sought out the direction of our gate and saw Bol Bol, already some ways ahead, going in some direction other than ours. He turned and looked behind him one last time. There was a hunted look to him, as though he were spooked at the thought a fan was onto him, and also a kind of longing, as though wishing I was a fan who knew exactly who he was, as opposed to someone who was staring at him because he was so tall, so slender. Maybe he was dreading the thought that I would approach him and ask, "Did you play in the league?"

I couldn't help but wonder if I would ever see him again—a sentiment both overblown and true to life, since so many young athletes who are fawned over, practically salivated over, in their youth, all the way up the draft, fade so quickly from sight. The flip side to the astonishing rise of

Nikola Jokić, the number-forty-one pick in the draft, to MVP is how many of the players drafted ahead of him vanished from the league.

For days in the immediate aftermath of this encounter, I attempted to verify that I had seen Bol Bol. Was he in the New York area in the days leading up to the moment on the escalator? Had he arrived somewhere, anywhere, on that day? I called his agency, CAA, where I was put through to the client services desk. There, a young woman, surely a summer intern, asked me to repeat myself when I explained my mission. Then she asked me to spell the name.

"Have you ever heard of Bol Bol?" I asked.

She only paused a moment. No, she said.

For a moment I teetered on the edge of obsession. But I recognized this as folly. To see Bol Bol on an escalator in an isolated part of an airport, or to imagine seeing him, amounts to the same thing, really—an opportunity to float in the enigmatic cloud space of Bol Bol.

My daughter's flight took off without a hitch. I watched her plane, the smallest on the runway, the whole time until it rose into the air and was out of sight.

—2021

Outscoring My Father

My father died of cancer when he was fifty-two. He wasn't, as far as I know, into sports or exercise of any kind. He was trim, about six feet. He smoked, he drank coffee, he combed his thick black hair into a tidy side part, slicked back, and knew how to knot a tie. He looked good in suits. Beneath his eyes, dark circles. To be a trim man in middle age whose main exertions involve lifting cigarettes and coffee to your well-shaped lips is, in a way, a kind of athleticism.

I must call myself out here for the tone with which I am discussing my father, which is ever so slightly patronizing. I don't mean to be. It's just that I have been aware of a change in the way I think of him in the months and years since I outlived him. He was younger than I am now when he died. I have become, in some way, the senior figure in the relationship. Instead of wishing he could console me, I want to console him. To put my arm around his shoulder and tell him he did a good job, all things considered. A great job, really. Surviving his childhood, escaping Vienna in 1938, getting through high school and college and medical school, making a life, meeting my mother, having a family, by which I mean having me. The cancer, and the early exit it portended, must have been so depressing. I shudder to think of it from his point of view.

The only time I ever recall discussing sports with him was when I went off to trophy day at the day camp I attended, age seven or so, turning in the apartment doorway to face my mother and father. I insisted to them, promised them, assured them that I was not going to be getting a trophy, while they beamed at me. I got one, for swimming, perhaps because I didn't sink. I still have it. Other than that, we didn't play, discuss, or watch sports.

I had been aware, as I approached the age of fifty-two, that I would soon outlive my father. Is that the word—*outlive*? If not, then what is the word? If one's age is a tally of years, months, days, hours, then one could say that outliving someone is the equivalent of outscoring them; in the terminology of NBA stats, you would rise above them on the minutes-played list. I had a vague notion the day would come around the halfway mark between fifty-two and fifty-three. I planned to commemorate it quietly. I was a little afraid of it. Perhaps that is why I never calculated the exact date. Then, as it approached, I forgot all about it.

My father was a psychoanalyst; once, when I was a teenager, I read some pages in one of the books lying around the house that had to do with the topic of latent compression. The term registered with me then and has stayed with me since, owing to a provocation: the idea, as I understood it, is that there is a period of time when a boy (Is it true of girls? It must be) is filled with all kinds of desires and urges, but then, when he is around seven or eight, the period of latency begins, and the memory of all these infantile desires and urges goes into the trash compactor. They are obliterated, more or less. Then comes puberty, during which all these desires reemerge with even more force and volatility. And they seem entirely new. You forgot about the earlier versions.

I think I focused on this idea because, at the time I read about it, I was post–trash compactor, but not by much. What memories was I suppressing? I wondered. What would it be like to remember them?

There must be an equivalent to latent compression when it comes to outliving your parents. Not in the sense of continuing to live after they die, but in the outscoring sense. Especially if your parents died young, as my father did. Your knowledge of its arrival becomes unacceptable, intolerable, and you make the event disappear.

All I remember from this time was my concern about hubris. I didn't want to think about outliving my father in the run-up to the moment I would outlive my father because it seemed to invite some hand of fate to smack me down just as I was arriving at … what? The logic of the sentence seems to suggest "the finish line." But what was being finished? I just sensed the possibility that I would feel guilty at the prospect of outliving him and then I would die in some freakish way just before I outlived him. This was the logic, or illogic, of the fear. But then even that was compacted. It all disappeared.

At some point in my life, maybe sometime in my early twenties, it occurred to me that although he was no longer here, with me, my father's life was like a map unfurling beneath mine. Up to the age of fifty-two, I could, if I wanted, pause and wonder, What was my father doing when he was my age? I wouldn't know the answer to this in any detail. And I rarely had this explicit thought. But it was the condition in which I lived.

Then I arrived at a point—the finish line or the starting line or just an arbitrary accumulation of days, a number—when this was no longer possible. A new era. I was on my own. In a way you could say I was without a father, again. But I forgot all about it in the months before this moment's arrival. And it continued to be forgotten for a couple of months afterward. And then one day I thought, "Wait a second, I think I missed something important."

I found a website that calculates the time between dates. I typed in my father's birthday in 1922 and the day of his passing in 1975. It turns out he lived for 19,239 days. I had an irrational pang of sadness that he didn't make it to 20,000 days, as though two more years would have made all the difference. Though to a nine-year-old, they would have made a big difference.

Then I input my birthday and the date of the search. A number appeared. Subtracting one from the other, it became apparent that I had outlived—outscored—my father a couple of months earlier.

I sat back and thought about what was going on around then. I scanned the horizon for ironies. Nothing came to mind. Then I remembered that crazy game. The strangeness of that night.

I play in a Wednesday night, half-court basketball league for the over-thirty age group. They call it Mellowball. Three-on-three. A ref, a clock, a scoreboard that buzzes loudly at the end of each quarter. And, as a bonus, unconnected to the official offerings of the league, a scorekeeper.

I checked the dates, did the math. And lo, it turns out that on the exact day I matched the life span of my father, I scored over a hundred points in a game of basketball.

The first person to whom I dared report this obscene point total was a friend I made playing pickup basketball on a playground in New York,